Lecture Notes in Computer Sc

T0237864

Commenced Publication in 1973
Founding and Former Series Editors:
Gerhard Goos, Juris Hartmanis, and Jan van Leeuwen

Editorial Board

David Hutchison
Lancaster University, UK

Takeo Kanade
Carnegie Mellon University, Pittsburgh, PA, USA

Josef Kittler
University of Surrey, Guildford, UK

Jon M. Kleinberg
Cornell University, Ithaca, NY, USA

Alfred Kobsa
University of California, Irvine, CA, USA

Friedemann Mattern
ETH Zurich, Switzerland

John C. Mitchell
Stanford University, CA, USA

Moni Naor
Weizmann Institute of Science, Rehovot, Israel

Oscar Nierstrasz
University of Bern, Switzerland

C. Pandu Rangan
Indian Institute of Technology, Madras, India

Bernhard Steffen
University of Dortmund, Germany

Madhu Sudan
Microsoft Research, Cambridge, MA, USA

Demetri Terzopoulos
University of California, Los Angeles, CA, USA

Doug Tygar
University of California, Berkeley, CA, USA

Gerhard Weikum
Max-Planck Institute of Computer Science, Saarbruecken, Germany

Ann Macintosh   Efthimios Tambouris (Eds.)

Electronic Participation

First International Conference, ePart 2009
Linz, Austria, September 1-3, 2009
Proceedings

 Springer

Volume Editors

Ann Macintosh
The University of Leeds
Institute of Communications Studies
Centre for Digital Citizenship
Chair of Digital Governance
Leeds LS2 9JT, UK
E-mail: a.macintosh@leeds.ac.uk

Efthimios Tambouris
University of Macedonia
Department of Technology Management
Periohi Loggou-Tourpali
59200 Naousa, Greece
E-mail: tambouris@uom.gr

Library of Congress Control Number: 2009932179

CR Subject Classification (1998): J.1, K.5.2, H.4.3, H.5.1, I.3.7

LNCS Sublibrary: SL 3 – Information Systems and Application, incl. Internet/Web and HCI

ISSN   0302-9743
ISBN-10   3-642-03780-1 Springer Berlin Heidelberg New York
ISBN-13   978-3-642-03780-1 Springer Berlin Heidelberg New York

This work is subject to copyright. All rights are reserved, whether the whole or part of the material is concerned, specifically the rights of translation, reprinting, re-use of illustrations, recitation, broadcasting, reproduction on microfilms or in any other way, and storage in data banks. Duplication of this publication or parts thereof is permitted only under the provisions of the German Copyright Law of September 9, 1965, in its current version, and permission for use must always be obtained from Springer. Violations are liable to prosecution under the German Copyright Law.

springer.com

© Springer-Verlag Berlin Heidelberg 2009
Printed in Germany

Typesetting: Camera-ready by author, data conversion by Scientific Publishing Services, Chennai, India
Printed on acid-free paper   SPIN: 12737628   06/3180   5 4 3 2 1 0

Preface

Welcome to the first in the ePart series of annual international conferences. ePart is dedicated to reviewing research advances in both social and technological scientific domains, seeking to demonstrate new concepts, methods and styles of eParticipation. ePart is dedicated to innovative and rigorous eParticipation research. It aims to bring together researchers from a wide range of academic disciplines and provide the scientific community with a platform for discussing and advancing research findings. The conference itself is preceded by a doctoral colloquium providing young researchers with the important opportunity to be part of the eParticipation research community.

This book brings together 16 papers representing the completed, comprehensive research of 41 authors with from countries ranging from Sweden to Australia. Reflecting on the highly complex and multi-faceted nature of eParticipation research undertaken by these authors, the papers are clustered under the three headings:

- Research Review and Outlook
- Evaluation and Assessment
- Tools, Techniques and Case Studies

Papers include those that consider future multi-disciplinary research directions, examine the potential contribution of social networking sites to political engagement, provide evaluation frameworks for both eParticipation policy and specific projects, and those that describe emerging tools and techniques with which to conduct and analyze eParticipation.

The ongoing research, projects, and general development issues, which have also been accepted for ePart 2009, are published in a complementary proceedings volume by Trauner Druck, Linz, Austria.

All papers were blind reviewed by at least three reviewers from the ePart 2009 Program Committee. We would like to acknowledge the valuable contribution that these reviewers have made to ePart 2009. They provided the authors with useful feedback to enable them to finalize their papers. We would also like to thank Gabriela Wagner of the DEXA organization and the DEXA staff for taking care of organizational issues of ePart. Thanks also to Konstantinos Parisopoulos of the University of Macedonia, who supported the administration of the review process, set up the program, coordinated author requests, and compiled the proceedings of ePart 2009.

ePart is closely aligned with the EGOV conference. The Program Chairs consider both conferences as sister conferences and are committed to co-locating the two events in the years to come. Our final thanks go to Maria Wimmer, without whose valuable support this conference would not have been possible.

The 2009 edition of DEXA and ePart was hosted by the Johannes Kepler University of Linz. We thank numerous local institutions for the support provided in the organization of the event. It was a pleasure to visit the wonderful city of Linz, the 2009 European capital of culture.

September 2009   Ann Macintosh
                                                                         Efthimios Tambouris

Organization

Executive Committee

Ann Macintosh   University of Leeds, UK
Efthimios Tambouris   University of Macedonia, Greece

Program Committee

Georg Aichholzer	Austrian Academy of Sciences, Austria
Kim Viborg Andersen	Copenhagen Business School, Denmark
Vincenzo Ambriola	University of Pisa, Italy
Kim Viborg Andersen	Copenhagen Business School, Denmark
Lasse Berntzen	Vestfold University College, Norway
Kathy Buckner	Napier University, UK
Yannis Charalabidis	National Technical University of Athens, Greece
Fiorella de Cindio	University of Milan, Italy
Clelia Colombo	Generalitat of Catalonia, Spain
Simon Delakorda	Institute for Electronic Participation, Slovenia
Arthur Edwards	Erasmus University Rotterdam, The Netherlands
Tony Elliman	Brunel University, UK
Sara Eriksen	Blekinge Institute of Technology, Sweden
Olivier Glassey	Institut de Hautes Etudes en Administration Publique, Switzerland
Tomas Gordon	Fraunhofer Institute for Open Communications Systems, Germany
Dimitris Gouscos	University of Athens, Greece
Jiri Hrebicek	Masaryk University, Czech Republic
Andrea Kavanaugh	Virginia Polytechnic Institute and State University, USA
Euripides Loukis	University of the Aegean, Greece
Ann Macintosh	Leeds University, UK
Ursula Maier-Rabler	Salzburg University, Austria
Peter Mambrey	Fraunhofer FIT, Germany
Rony Medaglia	Copenhagen Business School, Denmark
David O'Donnell	Intellectual Capital Research, Institute of Ireland, Ireland
Peter Parycek	Danube University Krems, Austria
Vassilios Peristeras	DERI, University of Ireland, Ireland
Alexander Prosser	Vienna University of Economics, Austria

Jeremy Rose	Aalborg University, Denmark
Oystein Saebo	University of Agder, Norway
Efthimios Tambouris	CERTH/ITI and University of Macedonia, Greece
Konstantinos Tarabanis	University of Macedonia, Greece
Ella Taylor-Smith	International Teledemocracy Center, UK
Thierry Vedel	Fondation Nationale des Sciences Politiques, France
Hilmar Westholm	IFIB Bremen, Germany
Maria Wimmer	University of Koblenz-Landau, Germany
Scott Wright	University of East Anglia, UK
Alexandros Xenakis	Panteion University, Greece

Table of Contents

Tools, Techniques and Case Studies

eParticipation: The Research Gaps

Ann Macintosh, Stephen Coleman, and Agnes Schneeberger

Centre for Digital Citizenship, Institute of Communications Studies, University of Leeds, UK
{a.macintosh,s.coleman,icsaih}@leeds.ac.uk

Abstract. eParticipation is a challenging research domain comprising a large number of academic disciplines and existing in a complex social and political environment. In this paper we identify eParticipation research needs and barriers and in so doing indicate future research direction. We do this by first setting the context for eParticipation research. We then consider the current situation and analyse the challenges facing future research. The future research direction was identified through conducting workshops and analysing published papers. The results are six main research challenges: breadth of research field; research design; technology design; institutional resistance; equity, and theory. These six challenges are described in detail along with the research direction to address them.

1 Shaping eParticipation Research

eParticipation is a hybrid term. Indeed, its hybridity is what makes it both fascinating and challenging to research. It relates to democratic theory (which is concerned with normative arguments for political participation), political science (which studies participation empirically), communication studies (which relate to channels and patterns of mediation), technology studies (which relate to the design and operation of e-tools), and information science (which explores the ways in which data and knowledge are socially produced and distributed). We recognise that in producing this list we are bound to have neglected a range of other academic fields and disciplines which might claim to have particular insights to offer in relation to eParticipation. Our starting point is to accept the value of having a wide range of disciplinary and methodological inputs into the study of eParticipation. We regard it as a research area that lends itself especially to an interdisciplinary approach.

The potential for technology to enhance democracy by increasing political participation has been the subject of academic debate for a number of years e.g. [1]. The arrival of more sophisticated forms of new media has produced a growing community of research and practice that is investigating the use of such technology to re-engage people with the democratic process [2]. Within eParticipation research a strict demarcation between the conduct of eParticipation and its study cannot be made, but nonetheless, while acknowledging the constitutive function of research, it is important for researchers to be sufficiently distant from the contingencies of practice to enable them to take a critical stance. In the case of eParticipation, this entails questioning the political, technological and cultural assumptions upon which projects are based, as well

A. Macintosh and E. Tambouris (Eds.): ePart 2009, LNCS 5694, pp. 1–11, 2009.
© Springer-Verlag Berlin Heidelberg 2009

as the empirical claims made by project managers, politicians, technology vendors, journalists and interest groups.

There are now a large number of real-world eParticipation applications in place. A recent survey conducted by [3] indicated that most of these applications were based at local and regional level of government as opposed to national and European levels. There are also a large range of tools are available to form the basis for such applications and nowadays it is well accepted that technical, social and political factors need to be considered when developing eParticipation applications [4]. However deterministic claims that new media technologies are bound to lead to more democratic consequences have been rightly criticised for neglecting the ways in which technologies are themselves socially shaped and for conceiving political relationships in an excessively functional and mechanistic fashion that misses the cultural and ideological dynamics of social power [5, 6]. Indeed the capacity of these technologies to simulate participation has not been as significant as was originally believed [7, 8].

Research in the field of the eParticipation is scattered and fragmented, and it is impossible to obtain a single point of access to the matter, due to a large extent the diversity of research disciplines involved [9]. Therefore our starting point is to accept the value of having a wide range of disciplinary and methodological inputs into the study of eParticipation but at the same time recognising that interdisciplinary research is not easy. However, the tensions and frustrations which relate to such integrated research are more likely to lead to good science and penetrating analyses than research which remains within isolated disciplines.

2 Study Approach

This study is based on our understanding of how eParticipation has progressed over the last decade. Through workshops and desk research we have identified eParticipation barriers and, therefore, future research direction for the academic community.

2.1 Workshops

To assist in identifying eParticipation barriers and associated research gaps we organised six research-intensive workshops held between May 2006 and March 2007. These were:

- Understanding eParticipation workshop, May 2006, San Diego, USA;
- eDeliberation workshop, October 2006, Leeds, UK;
- Knowledge and Semantic Technologies for eParticipation workshop, December 2006, Athens, Greece;
- eParticipation policy workshop, March 2007, Bergamo, Italy;
- Argumentation Support Systems for eParticipation workshop, March 2007, Berlin, Germany.

All the above workshops followed a similar format in that each considered the scope and characterisation of the main workshop topic, its current state within the eParticipation context and, having identified the major research gaps, some recommendations on how to start to address them. For example, the questions addressed during the Knowledge and Semantic Technologies workshop included the following:

- If eParticipation needs knowledge technologies, what exactly is the eParticipation knowledge that we have to manage?
- Are knowledge technologies mature enough in other domains, such as commerce, to demonstrate their usefulness in the eParticipation domain?
- Is there sufficient scope and are there sufficient difficulties in eParticipation that require knowledge technologies and new research in this area?

2.2 Publications

With regard to our study of publications, we restricted ourselves to recent reports and published papers that considered specifically the barriers or challenges for eParticipation.

The two most prominent project reports considered were [10] and [11]. The first of these set out to identify and respond to developing global research and innovation challenges in the field of eParticipation. The work involved analysing the European eParticipation research landscape in order to develop research agendas and roadmaps to govern the direction and future evolution of the research area. The recommendations listed in the report are based on findings from a global survey conducted during 2005 and 2006. The second report addressed the inter-disciplinarity of the research field and considered a framework to address the socio technical and political challenges of eParticipation. This paper was based on a survey of eParticipation researchers and fifteen position papers submitted by researchers across Europe from various academic disciplines.

With regard to published papers studied, these either attempted to characterise the research area [12, 13, 14, 15] or they specifically mentioned 'barriers' or 'challenges' in their title [16, 17].

3 Challenges, Barriers and Needs

Our analysis identified key challenges, barriers and needs associated with the conduct of effective eParticipation research. Also identified were concepts that lacked clarity and consistency and therefore required conceptual exploration and expansion. By comparing these challenges, barriers and needs we were able to characterise them under six main themes, the first two of which relate to the relative newness of the research area and its 'breadth of research field' and 'research design', while the other four (technology design; institutional resistance; equity and theory) relate to the social and political complexity of the domain.

The first theme, 'Breadth of research field' addresses problems resulting from the fragmented research field that constitute a real threat to the further development of eParticipation tools and integration of research. Achieving more integrated, multidisciplinary research is a key challenge and requires effective and critical dialogue between researchers to identify links between shared objects of research and ecologies of eParticipation. The second theme 'Research design' depicts methodological shortcomings of research designs that tend to focus upon government initiatives rather than other forms of more spontaneous online participation. The third theme 'technology design' summarises eParticipation barriers, challenges and needs from a predominantly socio-technical perspective. This includes issues such as the design of eParticipation tools and processes, and the representation and analysis of data. It also highlights the extensive consequences of technical determinism for eParticipation. The fourth theme 'Institutions resistance' concerns both institutional and political resistance to introduce, use and act on eParticipation applications. The theme draws attention to the relevance of digital media for politicians when faced with complex themes such as the distributed nature of contemporary governance, the nature of power and the problematics of power sharing and the diminished relevance of political institutions to citizens' life when faced with global economic forces. The fifth theme 'Equity' is concerned with the major divides which characterise the problem of political disengagement from political institutions among citizens and barriers deriving from demographic, social, economic and cognitive obstacles that limit access to eParticipation initiatives. The sixth theme 'Theory' highlights the need for a general discussion about the benefits and risks of (e)participation in the context of democratic theory, with particular emphases upon relationships between elected representatives, government executive and civil society, and the potential transference of power.

Each of these themes is now elaborated.

3.1 Breadth of Research Field

Fragmented research is an overarching barrier that is responsible for triggering a number of other obstacles to eParticipation research. Isolated eParticipation research lacks focussed discussion and shared concepts and is likely to produce idiosyncratic case studies fostering niche developments rather than supporting a comprehensive research framework. Researchers are tempted to hold firm to their traditional research disciplines, resulting in the eParticipation research domain suffering from a lack of a consistent terminology and language use, which poses a barrier to adequately identify and understand relevant sources. It also hinders scholarly communication causing misunderstandings among researchers from different disciplines.

The complexity of the research area means that it is difficult to understand what eParticipation research entails; to define and refine research agendas with concrete goals; and to move the field beyond its current fragmentation and theoretical underdevelopment.. The absence of coordinated research agendas leads to overlaps and even duplication of research activities, causing potentially unwanted competition, wasted resources and ineffective eParticipation applications. A consequence of this is the current plurality of definitions of eParticipation, resulting from contested views on democratic processes by government bodies, research institutions, or citizens. Finding definition(s) for eParticipation is a crucial process for mapping the field, defining boundaries and giving it an identity. This process however is at risk of having a biased foundation that can cause certain aspects to be excluded and other to be included automatically.

To address this fragmentation, it is necessary to foster an integrated interdisciplinary research culture through shared methods, tools and data which are agreed and disseminated through joint conferences and workshops. In this way we create common meeting places for researchers from different disciplines to share and exchange research results and to plan future cooperation. If research can be channeled into an overall framework, eParticipation will benefit from the rich epistemological and methodological approaches that are necessary to understand this multidisciplinary area. It is therefore important to support interdisciplinary translation and a commonly shared terminology. Establishing an eParticipation research domain requires scope, structure and conceptual clarity in order to combine existent sources of contributions from other disciplines into a useful eParticipation research pool.

3.2 Research Design

The immaturity of research methods and designs poses a barrier to the further development of eParticipation research and practice. Finding and assessing adequate methods is complicated by a lack of scope and agreed boundaries of the research field.

Currently employed research designs lack sensitivity towards self-representing strategies of political actors in their communicative practices, risking overlooking actual processes of participation. Addressing the problem of fragmented and asymmetrical orientated research agendas problematises the fact that government institutions are at the forefront in the development of participation on the Internet. This leads to a consequent undervaluation of the importance of spontaneous participation on the net, driven by citizens, voluntary organisations and pressure groups. There needs to be a stronger emphasis on maintaining reflection and problematisation to ensure the detection of methodological weaknesses and the evolution of research designs. eParticipation research designs need to be comprehensive, integrated and interdisciplinary in nature. There is a need for mixed and triangulated research designs. The combination of qualitative and quantitative methods will counterbalance deficiencies of individual methods, overcoming overconfidence in established methods within individual disciplines.

Two related methodological challenges concern quality and impact. Firstly, appropriate research design is needed to understand and measure the 'quality' of online discussion. Done well, this could lead to a value framework for eParticipation. Solutions need to take into account that electronic debates are often dominated by a relatively small number of participants who are contributing large numbers of contributions.

By concentrating upon the total numbers of contributions, the democratic value of such discussions could easily be overestimated, when in fact the number of participants is far from being representative. Similarly, it might also be misleading to interpret anonymity in online discussions as an indicator for low quality debate. There are cases where anonymity is intentional, in order to ensure participation of individuals that would otherwise be disadvantaged by identity requirements.

Secondly, appropriate research design is required to understand and measure eParticipation effects. While current research focuses on the analysis of activities and outputs it is still open how to evaluate the short and long-term impacts of eParticipation on democracy, institutions and individuals. The challenge of measuring effects opens the question which forms of communication should be included in eParticipation research. In order to grasp the full scope of politically fuelled communication research needs to look for it beyond traditional political forums in the virtual and offline sphere. The inclusion of everyday talk can bring the analysis of eParticipation effects to another level by connecting to everyday culture and would make the deliberation process more egalitarian There is a need to assess whether and how eParticipation activities effectively increase the opportunities of citizens to participate. These opportunities can evolve as a deepening of participation in the form of better informed citizens or as a broadening of political participation in the form of a maximum involvement of citizens in the political process.

3.3 Technology Design

Deterministic claims that new media technologies are bound to lead to more democratic consequences have been rightly criticised for neglecting the ways in which technologies are themselves socially shaped and for conceiving political relationships in an excessively functional and mechanistic fashion that misses the cultural and ideological dynamics of social power. Such technologies are neither inherently participatory nor exclusive, but depend upon cultural practices and policy contestations.

The social complexity that envelops eParticipation implies complex technology design that has to meet the requirements of a large heterogeneous stakeholder community. It has to take into account such issues as expectations, skills, contexts, and purposes, importantly, connecting with work practices and everyday culture. This design challenge is characterised by a holistic view of technology design that considers both participation and the governance structures it is embedded in.

The lack of effective and efficient technology design to support representation and analysis of eParticipation data poses a significant challenge to on-going research.

Unstructured information presented and gathered through eParticipation also affects researchers who express increasing concerns about information overload on the Internet that hinders navigation and focussed searches to find relevant information, adding to time and resources. This reveals a strong need to consider knowledge technologies to investigate how to make information available at the right time and place, and in the right form, quality and quantity. Demands on improved knowledge technologies include meeting the need to support rational and justified argumentation, establishing the best balance between a structured format, traceability of contributed information, its accountability in use and transparency about how much information is needed or used to inform policy debate. Additionally, technology design has to consider whether any structuring of information creates boundaries and borders that can limit the access to and understanding of content.

There is a need to move away from solely desk-top devices and consider how eParticipation technology designs are expanding to include communication devices such as mobile devices and the use of voice and text. Even though mobile technologies have been identified as a possible key technology for eParticipation, the actual potential of such technologies are yet not well understood. Challenges in this context include a better understanding what kind of mobile technologies can be employed to support which eParticipation processes.

The rapid growth of social networks suggests that political discussions and consultations are taking place away from formal government web sites. The relevance of these discussions and their potentially destabilising effects for traditional political communication needs to be investigated. Determining the space, scope and content of this outsider communication is crucial for understanding the interactions among citizens and the social contexts of everyday life. Social networking sites enable a new dimension for eParticipation. An important research challenge is to understand this dual nature of eParticipation – on the one hand sponsored and driven by administrations, on the other spontaneously conducted by citizens and special interest groups in their own way, using the many available Internet tools.

3.4 Institutional Resistance

eParticipation, including traditional forms of participation, can be perceived as a strategic political issue that addresses the distribution and access to power. This may cause some institutional and political resistance to the introduction and use of eParticipation applications. Without serious institutional involvement, the scope and potential of eParticipation remains extremely limited, at least at the official level of political democracy. It is therefore crucial to understand why political support is lacking and how it can be initiated. Increasing the involvement of elected representatives in eParticipation processes has been identified by researchers as a major challenge. The online visibility of policy makers in eParticipation activities is seen as an important factor for facilitating citizen's confidence. There is a need to better understand what online visibility means, when and how it can be applied.

Returning to the eParticipation barrier of institutional power, influential institutions often resist participative processes that could undermine their authority by interfering with their fields of activity and responsibility. eParticipation can cause a power shift with consequences for citizens, elected representatives and government executive. On the one hand, eParticipation will expand citizens' forms of participation from voting to more detailed input on particular policy issues which has consequences for their responsibility towards political outcomes. On the other side, policy makers will experience new forms of accountability to their constituency that requires them to consider citizen input in more regular intervals than only during election times. In this sense, power can stand in the way of realising eParticipation practice in case neither side wants to make a commitment to their changed roles and responsibilities. The goal is to find a balance between problem-solving and power-sharing that benefits both sides in the form of better informed political decisions and institutional trust that encourages sustainable future commitment.

The concern over time and resources is yet another recognised institutional barrier to eParticipation, for example, the considerable resources that can be required to provide adequate feedback on citizens' contributions. Online consultations on political debates can involve thousands of participants with individual contributions. The analysis and assessment of this large quantity of information cannot be made without additional resources, clarity and transparency of use and strong commitment from the institutional side.

3.5 Equity

The problem of engaging representative stakeholders from all groups of society in eParticipation is a major challenge. It has become a central priority because of the tendency of participation on the net to favour the technological and political elite. Without targeted inclusion, especially in relation to multi-cultural and multi-ethnic minority groups, eParticipation easily becomes a way of reinforcing existing democratic divides and deficits.

The civic divide describes the tendency of active citizens to make better use of eParticipation, creating a spiral of already active people that seem to be more prone to make use of eParticipation tools for expressing their political voice. They possess more resources in terms of time, political and technological skills, cultural and language abilities that enable them to take advantage of new technologies and forms of participation.

The digital divide describes unequal opportunities for people to access the Internet and eParticipation tools due to demographic, social, and economic segmentations. For research, the divide between Internet users and non-users poses a barrier to drawing generalisations and evaluating trends that are representative of the population. Apart from physical access to the Internet, including the affordability of hardware or the quality of the Internet connection in forms of broadband, other aspects such as language and culture, human capital in form of knowledge, skills and attitudes and social capital play an important role for eParticipation.

The dominance of English in supra-national political discourses poses a particularly far- reaching barrier to eParticipation, hindering the engagement of non-English speakers who lack comprehension, competence and confidence to participate and leading to group polarisation. This linguistic determinism can be described as the language divide. English is not only predominant in the use of supranational discourses but is the most common language used on the Internet. This means that the access to information and communication among citizens can suffer from a lack of diversified content provided in different languages.

As well as physical access to the Internet, citizens also require digital literacy skills such as the abilities to manage, integrate, evaluate and contribute information to an eParticipation environment. These skills are determined by the cognitive capacity of each individual to obtain, process, accumulate, and employ information in an efficient and effective way. Developing digital literacy skills through civic education is crucial to foster active citizenship and to provide citizens with the needs to engage in rational debate.

3.6 Theory

eParticipation research suffers from being seriously under-theorised. Analysis often lacks critical distance or conceptual clarity. This can sometimes lead to a 'consultancy' form of presentation which seeks to understand the functional working of processes rather than questioning actor motives, interests, values and outcomes. For example, the study of deliberation all too often proceeds as if there is a magical formula to be found (and technically facilitated) which can arrive at universal, consensually accepted truth. This underestimates the inherently contested nature of politics and the inevitability of interest conflicts, preference disagreements and trade-offs. eParticipation researchers need to develop a more sophisticated conception of deliberation, perhaps along a spectrum from everyday talk to structured decision-making discourses.

Overcoming theoretical barriers entails three strategies. Firstly, researchers must devote more attention to the contested nature of democracy. Actor network theory could be helpful in identifying competing political claims and the weight attached to them in the design and management of eParticipation exercises. Secondly, there is a need for more debate about the nature of concepts used regularly in eParticipation discourse. Particular attention should be paid to terms such as citizenship, deliberation, discussion, public and democratic. Thirdly, eParticipation researchers need to devote far more attention to meanings and methods of evaluation. Quite apart from the methodological difficulties of evaluating processes that are not discrete from other aspects of public life, there is a need to evaluate in terms that are informed by key works in democratic and political theory. Thus far the field has been particularly influenced by Habermasian theory,[i] but other theorists, from Marx and Weber to Foucault, Castells, Hardt and Negri, need to be brought into eParticipation literature. There is a huge debate taking place within democratic theory about the changing nature of the public sphere; deliberative democracy and counter-public strategies; eParticipation theory should not develop in isolation from these.

4 Future Research Direction

The findings summarised in this paper suggest that eParticipation plays an important role in reconciling contemporary conflicts between representative democracy and the participatory aspirations of citizens. Research and practice in this domain has already become very real and demonstrates significant development over a short period of time. But future research needs to be carefully theorised, planned, and strategically evaluated.

In order to take advantage of the breadth of the eParticipation research field it is essential to foster an interdisciplinary research culture that supports joined-up research and progresses eParticipation from different academic perspectives. Such an interdisciplinary environment requires shared methods, tools and data which are agreed and disseminated through joint conferences and workshops allowing planning of future collaborations. Research projects should be populated with the relevant range of academic disciplines and be able to take suitable advantage of results already attained in other disciplines. Therefore, a major consideration for the future eParticipation research must be to ensure cross communication and interdisciplinary projects that allow researchers from the different disciplines to come together and transfer methods and translate their vocabularies.

eParticipation research methods and design need to be more comprehensive, integrated and interdisciplinary in nature in order to overcome their current immaturity. There needs to be an appreciation of which methods to use in which context based on a portfolio of appropriate quantitative and qualitative methods identified for eParticipation. Two critical methodological challenges are to measure eParticipation effects and the quality of online discussion.

The choice of technology, its design and application for research are dependent on a limited understanding of the needs of isolated actors and dependent on the skills of available researchers. To resolve this issue there needs to be a change of emphasis, away from a purely technological solution to a more holistic view of design and application where social, political, organisational and technology issues are integrated to reflect public engagement contexts. Additionally, suitably configured knowledge technologies should make information more searchable and understandable and, therefore, contribute to more informed online public discussion.

There is currently much institutional and political resistance to eParticipation in practice, therefore we need to move to an environment and culture where there is clear commitment and willingness of political and administrative representatives to engage with eParticipation. eParticipation processes need to address the inter-connections between government consultations and other, nongovernmental, discussion sites on the same policy issues. For all this to happen we need to gain a better understanding of the tentative relationship between problem-solving and power-sharing that benefits all sides which is critical to ensure commitment and trust in eParticipation.

Future eParticipation research has to take into account the multi-cultural and multi-ethnic society we live in; appreciating the fact that citizens have different needs and preferences; have diverse interests and backgrounds; and have differing linguistic and technical capabilities. This requires an understanding of how to recognise and take into account the various factors that exclude different sectors of society from becoming motivated and engaged in issues of public importance. In this context there is also a need to recognise and understand the role of mass media, public-service broadcasters and other intermediaries in reaching the excluded sections of society. There is a need to explore the relationship between e-inclusion research and eParticipation research and how they can benefit each other. Added to this, there is a need to explore how eParticipation and offline participation can benefit each other. With the growing use of social websites to express political views, it is important for eParticipation researchers to investigate the divide between these trusted social websites and government websites.

Finally, the domain of eParticipation needs to be grounded in theory. This would provide a much needed opportunity for a more critical approach to eParticipation research and allow a questioning of eParticipation achievement so far. In assessing eParticipation there is a need to understand, for example, what level of participation is necessary; what type of accountability is required in the context of democracy. This implies research to explore different democratic norms and models in the context of eParticipation.

Acknowledgements. The collaboration and planning to write this paper was undertaken within DEMO_net. DEMO_net is a Network of Excellence funded under the European Commission's sixth framework programme: Information Society Technologies IST (FP6-2004-27219).

References

1. Dutton, W.H.: Political Science Research on Teledemocracy. Social Science Computer Review 10(4), 505–522 (1992)
2. Weber, L., Loumakis, A., Bergman, J.: Who Participates and Why? An Analysis of Citizens on the Internet and the Mass Public. Social Science Computer Review 21(1), 25–32 (2003)
3. Panopoulou, E., Tambouris, E., Tarabanis, K.: eParticipation initiatives: How is Europe progressing? European Journal of ePractice, 7 (March 2009)

4. Mambrey, P.: Networked ICT to Foster e-Democracy? In: Traunmüller, R. (ed.) EGOV 2004. LNCS, vol. 3183. Springer, Heidelberg (2004)
5. Willhelm, A.: Virtual sounding boards: how deliberative is on-line political discussion, Information. Communication & Society 1(3), 313–338 (1998)
6. Coleman, S.: E-Democracy: The History and Future of an Idea. In: Quah, D., Silverstone, R., Mansell, R., Avgerou, C. (eds.) The Oxford Handbook of Information and Communication Technologies, pp. 362–382. Oxford University Press, Oxford (2007)
7. Becker, T., Ohlin, T.: The improbable dream. Measuring the power of Internet deliberations in setting public agendas and influencing public planning policies. Journal of Public Deliberation 2(1), article 2 (2006)
8. Lusoli, W., Ward, S., Gibson, R. (Re)connecting politics? Parliament, the public and the Internet. Parliamentary Affairs 59(1), 24–42 (2006)
9. Macintosh, A.: eParticipation and eDemocracy Research in Europe. In: Chen, H., Brandt, L., Gregg, V., Traünmuller, R., Dawes, S., Hovy, E., Macintosh, A., Larson, C.A. (eds.) Digital Government: eGovernment Research, Case Studies, and Implementation, pp. 85–102. Springer, Heidelberg (2007)
10. Macintosh, A., Coleman, S.: Demo-net D4.2: Multidisciplinary roadmap and report on eParticipation research (2006),
    http://www.demonet.org (accessed January 28, 2009)
11. Westholm, H., Wimmer, M.: Demo-net D6.2: Interdisciplinary framework to address the socio technical and political challenges of eParticipation (2007),
    http://www.demonet.org (accessed January 28, 2009)
12. Andersen, K.V., Nørbjerg, J., Secher, C., Wimmer, M.: Coach class or Red carpet Treatment: Strategic choices for eParticipation in Local Government. In: eChallenges 2007, Den Haag (2007), http://echallenges.org
13. Saebø, Ø., Rose, J., Flak, L.S.: The shape of eParticipation: Characterizing an emerging research area. Government Information Quarterly 25(3), 400–428 (2008)
14. Dahlberg, L.: Computer-Mediated Communication and the Public Sphere: A Critical Analysis. Journal of Computer-Mediated Communication 7(1) (2001)
15. Wiklund, H.: A Habermasian analysis of the deliberative democratic potential of ICT-enabled services in Swedish municipalities. New Media & Society 7(2), 247–270 (2005)
16. Rose, J., Sanford, C.S.: Mapping eParticipation: Four Central Research Challenges. Communications of the AIS 20(55), 909–943 (2007)
17. Wimmer, M.A., Schneider, C., Shaddock, J.: Framework and Methodology to Turn Barriers and Challenges of eParticipation into Research Themes and Actions. In: eChallenges 2007, The Hague, The Netherlands, October 24-26 (2007)

ICT Is Not Participation Is Not Democracy – eParticipation Development Models Revisited

Åke Grönlund

Örebro University, 701 82 Örebro, Sweden
ake.gronlund@oru.se

Abstract. There exist several models to describe "progress" in eParticipation. Models are typically ladder type and share two assumptions; progress is equalled with more sophisticated use of technology, and direct democracy is seen as the most advanced democracy model. None of the assumptions are true, considering democratic theory, and neither is fruitful as the simplification disturbs analysis and hence obscures actual progress made. The models convey a false impression of progress, but neither the goal, nor the path or the stakeholders driving the development are clearly understood, presented or evidenced. This paper analyses commonly used models based on democratic theory and eParticipation practice, and concludes that all are biased and fail to distinguish between the three dimensions an eParticipation progress model must include; relevance to democracy by any definition, applicability to different processes, (capacity building as well as decision making), and measuring different levels of participation without direct democracy bias.

1 Introduction

In the field of eParticipation there are several models to describe progress. Models are typically of ladder type and hence one-dimensional. This is problematic as there are several dimensions involved. One is "participation", the specific activity of doing things together. Another is *democratic* participation, which is not the same as participation is valued differently by different democracy models. There is also the dimension of "e", use of ICT tools, which cannot be directly linked to either participation or democracy. While the sophistication of ICT tool use is important for quality of communication it does not in itself induce any particular level of participation or type of democracy. There is also the problem of relating the models to reality. In practice the term eParticipation is used for many government activities involving contact with citizens. Many of these are not directly, or even clearly, related to democracy as a decision making system. Many take place at a very early, non-committing, stage of the policy process which is best called visionary. Others take place within the bureaucracy, such as when comments are invited to government initiatives such as planing for a new highway. The EU-initiated European Participation project (www.european-eparticipation.eu) undertook a comprehensive inventory and analysis of eParticipation projects in Europe. Among the 216 cases investigated (at local, national and EU level) they found, consistent with all research on the topic, that most projects under the label of participation mainly concerned information provision, not interactivity

A. Macintosh and E. Tambouris (Eds.): ePart 2009, LNCS 5694, pp. 12–23, 2009.
© Springer-Verlag Berlin Heidelberg 2009

(Panopoulou et al, 2008). Citizen input, when allowed, was often about commenting on reports and such, i.e. not directly concerning democratic decision making. This means the eParticipation field in practice is quite broad and covers many contexts with different relation to democracy as a decision making system. To understand and improve practices it is important to be able to use quality measures of participation in all such contexts even if the value for democracy is indirect.

A problem with existing eParticipation models are that central concepts are not clearly defined and measurement scales are, consequently, not clear and often confuse different meaures. There are also underlying assumptions which influence the way scales are constructed. Examples of such assumptions, or values, are that direct democracy is the ideal value for eParticipation, that there is a trend towards that ideal or that development can be measured as a trend, and that increased sophistication in technology use leads to increased sophistication of participation. Because of such bias and confusion, the models convey a false impression of "progress" towards a vague goal of "better and more participation", but neither the goal, nor the path or the stake-holders driving the development are clearly understood, presented or evidenced.

This paper analyses some commonly used models based on democratic theory and eParticipation practice. For reasons of space, but also due to the need to thoroughly examine existing models, we do not present a new model at this time. We do, how-ever, conclude by presening and discussing the criteria such a model must meet. The paper contributes to the eParticipation field by doing away with the commonly used oversimplification and unreflected mix of factors that do not covariate. The criteria presented are compatible with any democratic theory and with any area of application of eParticipation tools and methods, and can hence be used to analyze democratic progress even outside strictly political contexts, for example in all applications of eGovernment.

2   Method

This paper is purely analytical. It exhibits some commonly used models for participa-tion and eParticipation and analyzes them based on their inherent consistency and orientation, democratic theory, and eParticipation practice. Regarding internal orienta-tion, in the analysis the models are tested against a number of underlying assumptions leading to bias, specifically the following:

A1: direct democracy is the ideal value for eParticipation (ideology),
A2: There is a trend in eParticipation practice towards that ideal,
A3: Development can be measured on a single scale, i.e. technology use, participa-tion and democracy covariate strictly, and
A4: Increased sophistication in technology use leads to increased sophistication of participation.
A5: Increased sophistication in technology use leads to better democracy.

Based on the total analysis a new model is proposed which overcomes the weaknesses of the existing ones. The proposed model is tested on some exemplar eParticipation application fields and shown to improve on the existing ones.

3 eParticipation Stage Models

There are several models designed to describe and estimate progress in eParticipation. Although most of them do not explicitly mention democracy, it is clearly understood that democracy is a basic value implied. First, the very definitions of the field of eParticipation have to do with improving democratic processes. The EU definition of eGovernment, for example, reads:

> eGovernment is the use of Information and Communication Technologies in public administrations combined with *organisational change* and new skills in order to *improve public services and democratic processes* (EU, 2009) [italics by the author]

The EU definition makes clear that participation in intrinsically a part of the wider field of eGovernment – which is then not narrowly considered as services to citizens from government but see these services as an integral part of a democratic society. Second, many ladder models are derived, if not always explicitly, from the "mother model" of Arnstein (1969). Most authors do not refer directly to Arnstein but to other ladder models used in policy documents and eParticipation papers (which then lack a historical dimension by forgetting the origin of the models). Let us now look at some ladder models and consider their motivations and shortcomings. There are many models, but while the sample discussed below is not very large it covers some of the most commonly used and the most authoritative models and indeed the crucial aspects. Criteria for inclusion include frequent citation (such as the Arnstein model), use by important authorities such as the EU (the Macintosh and Tambouris models), or the OECD (own model), and stakeholder representation (the partisan IAP2 model).

3.1 Participation as Power Struggle

The "mother model" for eParticipation, underlying many others, is the Arnstein (1969) model of participation. This model is a ladder of eight rungs designed to define stages of citizen influence over policy. The model is clearly, and explicitly, based on a direct democracy model as on the top rung power is no longer "delegated" (as it is on the 7th) but directly in the hands of citizens.

The Arnstein model describes levels of participation in view of public policy. This means it makes it possible to identify various forms of false participation, such as manipulation, mere informing, or therapeutic activities aimed at calming people rather than making them truly influential. The model does not have anything to do with ICT or "e", but it has a great potential in analyzing also eParticipation cases as it distinguishes between true and false participation, and labels some of the common implementation distractions used. However, it is not analytical in terms of democracy in general, because the role of participation is different in different democracy models. Arnstein's model has been critized for its focus on direct democracy. For example, Collins and Ison (2006) suggest "social learning" to replace participation, and Fung (2006) discusses Arnstein's ladder in the context of representative democracy, asking "How much, and what kind, of direct citizen participation should there be in contemporary democratic government?"

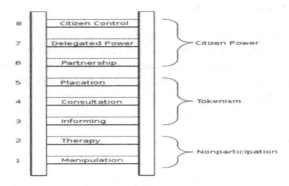

Fig. 1. The participation ladder of Arnstein (1969)

3.2 Participation as Evolution

Many have followed in the wake of Arnstein. The International Association for Public Participation (IAP2), a non-profit organisation advancing the practice of public participation, suggested the following five stages of a "participation spectrum" to describe the participation levels.

1. Informing. Provide the public with balanced and objective information.
2. Consulting. Obtain public feedback.
3. Involving. Work directly with the public throughout the [policy] process to ensure that public concerns and aspirations are understood and taken into consideration
4. Collaborating. "Partnering" with the public in each aspect of decision making. Enhanced two-way channel; citizens and governments cooperate and citizens are actively participating in the development of alternatives and the identification of preferred solutions.
5. Empowerment. Place final decision making authority in the hands of the citizens. (iAP2, 2002)

Similarly to the Arnstein model the IAP2 one targets direct public involvement, i.e. only direct democracy projects can reach the highest level. Unlike Arnstein, however, this model does not include the various methods for manipulating participation. The IAP2 model starts at level 3 of the Arnstein model, and bypasses level 5 (placation). This means it is more neutral with regard to use, but it also means it is a little naïve; while Arnstein explicitly recognizes potential misuses the IAP2 model conveys a picture of development from good (objective information) to better (eventually empowerment). While Arnstein depicts democracy as a power struggle among stakeholders with different stakes, in which participation is a contested ingredient, the IAP2 sees it as a less conflict-prone development. This means the IAP2 model draws on three of the five assumptions in our test, namely A1 (direct democracy is the ideal), A2 (there is a trend towards that ideal) and A3 (development can be measured on a single scale). Assumptions 4 and 5 are not applicable as IAP2 does not specifically address ICT.

3.3 ICT Use as Sophistication Measure

The IAP2 categories were adopted by Tambouris et al (2007) for the eParticipation domain. Similar to many eGovernment measurment models, such as Layne and Lee (2001), Tambouris et al try to provide a scale of increasingly sophisticated ICT use to indicate progress in what has now moved from the Arnstein and IAP2 notion of participation to *eParticipation*. Originally framed as "an attempt to produce a framework for assessing not only eParticipation projects but also eParticipation tools" (Panopoulou et al, 2008b) its use has been extended to evaluating particpation per se, for example by an EU project charged with the task of evaluating eParticipation in Europe (Panopoulou et al, 2008c). The stages are,

1. *E-Informing* is one-way communication that provides citizens with information concerning policies and citizenship online.
2. *E-Consulting* is a limited two-way channel that has the objective of collecting public feedback and alternatives.
3. *E-Involving* is about working online with the public throughout a process to ensure that public concerns are understood and taken into consideration.
4. *E-Collaborating* is a more enhanced two-way communication between citizens and government, a full partnership enabling citizens to actively participate in the development of alternatives and the identification of preferred solutions.
5. *E-Empowerment* is the delegation of final decision-making rights to the public, and implementing what citizens decide.

Again, we see a conflict-free model gradually evolving towards the final good (assumption A2). But while both the Arnstein and the IAP2 models are neutral towards technology, the Tambouris et al model – in its extended use – confuses the picture by using the "e". Clearly "empowerment" as of the highest step in the ladder is not in any way depending on technology, it is merely a political decision of involving citizens directly in decision making. This means the 5th step of the Tambouris model is incongruent with the others. Levels 1-4 all require ICT, in increasingly technically complex ways. The model hence introduces the complication that some but not all of the steps are dependent on a variable (technology use) which is not necessary for reaching the highest level. This means a specific project can be at more than one level at the same time. A project actually including citizen decision making (level 5) can in terms of ICT use be at any of the preceeding levels. On the other hand, levels 1-4 say nothing about the nature of the participation in terms of Arnstein and the model hence lacks any measure of improved participation. For example, projects meeting the Tambouris level 4, "enabling citizens to actively participate" may still include measures of manipulation, therapy and placation.

Such "e"-focused measures hence fail to connect the "e", ICT use, to participation. While there is a point in measuring the sophisitication of the "e" channels used, this must be detached from the notion of participation as a democratic practice, empowerment. It could be used to measure participatory activities taking place in the ICT medium, however.

This means the Tambouris et al model draws on all of the five assumptions in our test, namely A1 (direct democracy is the ideal), A2 (there is a trend towards that ideal), A3 (development can be measured as a trend on a single scale), A4 (increased sophistication in technology use leads to increased sophistication of participation), and A5 (increased sophistication in technology use leads to better democracy).

3.4 Representative Democracy Extended by Public Interaction

While the above models are designed for the ideal of direct democracy there are also models designed to improve representative democracy by introducing participation with the public. We shall here consider three such models, by the OECD, Lukensmeyer and Torres, and Macintosh respectively.

While taking up participation as a tool for democracy, the OECD (2001) model for government to citizen communication is open to different models of democracy. The three stages proposed end with "active participation", but not direct participation in decision making. The stages are:

1. *Information*: a one-way relationship in which government produces and delivers information for use by citizens.
2. *Consultation*: a two-way relationship in which citizens provide feedback to government. It is based on the prior definition of information. Governments define the issues for consultation, set the questions and manage the process, while citizens are invited to contribute their views and opinions.
3. *Active participation*: a relationship based on partnership with government in which citizens actively engage in defining the process and content of policymaking. It acknowledges equal standing for citizens in setting the agenda, although the responsibility for the final decision rests with government.

While more cautious than the previous models, the OECD step three is radical in terms of representative democracy. It is also vague; the term "partnership" does not have a clear meaning in terms of democratic decision making. The OECD model responds to the "democratic deficit" identified, to which engaging the citizens was seen a solution. The purpose is here to reinvigorate existing democracy rather than maximizing participation as the Arnstein and IAP2 models.

In terms of assumptions this model is clearer than the above ones. It avoids A1 by means of a more neutral definition of participation. It avoids technical determinism (A4, A5) by not specifying a determining role of ICT. As for A2 and A3 (a trend towards that ideal, and development can be measured on a single scale) the OECD model is somewhat vague. On the one hand, by offering stages there seems to be a single scale measurement, but on the other hand as the goal is only "active participation" it may be seen as not addressing wider goals, such as democracy. However, because the model is used in eParticipation discussions it may be argued that there are indeed concealed goals behind it that have to do with specific views on democracy. It also contains a fundamental weakness in this respect, namely that it ignores the fact that behind participation there must be a wish to take part, some engagement in the task. Where is motivation? This is a factor the next model at least points to.

Similarly framed within representative democracy Lukensmeyer and Torres (2006) proposed a ladder containing four levels of participation;

1. *Communication*; for the purpose of raising public awareness.
2. *Consultation*; to educate the public and stimulate debate.
3. *Engagement*; to involve citizens.
4. *Collaboration*; to represent stakeholders and involve experts.

While the categories are different than those of the OECD model, the genral scale is the same; using different participation tools to improve the *activity* of participation, but not the Arnsteinian *role* of it in decision making. Here, the role is instead to achieve public engagement. It is assumed, hence, that public engagement is detached from actual influence over decisions. This model shares the same assumptions as the OECD one, adds some confusion because of the factor "engagement" which must be interpreted as a factor underlying all the other three. Why at all collaborate, consult, or even communicate without a purpose that leads to engagement?

Responding to the same problem as the two above models, public engagement, but using a different model is Macintosh (2008) who after having worked extensively with eParticipation projects found the following three-step ladder model, which refers neither to participation nor to e-tools but to engagement, useful to describe the problem situation:

1. e-Enabling
2. e-Engaging
3. e-Empowering

Unlike the OECD model this one does not detail steps concerning either participation or democracy but rather takes a project approach; how to go about engaging people in politics using ICT? In this model all technical tools are contained in the first step while the second contains efforts to engage the public, and only after that comes the empowering. Macintosh does not discuss specifically what empowerment means, whether it is the weaker OECD form, influence over the agenda setting, or the stronger Arnsteinian "citizen control". The model as such is hence neutral with respect to democracy models and avoids assumptions A4 and A5. But because it is not detailed on either qualities or activities of participation it is not useful to describe progress on any of those crucial dimensions. Finally, enabling, engaging, and empowering are three different scales. Enabling refers to making tools available, engaging is a political agenda that can fit in any democracy model, and empowering is a political agenda where the scale takes on completely different values under different democracy models, as we shall see in next section.

Unike the Arnstein and the IAP2 models all three models in this section are placed within the representative democracy framework. Let us now turn to models of democracy in a comprehensive perspective.

4   Democratic Models

We have seen above that some but not all models of participation or eParticipation relate to the direct democracy model where citizens participate directly in decision making. Let us briefly consider democracy models. There are many, and one of the crucial dimensions on which they differ is the role of participation. Table 1 illustrates a taxonomy of democratic models using three categories, strong, quick, and thin, which are traced back to Barber (1984, the "strong" and "quick" models) and Prem-fors (2000, the "thin" model). The category names are chosen so as not to disturb the taxonomy by directly pointing to any particular model. However, clearly direct de-mocracy belongs to the realm of "quick", where voting is the central citizen activity. Representative democracy can contain various mixes of activities but in general it falls under the "thin" label as the involvement of citizens is indirect. The "strong" democracy is based on direct citizen involvement but unlike the quick type of models it is based on deliberation rather than voting.

Table 1. Categories of democracy models versus dimensions of democracy (Åström 1999, author's translation)

	Quick democracy	**Strong democracy**	**Thin democracy**
Goal	Sovereignty of the people	Autonomy	Individual freedom
Base for legitimacy	Majority decision	Public debate	Accountability
Citizen role	Decision maker	Opinion former	Voter
Representatives' mandate	Bound	Interactive	Open
Focus of IT use	Decision	Discussion	Information

Table 1 shows that participation as discussed by the various ladder models above comes out differently depending on the democratic model. Some – Arnstein, IAP2 – seem to fit best to the "strong" model (as discussion is involved), but there is also a potential fit with the "quick" model; voting, or e-voting, may be included as a way of implementing "empowerment". Table 1 shows why models such as the Tambouris one are confusing. They claim that there is a qualitative progression to the "focus of IT use" variable in Table 1, as the stages information – discussion – decision corre-spond to stages 1 – (2-4) – 5 in the Tambouris model, i.e. using ICT for decisions is considered "better" than using it for information. But there is clearly no progression among the democracy models, they are based on different world views, including views of man, society, and decision making practice, as a study of democratic theory shows (Pateman, 1970). So while tools and techniques – such as ICT tools, consulta-tions and various forms of collaboration – can be used within all models this would be for different purposes, with different focus and using different measures of success. Using ICT for information is indeed better than using it for decisions under the repre-sentative, thin, model.

4.1 Why Ladder Models Fail

As the brief review above has shown, no ladder model succeeds in measuring all the dimensions involved in eParticipation. These dimensions are, at least, participation, democracy, and practice (for example ICT use). All of these are relevant to ePartici-pation, but not all can be described on a scale, and the relations among them can not be simplified to be measured along one dimension only. There are different models

Table 2. The methods reviewed, their respective focus, bias, and unclarities

Model	Focus	Incompleteness	Unclarity	Bias
Arnstein	Participation	Does not relate to other democracy models		Direct democracy is the ideal value
IAP2	Participation	Does not relate to other democracy models		Direct democracy is the ideal value
Tambouris	ICT use	ICT use scale covers only 4 of 5 steps. Participation covers only 1 of 5 steps. Does not relate to other democracy models	ICT use scale implicitly coordinated with participation scale and democracy scale	Direct democracy is the ideal value Technological determinism – more ICT use leads to better democracy
OECD	Improving democratic decision making	Role of participation not defined	Role of key words like government-citizen partnership not defined	Representative democracy is the ideal value
Lukensmeyer and Torres	Improving democratic decision making	Role of participation not defined	Role of key words like government-citizen collaboration not defined	Representative democracy is the ideal value
Macintosh	Improving citizen engagement	Does not cover participation or democracy	Steps in ladder are not on the same scale	

for democracy which can not be placed on a progressive scale. This means any ladder is too simplified to describe the problem area. Further, the models to different extent draw on assumptions often not clearly stated. This means each of them is either incomplete, confusing (mixing scales), or biased (implements a hidden agenda, an implicit assumption). Table 2 lists the methods, their focus and biases.

There is much talk about "incentives and barriers" in the eParticipation literature. As we saw in Table 1, according to democratic theory, different models of democracy give different roles to different stakeholders. eParticipation is in this perspective not a discussion of incentives and barriers but about different world views, for example direct vs representative democracy. If participation is seen as a tool within democratic processes, imbalances among stakeholders are dealt with in political assemblies, representative for the electorate. But if eParticipation is equalled to direct democracy then there are no such forums. Stakeholders are left to competition and "societal objectives" are left undefined. Unless, that is, some actor (or set of actors in agreement) is recognized – by all stakeholders, not just themselves – as the sole bearer of those values. Clearly this cannot always be the case. In a representative democracy, the parliament is such an outstanding actor, but in eParticipation projects many others are stakeholders; individual politicians, municipalities, citizens, NGOs, etc. Neither of these can claim to be the sole bearer of societal values. But they can produce both outcomes and impacts. If eParticipation is not defined with respect to democracy then how can we know these outcomes are "good"?

5 Conclusion and Discussion

This paper has analyzed several models used in the eParticipation field to describe "progress". We have seen that models are typically one-dimensional ladders and share some often implicit, assumptions. In particular, progress is equalled with more sophisticated use of technology ("interaction" is considered better than "information"), and direct democracy is seen as the most advanced democracy model. From the model analysis and by reference to democratic theory we have seen that a useful eParticipation model needs to fulfil three criteria:

1. It must be *neutral towards democracy models*. Most eParticipation projects take place within representative democray so it must be possible to show progress within that model. Decision making is not the only important role of participation in democracy, capacity building is another.
2. It must cater for *different application areas*. Many eParticipation projects concern allowing the public to comment to EU reports, local government plans like "building a green city", etc. and/or regard early visionary stages with no direct coupling to decision making. Such application areas will rank very low on any of the participatory scales reviewed above, but this does not mean they are not important. They in fact allow for citizen input, they may make a difference in government organizations' operations, and they do contribute to producing workable methods for eParticipation.
3. It must allow for *distinguishing between different levels of participation* in a way that does not, like the Arnstein model, blur the border between participation as an activity (which is what should be measured) and the role of it in democracy.

The model needs not, however, explicitly relate to specific ICT uses by some measurement scale. Most ICT can be used in more than one way; they are "interpretatively flexible" (Bijker et al, 1987), so there is no causal relation between specific ICT tools and improved participation. For example, email can be used for delivering "balanced and objective information" as well as desinformation for the purpose of "manipulation", two of the very different steps in Arnstein's ladder. Also, earlier research shows that a mix of online and offline activities is most conducive to e-consultation success (Grönlund & Åström, forthcoming). This means there is no evidence that more sophisticated ICT tools by themselves lead to improved participation. Finally, ICT are so ingrained in most processes today that it is hard to distinguish the "e" component. Most government services exist online as well as offline, and citizens can use different media in different combinations for each step of a process. This means that it is in practice hard to distinguish between the role of ICT components and manual ones, just like it is hard to specify the relative importance of a pen and a telephone in communication.

Based on the above analysis and arguments, and on the fact that the 12 page limit is now close, let us conclude by just suggesting three dimensions which an eParticipation progress model should include; participation, the activity (point 3), democracy relevance (point 1), and process relevance (point 2).

References

Arnstein, S.R.: A Ladder of Citizen Participation. JAIP 35(4), 216–224 (1969)

Barber, B.: Strong Democracy. University of California Press, Berkeley (1984)

Bijker, W.E., Hughes, T.P., Pinch, T.J. (eds.): The Social Construction of Technological Systems: New Directions in the Sociology and History of Technology. MIT Press, Cambridge (1987)

Collins, K., Ison, R.: Dare we jump off Arnstein's ladder? Social learning as a new policy paradigm. In: Proceedings of PATH (Participatory Approaches in Science & Technology) Conference, June 4-7, 2006, Edinburgh (2006)

EU (2009), http://www.euser-eu.org/Glossary.asp?GlossaryID=12, eUser Glossary (retrieved March 19, 2009)

Fung, A.: Varieties of Participation in Complex Governance. In: Public Administration Review, ABI/INFORM Global, December 2006, p. 66 (2006)

Grönlund, Å., Åström, J.: DoITright: measuring effectiveness of different eConsultation designs. In: Forthcoming in Proceedings of the 1st eParticipation Conference. Springer, Berlin (2009)

IAP2, Spectrum of Public Participation. International Association for Public Participation (2002), http://www.iap2.org/associations/4748/files/spectrum.pdf

Lukensmeyer, C.J., Torres, L.H.: Public Deliberation: A Manager's Guide to Citizen Engagement. IBM Center for the Business of Government (2006)

Macintosh, A., Whyte, A.: Towards an Evaluation Framework for eParticipation Transforming Government: People, Process & Policy, vol. 2(1) (2008)

Tambouris, E., Liotas, N., Tarabanis, K.: A framework for Assessing eParticipation Projects and Tools. In: 40th Hawaii International Conference on System Sciences (2007)

OECD Citizens as partners: Information, Consultation and Public participation in policy-making (2001),
http://www.oecd.org/document/48/0,3343,en_33873108_33873376_2
5_36048_1_1_1_1,00.html (retrieved January 25, 2009)

Panopoulou, E., Tambouris, E., Tarabanis, K.: eParticipation good practice cases. Deliverable D4.1b, European eParticipation (2008),
http://www.european-eparticipation.eu

Panopoulou, E., Tambouris, E., Tarabanis, K.: Framework for eParticipation. Study and supply of services on the development of eParticipation in the EU. European eParticipation, Deliverable D4.1a (2008b), http://www.european-eparticipation.eu

Panopoulou, E., Tambouris, E., Tarabanis, K.: Framework for eParticipation. Study and supply of services on the development of eParticipation in the EU. European eParticipation, Deliverable D4.1a. (2008c), http://www.european-eparticipation.eu

Pateman, C.: Participation and Democratic Theory. Cambridge Univ. Press, Cambridge (1970)

Premfors, R.: Den starka demokratin (The strong democracy). Atlas, Stockholm (2000)

Tambouris, E., Liotas, N., Tarabanis, K.: A Framework for Assessing eParticipation Projects and Tools. In: Proc. 40th Int. Conf. on System Sciences, Hawaii, p. 90a (2007)

Åström, J.: "Digital demokrati?" Idéer och strategier i lokal IT-politik" (Digital Democracy? Ideas and Strategies in Local IT policy). In: IT i demokratins tjänst, SOU, p. 117. Fakta info direkt, Stockholm (1999)

Public Policies on eParticipation in Austria

Georg Aichholzer and Doris Allhutter

Institute of Technology Assessment, Austrian Academy of Sciences,
Strohgasse 45/5, 1030 Vienna, Austria

Abstract. This paper assesses the status of eParticipation within the political system in Austria. It takes a top-down perspective focusing on the role of public participation and public policies on eParticipation. The status of eParticipation in Austria as well as of social and political trends regarding civic participation and its electronic embedding are analysed. The results show a remarkable recent increase of eParticipation projects and initiatives. A major conclusion is that eParticipation is becoming a subject of public policies in Austria; however, the upswing of supportive initiatives for public participation and eParticipation goes together with ambivalent attitudes among politicians and administration.

Keywords: eParticipation, eDemocracy, institutional actors, public policy, government initiatives.

1 Introduction

The aim of enhancing public engagement by offering electronic tools includes the vision that ICTs have the potential to reinvigorate democracy, to be a useful remedy against declining voter turnout and increasing disengagement of citizens from politics and political organisations. But foremost, as stated by the United Nations' eGovernment survey, eParticipation "is one tool that enables governments to dialogue with their citizens. By enhancing government's ability to request, receive and incorporate feedback from constituents, policy measures can be better tailored to meet the needs and priorities of citizens" [1:58]. eParticipation denotes initiatives implemented by institutional and administrative actors as well as political activities initiated by civil society. Our paper takes a top-down perspective focusing on the policy framework related to civic participation and eParticipation in particular. The central research question is: how are eParticipation and its significance for public policy evolving in Austria? This links to theoretical assumptions of a reinforced role for civic participation along with changing forms of governance towards "interactive governance". The methods used for the empirical investigation include a review of the relevant literature, research reports, government documents and websites, complemented by personal communication with national experts in the field. After a sketch of the actual state of eParticipation in Austria section two outlines recent social and political trends regarding civic (e-)participation. Section three focuses on main institutional actors and policy initiatives in eParticipation, before section four summarises the main conclusions.

A. Macintosh and E. Tambouris (Eds.): ePart 2009, LNCS 5694, pp. 24–35, 2009.
© Springer-Verlag Berlin Heidelberg 2009

2   The Status of eParticipation in Austria

During the past ten years, the Austrian government has made considerable efforts to modernise its public administration and other state institutions with an advanced information and communication technology (ICT) infrastructure and online services. This has brought a leading position in eGovernment in Europe [2]. However, the focus has certainly been on administrative functions [3] while initiatives that aim at deploying electronic channels for public participation are still in their infancy. Online information services were the first to be implemented [4]. These have some relevance for political involvement of civil society as public information is essential for exerting citizen rights and enabling democratic participation. On the whole, also an earlier study on eDemocracy [5:3] pointed out that the eGovernment strategy had disregarded the electronic support of democratic processes. Interactivity tests by sending e-mails to political parties and members of parliament were disappointing. More recently, Fuchs [6] found that still e-mail practically remains the only online communication channel offered by national government and parliament. Among the political parties merely the Green Party's website provides a blogportal and the Social Democratic Party invites to online discussions on issues such as the ongoing reform of the Austrian education system.[1] In contrast to parties other interest groups and issue based initiatives have discovered the advantages and used various forms of eParticipation earlier. NGOs like Greenpeace Austria or Attack Austria offer tools like mailing lists, discussion boards, wikis, blogs and ePetitions. Filzmaier [5:12] notes that in early 2000 online platforms played a key role for organising civil protest movements against the coalition of the Conservative Party with the so-called Freedom Party. Since this time, Austria also experienced various forms of negative eCampaigning (satirical e-cards, mail bombings, fake websites). According to Mahrer and Krimmer [7] there were still only a limited number of Austrian eDemocracy examples, some of them initiated as local pilot projects in the academic sector. Currently, activities in the field of eParticipation and experiments with pilot applications are significantly expanding.

Traditional media do not play a major role in the promotion of eParticipation. Nevertheless, the Austrian public broadcasting service ORF provides online fora for discussion on topics of public interest.[2] Until recently, the role of the private sector in eParticipation has largely been restricted to being a partner in the development of standards and applications and a contractor for specific competences [8:125pp.]; e.g. the Austrian Federal Computing Centre is important here. As far as civic initiatives are concerned, the election to the national parliament in September 2008 has triggered some new eParticipation projects. Generally speaking, administrative and civil society initiators as well as academic researchers are major driving forces in eParticipation.

Despite the initial state of eParticipation in Austria, significant steps taken at government level signal the turn to an advancement and a more strategic coordination of both offline and online citizen engagement. Three such initiatives deserve special mentioning: the *Democracy Initiative of the Austrian Federal Government* with the online platform "entscheidend-bist-du.at" (YOU are Decisive) launched in early

---

[1] See http://www.gruene.at/blog_portal/> and <http://mitreden.spoe.at/index.php?
[2] See http://futurezone.orf.at/

2008;[3] the *Standards for Public Participation* elaborated by an inter-ministerial working group and adopted by the Council of Ministers in July 2008;[4] and the implementation of a *Working Group on E-Democracy and E-Participation* within the Austrian Federal Chancellery in 2006.[5]

2.1 Direct Democratic Rights and Political Participation

A look at the institutional and legal frameworks can help to understand the role of public participation and the potential for eParticipation in the Austrian political system. Austria is a representative democracy with direct democratic elements and a federal system of government. Political culture is characterized by a tradition of top-down political communication and consensus democracy with strong co-operation between major economic interest groups and the state, known as "Social Partnership". The Austrian constitution includes participation rights and provides for direct democratic procedures, namely petitions, referenda, and official opinion polls. Which legal regulations apply to a participation process depends on the actual case in question [9:13]. Participation processes can take effect at the level of policies and legislation, in planning activities and program development and in concrete projects. Examples of Austrian acts and statutes that feature arrangements for public participation include trading regulations, the statute on water and waterways or the individual provinces' statutes on land use.

In 2003, the so-called "Österreich-Konvent" (Austrian convention) was convened to decide upon a reform of the Austrian Federal Constitution. Propositions on extending plebiscitary components – like strengthening the position of citizens' initiatives in referenda and official opinion polls – have been declined [10:113]. However, some important parts were agreed upon to be implemented. Direct democratic rights were extended by reducing the minimum age for participating in referenda and public opinion polls to the age of 16 [11]. With respect to inclusion and legal equality Schaller [12:77pp.] stresses the need to extend the entitlement to vote as well as the right to participate in referenda, petitions and public opinion polls to a wider portion of Austrian residents, about nine percent of which are currently excluded because they do not hold the Austrian citizenship [12:68pp.].

Several studies have researched the actual extent and forms of public involvement of civil society in Austria [13, 14]. Recently, Walter and Rosenberger [15] described the historical development of participation in Austria and compared it with international data. They differentiate between voter turnout, elite-directed activities (e.g. working in a political party) and elite-challenging forms of participation (e.g. signing petitions, protest). This classification "provides a differentiation between the affirmative, hierarchically structured, and representative elite-directed, and the confrontational, egalitarian, and self-determined elite challenging forms of political activity" [15:10]. In comparison to other Western European countries Austria records high turnout rates[6] and a huge proportion of party members relative to the electorate.

---

[3] See http://www.entscheidend-bist-du.at/

[4] See http://www.partizipation.at/standards_oeb.html

[5] See http://reference.e-government.gv.at/E-Democracy.981.0.html

[6] Since the 1950ies, Austria's average turnout level at national parliament elections comes in second (behind Belgium) with 90.2 percent [15:17].

Whereas it ranks among the top European countries regarding voter turnout and elite-directed activity, it shows comparatively low levels of elite-challenging activity. The authors conclude that "in Austria, hierarchical and institutionalized participation is traditionally more widespread than protest behaviour. This has to be seen as a major characteristic of the Austrian political culture, where political parties have played a comparatively strong role in both politics and society" [15:18]. Nevertheless, Austria has been facing a decrease in voter turnout at all electoral levels (first and second order elections as well as European Parliament elections) and in elite-directed activities during the past 30 years. In contrast, surveys diagnose a significant growth of activities in the area of elite-challenging participation. Thus, Walter and Rosenberger [15:17] assume, "that there is less a decline of participation but rather a shift among different forms of political activity". The analysis on socio-demographic factors shows that the impact of education on political activity is channelled through intervening variables like age, gender and immigrant background: e.g. middle age groups are politically more active than young and elderly people and there is "a weak but significant effect of German as the first language spoken at home" [15:26]. Often women report being less interested in politics and tend to think that they cannot change things through their engagement. Other studies suggest this "disengagement of women mainly refers to a conventional notion of politics" [16:23]. Walter and Rosenberger, however, come to the result that gender does not have a significant impact on political participation in Austria [15:27].

2.2 Current Trends

Existing eParticipation offerings from government are still in a developing stage. This is suggested among others by Austria's ranking only 20th in the UN's eParticipation Index 2008 [1]. Early examples of citizen participation comprise initiatives like URBAN, an urban development project in Graz[7], the Viennese urban development project EDEN ("Electronic Democracy European Network"[8]) or the online platform "klasse:zukunft"[9] operated by the Federal Ministry for Education, Arts and Culture. Especially since 2007 many new eParticipation projects including several regional initiatives have been launched; many of them address young people[10]. Some projects have been triggered by significant events such as national elections. An example is the online platform "meinparlament.at" (My Parliament) which facilitates direct contacts between citizens and their representatives in parliament. Another site for questions to politicians is "wahltotal.at". A site which allows testing the congruence of oneself's political profile with that of a specific political party is "wahlkabine.at"

---

[7] See http://www.urban-link.at/

[8] See http://www.wien.gv.at/stadtentwicklung/eu/eden/index.htm; see also the digital land utilisation plan of the City of Vienna (http://www.wien.gv.at/flaechenwidmung/public/), and discussion boards of the City of Vienna (http://www.wien.gv.at/index/foren.htm).

[9] See http://www.klassezukunft.at/

[10] Examples are www.salzblog.at initiated by the City of Salzburg, www.cyberjuz.at initiated by the "Landesjugendreferat" of Upper Austria, www.jugendbeteiligung.cc initiated by the "Working Group Participation", www.mitmachen.at initiated by the Federal Computing Centre, www.entscheidend-bist-du.at initiated by the Austrian Federal Ministry for Education, Arts and Culture and the Ministry of Science and Research.

(Polling Booth). Already introduced with the national election in 2002, it has become quite popular, attracting over two million individual uses since then. The same function is offered by "politikkabine.at".[11]

As yet there is hardly any data on the number of participants and further socio-demographic characteristics of these projects. An investigation on eParticipation among youth undertaken by the former Ministry of Health, Family and Youth [17] provides an overview on some 40 projects surveyed between 2007 and 2008. The projects fall into three categories of participation: (1) the creation of websites; (2) planning of youth activities; and (3) discussions of political issues. Some projects of the second category included engaging youth via discussion fora, sometimes leading to quite vivid online interaction. However, this was hardly the case with top-down initiated projects. The third category gains increasing importance: e.g., discussion fora in connection with youth parliaments, interactions with politicians on youth-specific issues, engaging young people in developing youth policies in their home towns via wikis, and provision of information on elections and political parties, often in combination with games and interactive elements. Local level projects prevail and a large variety of technologies is employed (e.g. content management systems, weblogs, wikis, geo tagging). The study shows that eParticipation offerings targeting young people have to face strong competition from successful web 2.0 sites and makes it especially difficult for top-down initiated projects.

A further application area of growing importance is eParticipation in environmental issues. A recent study identified a dozen of such projects [18], many of them stipulating mandatory participation from civil society. Most of them targeted the general public, some the organised public and included formal as well as informal procedures. The majority of eParticipation cases are initiated by public administration and political institutions; invitations to participate mainly concern subjects at a strategic level, less often at concrete project levels; the dominating form is consultation and very often discussions among participants are intended as well. Outcomes contributed to opinion formation on behalf of decision-makers, only in some cases they were implemented in policy decisions. No justification was provided for non-consideration and evaluations of eParticipation were generally missing.

A general problem is the lacking overview on eParticipation possibilities and integrative tools for accessing political information on the Internet. This lack is not the only factor impeding electronic public engagement. Barriers to the use of eGovernment as well as eParticipation are connected to socio-demographic factors concerning political participation in general (see section 2.1) and to technology-specific aspects and digital divides in particular. In Austria the divide due to the lack of area-wide broadband access has received special attention. In 2003 a federal broadband initiative has been launched with support by similar initiatives at provincial level. An average of 55 percent of households had a broadband connection by 2008,[12] but strong imbalances between urban and rural areas persist [19:42]. Another initiative ("eAccessibility") deals with problems concerning people with special needs [20:12]. Austria has committed itself to the implementation of guidelines developed by the Web

---

[11] See http://www.meinparlament.at/, http://wahltotal.at/ and http://politikkabine.at

[12] See statistic "Haushalte mit Breitbandverbindung 2008 nach Bundesländern", Download: http://www.statistik.at/web_de/suchergebnisse/index.html

Accessibility Initiative (WAI) which envisages that all websites of public administrations are accessible to people with disabilities. In April 2007, the Austrian Federal Chancellery and all Federal Ministries have launched an accessibility survey in order to report on the situation in this area [21].

A separate strand of eParticipation which has been a research subject and a field of pilot projects in Austria for already a number of years with proponents in academia, IT industry and politics is eVoting [22]. Starting in 2004, working groups of the Ministry of Internal Affairs particularly discussed legal and technical aspects as well as international developments and experiences. eVoting is not part of the existing electoral law in Austria, but has been applied in specific sectors such as the Austrian Chamber of Commerce and the Board of Listeners and Viewers of the Austrian Broadcasting Corporation. In May 2009 eVoting was offered as an optional channel for the casting of votes at the election to the Austrian National Students Union and aroused a controversy on trust and security issues.[13]

3 The Austrian Policy Framework for eParticipation

3.1 Actors Promoting eGovernment and eParticipation

At the EU-level eParticipation is closely interlinked with policy documents on eGovernment. Also in Austria the domain of eGovernment has become a major driver to explore new tools based on ICT for involving citizens in public debate and decision-making. The overall coordination of eGovernment policies and activities lies within the competence of the *Federal Chancellery* in Austria. The *platform "Digitales Österreich"* (Platform Digital Austria) operates as a strategic umbrella of an elaborated organisational structure providing for central coordination across all levels of government. Its top management level is represented by the CIO of Federal Government, the head of the Federal ICT Strategy Unit and the speaker of the Platform. The *E-Government Working Group* organises the cooperation of federal, regional and local authorities. The *E-Government Innovation Centre* (EGIZ) serves as a competence centre for innovative technologies and solutions. A number of organisations contribute to implementing eGovernment and eParticipation respectively. The *Austrian Federal Computing Centre* (Bundesrechenzentrum – BRZ) offers solutions for eParticipation and has initiated various pilot projects [23]. The *Working Group on E-Democracy and E-Participation*, an inter-ministerial and expert forum at the Federal Chancellery contributes to drafting an eDemocracy strategy.[14] The *Data Protection Commission* is responsible for privacy issues. The *Secure Information Technology Centre* (A-SIT) is in charge of the Citizen Card for identification and authentification of citizens in online procedures.

Regarding the commitment of political actors towards implementing new concepts of digital democracy, empirical studies suggest some sceptical views on the current state in Austria and on its prospects. Mahrer and Krimmer [7] found a high level of scepticism towards eDemocracy among members of parliament from all political parties. Objections were formulated as concerns about unequal conditions, security and

---

[13] See http://papierwahl.at/
[14] See http://reference.e-government.gv.at/E-Democracy.981.0.html

privacy issues, and potential manipulation. Politicians were well informed about different concepts of eDemocracy but very actively opposed it. Pretending that "the ordinary citizen was 'uninterested' in politics and 'unqualified' to participate" [7:36], politicians tended to oppose change on different grounds in collective agreement. The study concludes that the scepticism against enlarged citizen engagement "is driven by the fear of a lasting loss of power for the political elite when supporting e-democracy" [7:38]. Another research project [24] investigated the Austrian discourse on eGovernment and its democratic potential. Analysing the process of the Austrian E-Government Act, Bargmann [8:113] found that even though the European Commission points out the aim of eGovernment to enhance democratic processes and to improve the development and implementation of government policies, this aspect has been neglected in the Austrian political debate. Most of the political parties seem to have delayed this topic to an undefined future point in time; only the Green Party criticised that the chance to include elements of participatory democracy and to develop public information has been passed up.

Contrary to these indications of a neglect of options for public engagement and barriers to its advancement, initiatives in some sections of government in Austria point towards a supportive attitude. Policy developments at European level were certainly major stimuli. In particular, the *Renewed EU Sustainable Development Strategy* stressing involvement of citizens as well as involvement of businesses and social partners as policy guiding principles, together with principles of Good Governance [25] had an influence. The linkage between sustainable development, governance and greater involvement of the civil society has been established in the Austrian Strategy for Sustainable Development of 2002 [26]. In the same year a *Strategic Group on Participation*[15] was set up on the initiative of the Ministry of the Environment and the Austrian Society for Environment and Technology (ÖGUT). The group aims at promoting awareness of participation in the public eye and among decision-makers in politics, public administration and business. It elaborates participation strategies for policies, especially those relevant to the environment and to sustainability. An important recent step was taken with a project by order of the Federal Chancellery and the Ministry of Agriculture, Forestry, Environment and Water Management: An interministerial working group in co-operation with chambers, NGOs and external experts elaborated a manual on *'Standards for Public Participation'* [26, 27]. Approved by the Council of Ministers in July 2008, it is to serve as a practical guide for public administration officials.

Also in the context of law-making at the federal parliament there are developments towards some form of eParticipation [28]. While law making has been transformed with the implementation of the eLaw workflow system[16], including the promulgation of laws on the Internet, the process of evaluating draft legislation still lacks an electronic consultation environment. Options for extending participation in the legislative process supported by electronic tools are being studied. They include the question of suitable designs for eParticipation in the legislative process, in particular on bills

---

[15] See http://www.partizipation.at/index.php?english
[16] See http://www.parlament.gv.at/SK/VLESESAAL/PUBLPD/
ERECHT/2006-04-18_Publikation-Englisch.pdf

proposed by ministries [29] and reflections on political rationales as well as functional requirements of an electronic platform for evaluating draft laws [28:49pp.].

3.2 Policies on eParticipation and eDemocracy

Specific policies addressing eParticipation in Austrian political practice are just about to be initiated. In June 2008, the *Working Group on E-Democracy and E-Participation* within the Federal Chancellery has released a position paper on "E-Democracy & E-Participation in Austria" [30] which accomplishes first clarifications on basic topics of eParticipation like different forms, potentials and questions of its institutional embedding. It provides a set of suggestions and recommendations serving as starting point for developing a national eParticipation strategy. The objective is not to install plebiscitary, direct democracy or to compete with the representative model of democracy, but to complement it and to foster civil society participation according the ideal of the "interactive state" [30: 4pp.]. The model stands for an evolutionary transformation of governance from a monolithic state to a pluralistic networking with the business sector and civil society. The future is seen as "governance webs" delivering public services and also forming political processes. Participation in the narrower sense is understood as making use of (at least) two-way communication, i.e. consultation and cooperation. Most current eParticipation initiatives[17] go beyond merely providing information and offer participation via discussion fora, weblogs, and opinion polls. Nevertheless, the projects are hardly ever connected to actual political decision-making. The position paper emphasises the necessity of multiple channels of participation [30:18]. These should also help to adjust the strong media concentration in Austria. Furthermore, e-tools are seen as complementary to formal procedures. Synergies with already existing eGovernment services shall be sought, e.g. with the Citizen Card [30:19pp.]. The *'Standards for Public Participation'* and the *'Recommendation of the Committee of Ministers to member states on electronic democracy'*[18] offer some input when elaborating an eParticipation strategy comprising principles, measures and instruments (the latter document has been produced under the Austrian chair of CAHDE, the Ad hoc Committee on eDemocracy of the Council of Europe).

National policies such as Austria's Strategy on Sustainable Development or the implementation of the EU directive on establishing a framework for Community action in the field of water policy are another field of activities where eParticipation is getting relevant. Mandatory civic participation is stipulated at various levels, including strategy, program and project levels, and invites the support by electronic means. The "Common Declaration on the Local Agenda 21 in Austria" enacted in 2003 stimulated a multitude of local and regional participatory processes aiming at sustainable development, including the use of electronic tools in various forms.

The active Government Programme for the period 2008-2013[19] contains plans for initiatives in advancing eGovernment and the chapter on state and administrative

---

[17] See table of Austrian participation projects in the Federal Chancellery's "Portal:EDEM", http://www.ag.bka.gv.at/index.php/E-Participation_Projekte
[18] See http://www.bmeia.gv.at/fileadmin/user_upload/bmeia/draft_Reco_as_adopted_08114.pdf
[19] See http://www.bka.gv.at/DocView.axd?CobId=32965

reform envisions increased citizen orientation. However, as regards the legal situation in Austria, there are no specific policies setting out citizens' rights in eParticipation.[20] Various policy measures had relevant catalyst or infrastructure functions for the implementation of eParticipation: The *E-Austria in e-Europe Programme (2002)* by the Federal Chancellery is the Austrian equivalent to the European Commission's e-Europe initiative. The *Decision on Electronic Law-Making (2001)* aimed at facilitating and accelerating Austrian law-making by implementing a completely electronic process for creating legislation. A number of initiatives have been launched earlier to foster diffusion of and equal access to ICTs, e.g. the *Information Society Action Plans* of 1997 and 1998 which started to define a legal framework for the information society and aimed at implementing new public information services. The *Information Society Programme* had addressed the topic of eDemocracy for the first time. More recent activities include the *Austrian electronic network (AT:net) initiative (2007)* supporting the introduction of innovative services and the further diffusion of broadband access, the survey on barrier-free web accessibility [21], and the *Internet Offensive*,[21] initiated by the Federal Government in 2008.

The recent government initiative "Entscheidend-bist-du" (YOU are decisive) aims at raising interest in politics and democratic involvement. Measures to increase awareness of the various electronic forms of political engagement include the support of eVoting by the science ministry. The whole initiative was launched in 2007 as an accompanying measure of the reduction of the minimum age for participation in elections to the age of 16 and lies in the hands of the Ministry of Science and Research together with the Ministry of Education and Culture.[22] One of the various types of measures within this initiative, a so called DemoLAB, has been explicitly dedicated to eDemocracy and involved the Minister of Science and Research in discussion with college students.

Finally, a very recent indication of increased attention to eParticipation in public policy concerns the awareness of information barriers mentioned earlier. Up to now there has been no overview on eParticipation offerings and citizens lack information on opportunities for engagement in matters of public interest. This barrier is supposed to be reduced as the Federal Chancellery has taken the initiative in creating an integrative portal for eParticipation offerings.

4 Conclusion

This paper aimed at assessing the status of eParticipation in Austria from a top-down perspective, focusing on the policy framework and emerging public policies on eParticipation. It intends to offer a tentative assessment of relevant developments against the background of changing forms of governance which has to be followed by further, more directed and thorough analyses.

---

[20] A number of relevant legal documents refer to eParticipation more generally, such as the *E-Government Act (2004; 2008)*, the *Electronic Signature Act (2000)*, the *Data Protection Act (2000)*, the *Information Re-Use Act (2005)* and the *Environmental Information Act (2004)*.

[21] See http://internetoffensive.at/

[22] See http://www.entscheidend-bist-du.at/?pg=content2&id=3

A major outcome is that citizen participation and eParticipation in particular have been playing a marginal role within the Austrian political system with its culture favouring governance by state and corporatist actors. But both public participation as such and participation in electronic ways seem to be gaining increased importance in public policies in more recent years. The enhancement of public participation by principles of good governance and in policy documents such as the Austrian Strategy for Sustainable Development of 2002, the establishment of a Strategic Group on Participation with support by the Ministry of the Environment, the approval of 'Standards for Public Participation' by the Council of Ministers in 2008, the preparation of a national eDemocracy strategy and a recent governmental democracy initiative aimed at young people are signs that participation plays an increasing role for government. At the same time this does not mean that eParticipation and citizen engagement are promoted throughout government as research has also shown rejection of citizen participation by politicians and public administration officials.

While Austria's political institutions have been laggards in experimenting with and adopting eParticipation, in comparison with forerunners like the USA or the UK, Italy and Germany in Europe, there are a number of recent initiatives and projects, particularly in the field of youth participation and participation in environmental issues. Institutional actors actively dealing with eParticipation and promoting it, respectively, include those responsible for eGovernment around the Federal Chancellery, the Federal Computing Centre, and ministries such as those for Agriculture and Environment, Education and Culture, Science and Research. The Working Group on E-Democracy and E-Participation at the Federal Chancellery drafting an eDemocracy strategy is a further indicator that eParticipation has become a subject of public policy in Austria. However, it has to be noted that the recent upswing of supportive initiatives for public participation and eParticipation go together with ambivalent attitudes among politicians and administration. Overall, a hesitant attitude among policy-makers towards eParticipation still prevails and indications of a gradual change towards a more "interactive governance" style are patchy rather than expressing a coherent policy change.

Given the initial state of eParticipation initiatives in Austria, a systematic evaluation of results and consequences has not yet been conducted. From available evidence only first trends and some lessons can be outlined. As our collaborative research within the EU-funded Network of Excellence DEMO-net[23] showed, some patterns are shared with other countries: Experimenting, testing and learning are still in the foreground; top-down initiated projects often have problems to attract larger numbers of participants; information dissemination and gathering, rather than deliberative forms of participation and integration into decision-making, prevail. At what pace, in which direction eParticipation will develop and which functions to which extent it will fulfil, e.g. regarding two poles such as instilling democracy through greater citizen empowerment or keeping the growing potential of elite-challenging citizen activities within the limits of representative democracy through greater acquiescence with government policies, is still open.

---

[23] See http://www.demo-net.org/

References

1. United Nations: UN E-Government Survey 2008. From E-Government to Connected Governance. United Nations, New York (2008)
2. Capgemini: The User Challenge. Benchmarking the Supply of Online Public Services, 7th Measurement (September 2007),
   http://ec.europa.eu/information_society/eeurope/i2010/docs/benchmarking/egov_benchmark_2007.pdf
3. Rupp, C.: E-Democracy in E-Austria. In: Prosser, A., Krimmer, R. (eds.) Electronic Voting in Europe. Technology, Law, Politics and Society, pp. 17–20. Köllen Druck + Verlag, Bonn (2004)
4. Aichholzer, G., Spitzenberger, M.: E-Government in Österreich: Entwicklungsstand, Nutzung und Modellprojekte, Bericht 1: Stand des Diensteangebots. In: Study report commissioned by the Federal Chancellery. Austrian Academy of Sciences, Institute of Technology Assessment, Vienna (2004)
5. Filzmaier, P.: E-democracy in Austria: Country report and analysis of legislatures' and political parties' web sites, Research report, Florence: European University Institute, EUI (2003), http://www.europarl.eu.int/stoa/publi/default_en.htm
6. Fuchs, C.: eParticipation Research: A Case Study on Political Online Debate in Austria, Research Paper No. 1, June. ICT&S Center at the University of Salzburg, Salzburg (2006)
7. Mahrer, H., Krimmer, R.: Towards the enhancement of e-democracy: identifying the notion of the 'middleman paradox'. Information Systems Journal 15(1), 27–42 (2005)
8. Bargmann, M.: Der österreichische Diskurs über E-Government: Intentionen, Argumente, Hintergründe. In: Wimmer, M.A., Traunmüller, R., Orthofer, G. (eds.) Knowledge transfer across Europe: 4th and 5th Eastern European eGov Days, pp. 106–129. OCG, Vienna (2006)
9. Arbter, K., Handler, M., Purker, E., Tappeiner, G., Trattnigg, R.: Shaping the future together. The public participation manual, Vienna (2007),
   http://www.partizipation.at/fileadmin/media_data/Downloads/Publikationen/participationmanual_en.pdf
10. Heindl, P.: Partizipation und demokratische Kontrolle: das Spannungsfeld zwischen BürgerInnenmitbestimmung und repräsentativer Demokratie – wer darf wo und wie mitgestalten? In: Graf, D., Breiner, F. (eds.) Projekt Österreich: In welcher Verfassung ist die Republik?, pp. 107–120. Czernin Verlag, Wien (2005)
11. Österreich-Konvent: Bericht des Österreich-Konvents, 31.01.2005 (2005),
    http://www.konvent.gv.at/K/DE/ENDB-K/ENDB-K_00001/pmh.shtml
12. Schaller, C.: Zur Demokratiequalität politischer Partizipation. In: Campbell, D., Schaller, C. (eds.) Demokratiequalität in Österreich. Zustand und Entwicklungsperspektiven, pp. 69–88. Leske + Budrich, Opladen (2002)
13. Plasser, F., Ulram, P.A.: Politische Involvierung und politische Unterstützung in Österreich. In: Plasser, F., Gabriel, O., Falter, J.W., Ulram, P.A. (eds.) Wahlen und politische Einstellungen in Deutschland und Österreich, pp. 241–262. Peter Lang, Frankfurt am Main (1999)
14. Ulram, P.A.: Civic Democracy. Politische Beteiligung und politische Unterstützung. In: Pelinka, A., Plasser, F., Meixner, W. (eds.) Die Zukunft der österreichischen Demokratie. Trends, Prognosen und Szenarien, Signum, Wien, pp. 103–140 (2000)
15. Walter, F., Rosenberger, S.: Skilled Voices? Reflections on Political Participation and Education in Austria, EDU Working Paper No.11 (2007),

```
http://www.sourceoecd.org/rpsv/cgibin/
wppdf?file=514cpg4s1gtg.pdf
```
16. Inglehart, R., Norris, P.: Rising Tide. In: Gender Equality and Cultural Change, Routledge, New York (2003)
17. BMGFJ – Bundesministerium für Gesundheit, Familie und Jugend, Abteilung Jugendpolitik: Jugendbeteiligung und digitale Medien: e-Partizipation in der Jugendarbeit, Wien (2008),
```
http://www.bmgfj.gv.at/cms/site/attachments/4/4/7/CH0592/CMS
1227689792579/jugendbeteiligung_und_digitale_medien.pdf
```
18. Heckl, F.: Projekt: eParticipation im Umweltbereich (ePU). Zusammenfassung und Schlussfolgerungen. Umweltbundesamt (unpublished manuscript), Wien (2008)
19. IDATE Consulting & Research: Broadband Coverage in Europe, Final Report, 2007 Survey, Data as of December 31, 2006 (2007),
```
http://ec.europa.eu/information_society/eeurope/i2010/docs/
benchmarking/broadband_coverage_10_2007.pdf
```
20. eGovernment Factsheets, eGovernment in Austria, Version 10.0 (July 2008), http://www.epractice.eu/factsheets
21. Bundeskanzleramt: Erhebung Barrierefreiheit, Endbericht – Version 1.3 (2007), http://www.digitales.oesterreich.gv.at/DocView.axd?CobId=24558
22. Prosser, A., Schiessl, K., Fleischhacker, M.: E-Voting: Usability and Acceptance of Two-Stage Voting Procedures. In: Wimmer, M.A., Scholl, J., Grönlund, Å. (eds.) EGOV 2007. LNCS, vol. 4656, pp. 378–387. Springer, Heidelberg (2007)
23. Piswanger, C.-M.: The Participatory E-Government Strategy of the Austrian Federal Computing Centre. In: Proceedings eGov-Days 2007: Best Practice and Innovation, pp. 205–210. OCG, Vienna (2007)
24. Betz, F., Bargmann, M., Lippmann, A.: How Democratic is e-government? Public Knowledge Management and Governmentality in Europe, Research report within research programme >node< – new orientations for democracy in Europe. FH-Studiengänge Burgenland, Eisenstadt (2006)
25. CoEU – Council of the European Union: Renewed EU Sustainable Development Strategy, DOC 10917/06, Brussels, June 9, 2006 (2006),
```
http://ec.europa.eu/sustainable/docs/renewed_eu_sds_en.pdf
```
26. Trattnigg, R.: Sustainable development and public participation. In: Brix, E., Nautz, J., Trattnigg, R., Wutscher, W. (eds.) State and Civil Society, pp. 197–220. Passagen Verlag, Vienna (2008)
27. Arbter, K., Trattnigg, R.: Standards zur Öffentlichkeitsbeteiligung: Auf dem Weg zu effizienter und effektiver Partizipation. In: Bauer, H., Biwald, P., Dearing, E. (eds.) Public Governance – Öffentliche Aufgaben gemeinsam erfüllen und effektiv steuern, pp. 295–307. Neuer Wissenschaftlicher Verlag, Wien/Graz (2005)
28. Schefbeck, G.: Auf dem Weg zur E-Konsultation. Zur Praxis "deliberativer Politik" in Österreich. In: Prosser, A., Parycek, P. (eds.) Elektronische Demokratie in Österreich. Proceedings der EDem 2007, September 27-28, pp. 43–59. OCG, Wien (2007)
29. Weber, B.: Elektronische Partizipation im österreichischen Bundesgesetzgebungsprozess unter besonderer Berücksichtung von E-Bürgerinitiativen und der elektronischen Abgabe von Stellungnahmen zu Ministerialentwürfen, PhD thesis. University of Graz, Graz (2008)
30. E-DEM: Positionspapier zu E-Democracy and E-Participation in Österreich, Whitepaper of the Working Group on E-Democray, v.1.0.0 (2008),
```
http://reference.e-government.gv.at/uploads/media/
EDEM-1-0-0-20080525.pdf
```

A Tale of Six Countries: eParticipation Research from an Administration and Political Perspective

Anna Carola Freschi[1], Rony Medaglia[2], and Jacob Nørbjerg[3]

[1] University of Bergamo, Via Salvecchio 19, 24129, Bergamo, Italy
anna.freschi@unibg.it
[2] Copenhagen Business School, Center for Applied ICT, Howitzvej 60, DK-2000,
Frederiksberg, Denmark
rm.caict@cbs.dk
[3] Copenhagen Business School, Department of Informatics, Howitzvej 60, DK-2000,
Frederiksberg, Denmark
jan.inf@cbs.dk

Abstract. This paper presents a cross-national analysis of eParticipation research in the administrative and political domain. It covers eParticipation research in six European countries (Austria, Denmark, France, Germany, Italy, and Sweden) focusing on several aspects of eParticipation research, including research questions, methods, disciplinary approaches, units of analysis, research findings. The paper also provides an overview of national research, and outlines overall research findings and future directions in eParticipation research.

Keywords: eParticipation; institutions; cross-national comparison.

1 Introduction

As the body of research knowledge on eParticipation keeps growing, a stronger need for outlining the current research scenario emerges. Although there are many different definitions of the concept, we will here refer to the definition of eParticipation as "the use of information and communication technologies to broaden and deepen political participation by enabling citizens to connect with one another and with their elected representatives" [1]. Given the widely acknowledged interdisciplinarity of the field, contributions in eParticipation research have increasingly included not only a multitude of disciplinary perspectives, but also different methodological approaches and normative stances [2], [3], [4]. The diversity of overall values underlying eParticipation research, the wide range of methods adopted, and the different disciplines embarking in studies related to eParticipation initiatives, all make the current eParticipation research scenario difficult to picture as a whole. In fact, the eParticipation research reflects the institutional variety of the research objects (the social and political systems) as well as the different research focuses and backgrounds. Moreover, the recent growth of studies published in different languages is largely undervalued at international level, with the effect of limiting the circulation of these research

A. Macintosh and E. Tambouris (Eds.): ePart 2009, LNCS 5694, pp. 36–45, 2009.
© Springer-Verlag Berlin Heidelberg 2009

findings. Of course an analysis of different national literatures is not sufficient to set any comparative analysis, because of the classical methodological problems of cross-national comparison. Although diverse characteristics, traditions, and even "natures" of eParticipation initiatives seem to be linked to the institutional peculiarities of each country, this approach is still rarely taken into account. A discussion of the empirical findings in different contexts can be a preliminary step towards a more solid comparative effort.

Such features of the current eParticipation research scenario – its steady growth, and its fragmentation – call for an effort to systematize the existing body of knowledge about eParticipation. A comprehensive view is needed regarding the nature of the research questions dealt with, the methods used, the scientific disciplines involved, and the units of analysis adopted.

The international research on eParticipation has been analyzed in a number of papers [2], [3], [4], but these works are mainly focused on research published in English. This paper provides a cross-national analysis of the existing research on eParticipation in the institutional domain in six European countries (Austria, Denmark, France, Germany, Italy and Sweden). Such a coverage aims at valuing a wider set of eParticipation research contributions, which otherwise would often remain hidden to the eParticipation research community.

This paper provides the main results of an extensive analysis [5] of the current body of research on eParticipation adoption and use in public institutions (assemblies, governments, administrations, political parties) within their political, organizational and institutional contexts at different territorial levels (from local to national), focusing on the effects on the decision making process and its implementation, and the participation of citizens/ groups/ associations.

A summary of the main research findings is provided on the basis of the results emerged from a review of the empirical literature about the six national cases. The main research focuses, units of analysis, methods used, main findings, and promising future research directions are identified. This analysis has resulted in a set of five overall groups of findings emerging from the national research, and four categories of future directions of research on eParticipation.

In the conclusions, these findings and future directions are summarized and discussed, and further challenges for the development of eParticipation research are outlined.

2 Method

A total of 262 research items (journal articles, books, conference papers, policy documents, etc.) were analysed by researchers of each of the six countries in the study. The sources have been selected on the basis of their methodological consistency. The review was focused on main research issues, units of analysis, methods, main findings, promising research directions.

Table 1. eParticipation research items included in the review (journal articles, books, conference papers, etc.) analysed

Country	Research items (N)
Austria	53
Denmark	10
France	67
Germany	22
Italy	61
Sweden	49
Total	262

3   Findings

The findings from the analysis [5] are summarized in table 2.

The national eParticipation research is varied in shape but quite convergent in the contents. Within the large and interesting variety of research perspectives and outputs as far as eParticipation is concerned, at this stage it is possible to highlight a number of common research focuses, trends, and results. These can be considered as the current "core" features of the overall eParticipation scenario, around which a large variety of other, "outlier" specific focuses revolve.

At a more general level of abstraction we can clearly observe that, overall, the *main research question* tackled in the national research environments concerns *understanding the changing relationships between citizens and authorities/ the political elites, brought about by on-line participation*. While such a focus encompasses a wide range of research subjects, some peculiar focuses emerge in the national analyses. Some Italian and Swedish studies underline the contrast between the rhetoric of democratic renewal and eParticipation implementation. In Germany there is a specific focus on the role of specific demographic groups, such as ethnic minorities. Finally, the Austrian research is mainly related to design issues, and the way certain designs affect eParticipation processes.

The *unit of analysis* in the national research is the most homogeneous category, as the core/main focus is on eParticipation at the local level of government.

The *research themes* vary across the national cases. Many contributions focus on the changing interactions between citizens, politicians and administration introduced by eParticipation. However, many "outliers" emerge. French and Austrian research features a focus on eVoting practices, with the former highlighting the role of eDeliberation, and the latter focusing more on eInformation. eParticipation research in Germany is greatly concerned with digital inclusion as a research subject, while Italian studies show a shift from a focus on the impact of ICT on local politics to studies on the institutional and cultural contexts affecting eParticipation and participation processes together. In Austria, on the other hand, there is a great focus on usability and legal issues raised by eParticipation adoption.

A wide variety of *methods* is adopted. A general trend of integrating qualitative and quantitative research emerges, and is linked to the scale of research, with an increasing emphasis on reconnecting analyses of the online and offline domains. The methods used in the national contexts include action research and experiments,

Table 2. Overview of eParticipation research in the institutional domain

Question	Austria	Denmark	France	Germany	Italy	Sweden
Main research focus	Options, potentials and risks in using new ICTs to enhance participation in democratic processes. Scope of inclusion and impact of eParticipation. Design issues. Evaluation issues.	Does eParticipation change/ improve citizens' interaction channels and levels of influence? What are the barriers for eParticipation?	The reshaping of traditional mediation systems and communication channels.	Scope of audience, specific user groups (e.g. youngsters, migrants). Combination of media, participation and communication about it, usage of governmental supplies, capacity building of governmental institutions regarding eParticipation. Interrelations between social context and technology in participation.	The impact of the new media on the relationships between political institutions and citizenship (individuals and organized). Relationship between political-social context and eParticipation models.	How do citizens, political parties and local government use the Internet?
Units of analysis (institutional level)	Political elites, grassroot movements, local communities. EU level.	Mainly local (municipal) level.	Political parties and all institutional levels. Local government-led initiatives dominate.	Mainly local (municipal) level. National level for state of the art, and user view	Civic networks, political parties, participation in public policies and practices.	Citizens, local government, political parties, and representatives.
Methods	N/A	Evaluation of eParticipation initiatives. Experiments.	Evaluation. Experiments with technology and	Case studies. Analysis of online communication	Case studies. Analysis of on-line communication	Exploratory and descriptive. Interviews, on-line

Table 2. (*continued*)

Question	Austria	Denmark	France	Germany	Italy	Sweden
		Empirical studies (content analysis, discourse analysis).	content delivery (process analysis, content analysis; logfile analysis, usability tests). Action research (online) surveys, (expert) interviews.	(websites, mailing lists and forums). Focus groups, interviews. Ethnography. Surveys.	(websites, mailing lists and forums). Focus groups, interviews. Ethnography. Surveys.	surveys, content and discourse analysis
Main findings	eParticipation potential is not exploited. Legal and institutional barriers. Politicians are reluctant towards increased civic engagement. Existing participation patterns are reinforced. Recently, new impulses for public participation and eParticipation .	No significant change in citizens' involvement and influence. The new media supplement existing means of interaction and influence.	Local level: Internet used for information provisioning and services. Interactive potential not realized. Politicians hesitant towards new communication channels and increased citizen involvement. Socio-cultural resistance to eVoting. The new media supplements existing channels.	Different means of communication and media supplement each other (if considered in planning). Socio-cultural context influences participation in the democratic process. eParticipation often strengthens exclusion (gaps regarding gender, education, status).	eParticipation failures in promoting new participation. Political inclusion/exclusion. Trend to de-politicization in government-driven eParticipation. Active citizens develop their own fora. Initiatives by political parties lack attention to deliberation.	Citizens' eParticipation is still limited. Off-line patterns are repeated on-line. Parties use the Internet as a campaign tool but do not engage with citizens in on-line debate. Local governments provide information and receive questions and comments. Cost, size, and technological determinants impact local govt. web-adoption.

Table 2. (*continued*)

Question	Austria	Denmark	France	Germany	Italy	Sweden
Promising directions	Lack of theoretical grounding and empirical analysis of eParticipation projects. Need for systematic analysis of wider impacts. Need of conceptual developments.	Research focus on government-initiated eParticipation. Need to focus on bottom-up citizen-initiated eParticipation initiatives.	The research is mainly based in the social sciences. Need for interdisciplinary research and industry-academia collaboration. Need to involve stakeholders (citizens) in research.	Double role of researchers: initiators *and* evaluators of eParticipation initiatives. Need for more transdisciplinary research. There are enough case studies, it is now time for general implementation.	Contextualization within the wider processes of transformation of democratic governance.	Few empirical studies. Need for more empirical research, contextual studies *and* better theoretical models. Focus on the role of the citizen. Need to move towards other institutional levels. Need of more comparative studies.

reviews, focus groups, ethnographies, web statistics and content analysis. Evaluation studies, independent or as part of an experiment, are quite common across all national research environments, together with the use of content and discourse analysis. The latter seems to be preferred in studies focusing on deliberation practices within eParticipation, as in France, Italy, and Austria.

Summarizing the findings from the national reviews, it can be observed that the current panorama of eParticipation research, however varied, is often fragmented and heterogeneous in nature. However, it suggests some core conclusions regarding eParticipation, that can be synthesized as follows:

- *eParticipation must be analyzed in the context of other forms of participation.* A shared assumption resulting from empirical research investigation in the different national scenarios regards the interaction between the new channels related to eParticipation activities and the traditional forms of participation. A common conclusion reached by a large share of the research contributions is that eParticipation is to be analyzed in the context of such other forms of participation, to be either considered as background, independent and/ or dependent variables of the processes included in eParticipation initiatives.
- *New media supplement traditional forms of participation.* A large number of research contributions from the different national cases reach the conclusion that new, eParticipation-based platforms prove to be complementary of traditional participation channels, rather than to replace them.
- *New media often reinforce existing off-line patterns of participation, rather than changing them.* When implemented and successfully operating, eParticipation processes seem to follow the path of processes occurring in traditional, off-line participation processes, as research has known them so far. Together with being complementary to the traditional channels of participation, eParticipation initiatives, especially those promoted by public institutions, seem to follow patterns that are are largely overlapping with those found in traditional means of participation. These patterns include the way and the extent of the influence on the decision-making processes and the actor composition of participatory groups.
- *Information dissemination and gathering, rather than deliberation and debate, dominate digital platforms initiated by parties and institutions.* eParticipation initiatives promoted by institutional actors and political parties tend to focus on information-oriented implementation of eParticipation platforms, rather than on platforms enabling deliberation and debate. This is widely reflected, for instance, in the cross-country research contributions on the adoption of eParticipation features in institutional websites. Basically all analyses focusing on web adoption of participatory devices, especially at the local level of government, bring evidence of a common neglect of deliberation-enabling features in on-line platforms, to the advantage of information-based implementations.
- *Politicians are generally reluctant to embrace new possibilities enabled by eParticipation.* Closely related to the above mentioned phenomenon, there is evidence of poor support of advanced eParticipation adoption by politicians across different countries. Many research contributions highlight the fact that behind a slow, or absent take-up of participatory features through digital means, there is an underlying reluctance of political decision-makers to engage in such activities and to support

them. Evidence of such a weak support is distributed across a wide variety of national research scenarios, at institutional and administrative level.

The review of national eParticipation research benefits from both mapping the research areas which are still currently overlooked in the different national eParticipation research contexts, and from suggesting a sketch for a new, European-wide agenda for the future of eParticipation research.

The main future directions in the research in eParticipation emerging from the international and cross-national analysis can be summarized as follows.

Conceptual development. As this review is mainly focused on empirical research, it is hard to reach solid conclusions about the conceptual backstage. The fragmentation of the empirical research does not support solid and coherent theory development. Non-coordinated methodologies or case studies, for example, make comparisons between data and findings difficult. Small-sized studies can propose exploratory hypotheses, but there is a need for wider studies to test theories. The development of theory can derive only from more coordinated efforts in empirical research, especially in a new research field such as eParticipation, also because of the complexity of eParticipation as a research object.

Empirical studies. Wider cross-national studies are needed in order to recombine the fragmentation of the empirical studies. In fact, in this field of research, the problem is not the lack of empirical studies but their narrow scale and ambition. The comparison of the national reviews still highlights the insufficient number of empirically-based, rigorous research contributions. The growing number of eParticipation initiatives in different countries should be an opportunity for wider, deeper and cross-country empirical studies, as well as for the development of a specific European level of eParticipation research. It is worthy of attention that bigger and more ambitious studies also imply a better coordination of ongoing work and resources.

Focus on relevant institutional levels of eParticipation other than the local one. The dominating focus on the local level of government reveals a gap as far as all other levels of government are concerned. Due to the widespread development of local eParticipation projects, the national and especially supranational levels (EU) of government are currently under-investigated, despite the importance of fostering citizen participation that characterizes the higher levels of government as such. Initiatives regarding, for instance, the use of ICT to foster citizen participation as a reaction to the so-called EU "democratic deficit" are worth a closer attention by the eParticipation research community.

Transdisciplinary research. Lastly, the review of national eParticipation research brings evidence of a situation of relatively isolated disciplinary approaches, with little cross-fertilization between them. eParticipation is studied from the perspective either of social sciences, including sociology, political science, policy analysis, etc., or of information systems – besides the more technical approaches. The different disciplines seem not to interfere with each other, and approaches that combine two or more disciplinary perspectives are still rare. Such a gap is even more challenging when considering the inherent degree of transdisciplinarity that characterizes eParticipation as such: a field that embraces a wide array of key processes related to technical infrastructures, with so many social, political and cultural implications.

4 Conclusion

This paper provides the main results of an extensive analysis of the current state of eParticipation research in six European countries (Austria, Denmark, France, Germany, Italy, Sweden). The main research questions addressed in the literature of each country are included, and the shared characteristics and differences between them regarding the main research questions, the units of analysis, the research subjects, the methods used, the results and the future directions are discussed. As a result of this analysis of the national scenarios, a common set of research findings and future directions of research are identified. The main research findings emerging are the following:

- eParticipation must be analyzed in the context of other forms of participation;
- New media supplement traditional forms of participation;
- New media often reinforce existing off-line patterns of participation, rather than changing them;
- Information dissemination and gathering, rather than deliberation and debate, dominate digital platforms initiated by parties and institutions;
- Politicians are generally reluctant to embrace new possibilities enabled by eParticipation.

A comprehensive analysis of the six national cases has also identified the following gaps in eParticipation research:

- Conceptual development;
- Wider cross-national empirical research;
- Focus on the emerging institutional levels (European, national, regional) other than the local one.

At a more scholarly level, a challenge to be faced in the near future of eParticipation research concerns breaking the boundaries between disciplines in approaching the analysis of eParticipation processes. Given that eParticipation as such is a complex social, technical, political and also economic and management process, the research community will have to move away from a relatively persistent division between different disciplinary approaches to the mushrooming number of eParticipation processes in Europe. This also brings us to a further need identified in the analysis: the development of more solid conceptual frames. The refinement of new tools of analysis, and of new research methods to be used for investigating eParticipation needs in fact to stem directly from the interaction between disciplines, including sociology, political sciences, law, information systems, psychology and other social sciences. Moreover, the need for transdisciplinary research underlines the practical necessity of further networking between researchers at the European level.

Building a relevant body of knowledge around eParticipation, although still somehow fragmented and with room for improvement regarding shared concepts and research tools, has been basically accomplished so far. The next challenge to be faced in the near future is to provide durable integration among different research communities in order to make this body of knowledge further flourish and cross-fertilize.

While the top-down and public institutions focus in eParticipation is still important, because it expresses the commitment of institutional decision-makers, citizen-initiated processes are becoming increasingly relevant in understanding what is going on in the "real world" of ICT-enabled new forms of democratic participation. At the level of promising research themes in the forthcoming eParticipation agenda, we have to highlight the fundamental importance of bottom-up, citizen-initiated eParticipation processes. The emergence of the Web 2.0 philosophy, the diffusion of social networking services and of entirely new platforms based on user-created content cannot be overlooked anymore as far as eParticipation research is concerned. Web 2.0 environments, such as YouTube, Wikipedia, Facebook, citizen blogging, etc., constitute now the new frontier of citizen interaction in the online world. We need to shift our focus from the top-down, institution-initiated eParticipation platforms, to the bottom-up, citizen-initiated ones, which are playing an increasingly relevant role in shaping the way citizens interact with decision-makers and the institutions. The new agenda of eParticipation research will have to include this focus shift in the immediate future.

Acknowledgments. This paper is based on the booklet "Analytical report on eParticipation research from an administration and political perspective. A review on research about eParticipation in the institutional domain", project deliverable 14.1 of the European eParticipation Network of Excellence DEMO_net (FP6-2004-27219). The booklet is authored by Georg Aichholzer, Doris Allhutter, Florian Saurwein (Austrian Academy of Science); Joachim Åström (Örebro University); Michela Balocchi, Anna Carola Freschi, Luca Raffini, Giovanna Tizzi (University of Bergamo); Rony Medaglia, Jacob Nørbjerg, Christine Secher (Copenhagen Business School); Thierry Vedel (Foundation National des Sciences Politiques); Hilmar Westholm (Institut für Informationsmanagment Bremen).

References

1. Macintosh, A.: eParticipation in Policy-making: the research and the challenges. In: Cunningham, P., Cunningham, M. (eds.) Exploiting the Knowledge Economy: Issues, Applications and Case Studies, p. 1. IOS press, Amsterdam (2006)
2. Medaglia, R.: The challenged identity of a field: The state of the art of eParticipation research. Information Polity: The International Journal of Government & Democracy in the Information Age 12(3), 169–181 (2007)
3. Rose, J., Sanford, C.: Mapping eParticipation Research: Four Central Challenges. The Communications of the Association for Information Systems 20(55), 909–943 (2007)
4. Sæbø, Ø., Rose, J., Skiftenes Flak, L.: The shape of eParticipation: Characterizing an emerging research area. Government Information Quarterly 25(3), 400–428 (2008)
5. Aichholzer, G., Allhutter, D., Åström, J., Balocchi, M., Freschi, A.C., Medaglia, R., Nørbjerg, J., Raffini, L., Saurwein, F., Secher, C., Tizzi, G., Vedel, T., Westholm, H.: Analytical report on eParticipation research from an administration and political perspective: A review on research about eParticipation in the institutional domain, DEMO_net Deliverable 14.1, IST Network of Excellence Project FP6-2004-IST-4-027219 (2009)

The Role of Social Networking Services in eParticipation

Øystein Sæbø[1], Jeremy Rose[2], and Tom Nyvang[3]

[1] University of Agder, Gimlemoen, 4604 Kristiansand, Norway
Oystein.sabo@uia.no
[2] Aalborg University, Selma Lagerlöfs Vej 300, 9220 Aalborg, Denmark
jeremy@cs.aau.dk
[3] Aalborg University, Selma Kroghstræde 1, 9220 Aalborg, Denmark
nyvang@hum.aau.dk

Abstract. A serious problem in eParticipation projects is citizen engagement – citizens do not necessarily become more willing to participate simply because net-services are provided for them. Most forms of eParticipation in democratic contexts are, however, dependent on citizen engagement, interaction and social networking because democratic systems favour the interests of larger groups of citizens – the more voices behind a political proposition, the greater its chances of success. In this context of challenges the study of social networking on the internet and social network theory offers valuable insights into the practices and theories of citizen engagement. Social network theory focuses on the chains of relationships that social actors communicate and act within. Some social networking services on the internet attract large numbers of users, and apparently sustain a great deal of interaction, content-generation and the development of loosely-coupled communities. They provide the forum for much discussion and interaction. In this respect social networking could contribute to solve some of the problems of engaging their users that eParticipation services often struggle with. This paper investigates the potential of Social Networking Services for the eParticipation area by defining social networking services, introducing the driving forces behind their advance, and discusses the potential use of social networking software in the eParticipation context.

Keywords: eParticipation, Social networking services.

1 Introduction

This paper focuses on social networking services (SNS) such as Facebook and MySpace in the eParticipation context. There are several reasons for SNS should be investigated and discussed. Many eParticipation projects are initiated to increase citizens' (particularly young citizens') participation in politics, but few are successful [1]. Citizens on their part also express interest in participation. They value being able to communicate opinions efficiently and having their opinions matter [2]. One reason for the failure of eParticipation projects is lack of involvement of citizens in developing and designing services [3]. SNS, in contrast, attract large numbers of users, and apparently sustain a great deal of interaction. Here users are no longer passive receivers

A. Macintosh and E. Tambouris (Eds.): ePart 2009, LNCS 5694, pp. 46–55, 2009.
© Springer-Verlag Berlin Heidelberg 2009

of predefined content. The development and design of these services are highly dependent on active participation. In this respect social networking could contribute to solve some of the problems of engaging citizens that eParticipation services often struggle with.

SNS are beginning to be used in an eParticipation context and by political stakeholders. EParticipation through SNS has not solved the democratic challenges posed by lack of participation. In order to understand the potential of SNS, it is necessary to look beyond *government-driven supplier oriented initiatives* - the major researcher focus in the existing literature [4, 5]. Here the object of study is a project or a policy which is (usually) sponsored by politicians and implemented by government institutions. Of course many other actors may be involved, such as software suppliers, researchers and citizen groups. However, government remains the driving force and normally provides the funding. Many research projects are sponsored and paid for by governments, and have to meet objectives which suit the purposes of politicians and administrators. Thus it is easy to develop the understanding (through reading this literature) that eParticipation is the responsibility of government and is also primarily enacted by government.

This understanding stands in rather sharp contrast to understandings developed through the study of related literatures. In the fields of technology innovation and technology and society, for instance, technology development and adoption is not primarily regarded as government-driven (though of course governments have a role to play). The wider interests of commerce and consumers (citizens) are also primary drivers of technology change. In modern social theory such as Castells' account of the network society [6], governments are regarded as a structure of society, where social movements made up of citizens and enabled by network technologies (such as the internet) provide the driving force for change. According to this perspective, much of the technological support associated with eParticipation (internet, blogs, virtual communities, discussion forums, wiki's, decision support, and podcasts) is developed in response to societal demand, rather than promoted by governments.

Inspection of the internet (in as far as this is possible) shows extremely widespread spontaneous political activity. Citizen blogging is a dominating form of political expression in highly developed European countries, far outstripping government-inspired political discussion forums in scope, use and dimension. SNS contribute to this trend since citizens are active participators in all aspect of developing the networks, the content as well as (in some respects) the design of the services.

A perfectly legitimate object of research study is therefore citizen-driven eParticipation. Here the focus is on citizens' demand for political expression and participation, rather than the comparatively unimaginative services which governments supply. Widely-used technologies are high-jacked as political campaigning and influence tools, as subversion instruments, and for the promotion of the alternative ideals of sub-cultures. If governments are to provide effective eParticipation services in the future, then they will probably do it at the insistence of their citizens, using the tools and technologies that citizens have decided are appropriate and effective. Thus the extremely popular SNS are an important topic for eParticipation researchers.

This paper is organised as follows. The next chapter introduces the eParticipation area. Then we briefly describe social networking before we introduce driving forces and major characteristics of SNS and discuss how these could be used in the eParticipation area. We conclude by discussing future use of social networking software in the eParticipation area, seen from both citizens' and governments' perspectives.

2 eParticipation

The importance of arenas for a free democratic debate, where citizens and other stakeholders can meet and discuss political issues freely, has been emphasized by democratic theorists from Aristotle, via Rosseau [7], to Habermas [8]. Discussion concerning how communication technology could (or could not) be utilised is not new; Dewey cautioned that communication technologies could by no means replace face-to-face interaction for collective learning, education, problem solving and moral development [7] as early as 1927.

In the early days of the internet, this rather pessimistic view of ICT's value in supporting social network found support. The pessimism was, however, grounded in knowledge about traditional media like TV, radio, mail and newspapers and their inability to support social networks due to limited interaction and a high degree of central control open to abuse or manipulation by the elite [7]. Another critique argues that a genuine social and mutually engaging interaction can only take place in a face-to-face setting, because real interaction is based in a bodily presence [9].

Despite these scepticisms, the term eParticipation appears early this century, drawing on general development in computer supported cooperative work and groupware technologies, the drive towards ICT supported interaction between governments and citizens, and the general development in eGovernment towards more complex services [1]. eParticipation involves the extension and transformation of participation in societal democratic and consultative processes mediated by information and communication technologies [1], and the focus on eParticipation responds to a perceived decline in political engagement, a disconnection between citizens and their elected representatives, and a consequent decline in the legitimacy of political institutions [1].

EParticipation aims to increase the availability to participate in order to promote fair and efficient society and government support, by using the latest technology developments. Many forms of ICT with the potential to support participation are readily available (or in development). Examples include chat technologies, discussion forums, electronic voting systems, group decision support systems, and Web logs (blogs).

3 Social Networking in the eParticipation Area

Most forms of eParticipation in democratic contexts are dependent on social networking. This is because democratic systems favour the interests of larger groups of citizens – the more voices behind a political proposition, the greater its chances of success. Most political work involves mobilization of interests, community backing, deliberative discussion and other forms of activity enabled by social networks. An eParticipation site provides a mechanism for a network of interested parties to come together.

Though no comprehensive evaluation of eParticipation projects exists, it is clear that many initiatives are rather unsuccessful [1]. Though the technology platform appears deceptively simple and cheap to implement, many efforts fail to attract widespread interest amongst citizens or politicians, are unrepresentative [10], lead to poor information [11] or poor quality of debate [12], or are monopolised by a few vocal contributors. A serious problem with these forms of eParticipation is citizen engagement – citizens do not necessarily become more willing to participate simply because net-services are provided for them.

In this context the study of social networking on the Internet becomes interesting for eParticipation researchers. Some social networking services attract large numbers of users, and apparently sustain a great deal of interaction, content-generation and the development of loosely coupled communities. They provide the forum for much discussion and interaction – though not primarily the serious political deliberation and discourse targeted by eParticipation services. In this respect they seem to solve some of the problems of engaging their users that eParticipation services often struggle with.

3.1 Social Networking

Social networks and networking in different forms and shapes are not new inventions strictly related to SNS and Web 2.0. Comte, often regarded the founder of modern sociology, was among the first researchers to focus on the societal impact of social relations between individuals [13]. He did so in the first half of the 19th century, however sociologists following just after Comte, e.g. Simmel and Durkheim, are much more influential today. Simmel and Durkheim made substantial contributions to sociology by theorising about the relation between the individual and the structures of society. Among other issues Simmel focused on the interaction between individuals and the growing interdependency between individuals in modern society. According to Simmel this means that modern society to a much higher degree than the traditional society depends on honesty and trust between individuals [13]. Durkheim on his part wondered how modern societies survive when ethnicity and religion no longer are the common structures that hold a society together. His answer was that the glue is solidarity and he identifies two major kinds of solidarity: *mechanical* and *organical* solidarity. *Mechanical* solidarity is characterized by individuals that are all generalists and little division of labour, whereas *organical* solidarity is characterized by a high degree of specialization and division of labour. According to Durkheim it is the organical solidarity that holds modern societies together by increasing the interdependency between individuals [13]. Even though Simmel and Durkheim disagreed on many issues they supplement each other when it comes to understanding social networking today; by specializing and networking with others specialists we can accomplish more than we can on our own, but to hold the network together thrust and honesty between the members of the network (or society) are crucial.

After Simmel and Durkheim sociology has developed in many different directions. Over the past 50-70 years there has been an increasing interest in the role of communication and symbols in the social construction of reality when in comes to understanding relations between individuals and society in general (see for example Habermas [14], Giddens [15] and Luhmann [16]). Another important development is the one that focus specifically on social networks. The term social network has been used systematically since 1950s to denote patterns of connections in societies. Social network theory focuses on the chains of relationships that social actors communicate and act within. These relationships can be described in terms of nodes and ties - where nodes are the individual actors within the social networks, and ties are the relationships between the actors. Social network theory differs from some traditional sociological studies which take as their starting points the attributes and actions of individual actors. Social network theory produces an alternate view, where individuals are less important than their relationships, and their ties with other individuals.

Particularly interesting for participation studies are the role of social networks in producing social capital. According to Bourdieu and Wacquant social capital is "the sum of the resources, actual or virtual, that accrue to an individual or a group by virtue of possessing a durable network of more or less institutionalized relationships of mutual acquaintance and recognition" [17,p 119]. Following this definition it is reasonable to regard social networks and SNS a driver for development of social capital. It is however still a complex process of distributing information and negotiating knowledge and opinions in the network – once again development of trust in the network is important for the network to be valuable and thus give the individual social capital. When the network holds a significant amount of social capital it has a role in the formation of public opinion. Social networks with high social capital thus influence collective action, voting choices, and other aspects of political participation. Castells [6, 13] used the concept of network to capture both social relationships and the infrastructure of the emerging internet. His thesis was that society is altered by the emergence of the internet – in which commerce, governance, work, identity, change through social movements, gender and politics are partially transformed In this sociological account, the prime characteristic of modern society is social network, which are enabled by the technological network (the Internet).

The characteristics of participation may therefore also be altered by the emergence of the internet. Trust and ability to negotiate meaning among the members of the network does however still seem to be of importance when comes to judge the strength and impact of the network.

3.2 Driving Forces of SNS

SNS provide ways for people to locate each other, to provide information about themselves (and various other forms of content), to interact in various ways for various (often un-specified) purposes, to overcome networking barriers such as geography, different time zones and language, and to maintain contact over time. SNS has to some degrees, altered the role of users from more or less passive consumers of static websites, to "prosumers" (both consumer and producers) of dynamic online web-platforms [14, 15]. Social network services are not only (or primarily) a technological development, but should also be understood as a social evolution. They are characterised by the principles of free access to information, self-organisation, mass collaboration, non-exclusive services, and user participation – also reflected by other movements such as open source development.

The rapid growth of SNS is driven by technical, social, economic and institutional forces. The rapid uptake of broadband technologies is a major *technological driver*, which enable users to download, create and post online content. Earlier limitations in access restricted content creation to text and low quality graphics. Thus the uptake of broadband technologies is a prerequisite for the development and use of SNS allowing creation, uploading and downloading of larger media files. Hardware and software necessary to support SNS are widely available. Hardware such as storage devices and cameras, are getting cheaper and with improved quality. Software tools are more available, with a rapid growth in free (mainly open) software that allow users to find, edit and create media files without specialist knowledge [14].

The major *social driver* is the changed media consumption habits of Internet users, especially among young users. So far youngsters are core producers of online content [14]. These young people will soon grow up and can potentially change how the Internet is used in the education sector, professional life as well as the political sphere. Changes in cultural attitudes, like increased individualism, and in social and political values (e.g. privacy, or aspiration to more participative forms of governance) could also influence on the use of these Networking software.

Institutional drivers include new legal means to create and distribute content, and the rise of copyright licensing agreements to support distribution of user generated contents. Moreover, widespread distribution of online content are getting cheaper, and network effects, where the value of the service increases for every new user, are economic drivers for the development of social network services.

3.3 Characteristics of SNS

Social networking services can take different forms, but they share certain primary characteristics. Drawing on both analyses, theoretical and empirical, Medaglia et al [16] identify six characteristics of social networking services:

- *Digital Persona/Virtual Identity.* Social networking software facilitates the development of an on-line persona. A persona is, in this case, an image or representation of the user. The persona is controlled and developed by the user themselves (though the structure for that representation is given by the features of the software). The persona is always a projected image of the user and it may have more or less correspondence with the user's real identity (as they themselves understand it or as understood by other people). Digital identity presupposes a digital public or audience – a profile is first meaningful when experienced by another user.
- *Network Building.* The software offers tools and opportunities for building the social network(s) of the user. It facilitates searching for other users, recruiting tools for members of the user's off-line network, meeting or being introduced to other users, and grouping of users around themes and interests. Users build interlocking networks of friends, colleagues, work acquaintances, contacts with shared interests, family and so on. On-line networks can be independent, but they often overlap and interact considerably with users' off-line networks. The service is dependent upon achieving a critical mass – sufficient users to make it feasible to build up a meaningful network.
- *Network Maintenance.* The software provides features for persistence, such that the user's network can reach over time, and survive changes to their or other

users' persona. The software maintains the coupling between networked users ir-respective of other changes in their real or on-line circumstances.

- *Network Interaction.* The software provides ways for users to interact, through direct communication, shared activities, games, or exchange of virtual objects. The virtual environment minimises some difficulties connected with physical in-teraction, such as geographical or time separation, or mobility.
- *User Generation of Virtual Content.* Not only are users responsible for control-ling their own digital personas, but they have the opportunity to provide virtual content and digital objects. These can include text, pictures or video, music clips, three dimensional virtual objects, or programs or applications. This content is important both for the virtual identity of the user, but is also exchanged as a pri-mary component of network interaction.
- *Network Self-Governance.* The network displays observable social norms, social conventions, informal codes of behaviour, and (sometimes) formal rules and regulations. Governance structures are partly enforced by the service providers, partly written into the way the software functions (what is enabled or disal-lowed), but primarily reproduced by the on-line communications, actions and be-haviours of the network members.

4   Features of Citizen-Driven Use of SNS and Further Research

The networking features of social network building tools make them good candidates for use in the eParticipation area. Societal democratic and consultative processes involve developing networks with other stakeholders, and communicating, sharing interests and entering into alliances with others. Groups like the ICT4Democracy [17] and Citizens Empowerment Symposium 08 [16] are discussing issues directly related to the eParticipation area. There are some features of citizen-driven social networking which are relevant to eParticipation and are already becoming evident:

- *Social movements facilitated by networking software.* Social networking on the net facilitates social movements and political mobilisation. It has the potential ability to enable networks and networkers beyond geographical boundaries and language limitations – the globalisation of protest [18]. Location-based services help in finding like-minded individuals, whereas other social networking tools facilitate dialogue and the co-ordination of political action. It is not known whether these developments can alter the balance of power between actors in established political systems and the various interest groups in society.
- *The hyper-complex network.* Networking on the internet may alter the structure of social networking towards large constellations of many dense networks with many nodes made up of predominantly weak ties [19]. This tendency may be ex-tended by convergence of the technologies and the development of aggregators – software linking user-generated content for the various proprietary tools.
- *Community development.* "ICTs facilitate community participation and collective action (a) by creating large, dense networks of relatively weak social ties and (b) through the use of ICTs as an organizing tool" [19]. They do this by providing networking infrastructure, but also by supporting 'communicative mobility' - the

intellectual movement of people towards common understandings of a shared situation[20].

- *Viral dissemination of ideas and issues.* Large dense social networks allow the viral spreading of ideas or issues without large push investment – each networker sends them on. The many nodes and overlapping networks mean that an issue can be rapidly distributed - enabling unpredictable exponentially-exploding concentrations of ideas forcing attention from the media and action from decision-makers. Internet-enabled social networks can thus play a role in political agenda-setting.

- *Erosion of distinctions between real and virtual identity.* In principal, every social networker on the net can be identified - at least the contribution they make can be traced back to the computer it was made on. In practice social networkers can project their real life identity onto the net, or choose to be different (often protected by anonymity). Thus a conservative businessman (in real life) can be an anonymous animal rights activist practising civil disobedience (hacking) on the net. This extension of virtual identity and the eroding of boundaries between net life, virtual world life and real life raise issues for eParticipation where the evaluation of the participation is always tempered by an understanding of the participator's identity.

- *Participation in internal governance.* Social networking providers offer slim governance – usually confined to preventing overt and extreme anti-social behaviour. This means that much of the site governance is performed participatively by its members. An example is reputation management [21] –where networkers rate other networkers by the quality of their contributions or the nature of their networking ties (how many friends and who they are).

- *Extensions of commerce and government through social networking.* The principle form of networking at many networking sites is peer-to-peer network – networking between like-minded individuals. However individuals can also stand as representatives for the organisations they work for. Businesses, communities and interest groups are heavily represented in many forms of internet social networking. The virtual governmental presence is slower to emerge, but is clearly on the way. All social networking sites can potentially be used for networking between government institutions and businesses, interest groups and citizens.

4.1 Further Research Directions – SNS and eParticipation

Comparison of the existing research literature on citizen-driven SNS and eParticipation themes allows us to formulate some further research directions.

- *Cross cultural and national variations in using SNS for eParticipation.* The democratic context influence the use and influence of eParticipation projects [22]. The opportunity to add user-generated content and enforce some self-governance allow to adaptation of SNS to various eParticipation context. Research is needed to further understand how to adapt SNS to fit various purposes and democratic contexts.

- *The emergence of trans-national activism.* eParticipation strategies are mainly developed nationally, often focusing on a local municipality level [1].

Citizen-driven eParticipation projects, based on the use of SNS, are often focusing on specific issues or interests, independently of borderlines or government structures. More research is needed to explore how these citizen-oriented services, independent on traditional way of organizing politics and government, could be designed and managed to attract stakeholders and gain democratic influence.

- *Digital divide in the use of SNS for eParticipation.* Current growths in the use of SNS for eParticipation purposes increase the importance of conducting research on digital divide issues. SNS are by nature ICT-based, without any obvious offline counterparts, excluding the non-Internet users. On the other hand, more and more participators are attracted by SNS, expanding the potential to attract citizens by SNS-based eParticipation services. Research is needed to increase our knowledge on how to tackle the digital divide issues.

- *Social roles and interactions in internet-mediated eParticipation.* SNS are developed mainly to support activities initiated by members and networks. The software act as supplier of terms, by the restrictions made, whereas the networks define social roles and interactions. Government initiated eParticipation services are often grounded on an idea of control and moderation from the government itself, quite contradictory to the SNS' premises. Research is needed to explore the (potential) contradiction between the nature of SNS and the nature of government-initiated eParticipation services.

5 Conclusion

In this paper we introduced two forms of eParticipation – that driven primarily by governments and that driven primarily by citizens. We explored the close relationship between eParticipation and social networking, and described the emergence of modern internet-based social networking services which are used for various kinds of participation. Though already widely used by citizens for political participation, these tools have yet to be adopted by governments. We are therefore able to suggest both future research directions for the eParticipation research area related to SNS, and some SNS features governments can use to foster eParticipation amongst their citizens.

References

1. Sæbø, Ø., Rose, J., Flak, L.S.: The shape of eParticipation: Characterizing an emerging research area. Government Information Quarterly 25, 400–428 (2008)
2. Kolsaker, A., Lee-Kelley, L.: Citizens' attitudes towards e-government and e-governance: a UK study. International Journal of Public Sector Management 21(7), 723–738 (2008)
3. Macintosh, A., et al.: Electronic Democracy and Young People. Social Science Computer Review 21(1), 43–54 (2003)
4. Helbig, N., Ramón Gil-García, J., Ferro, E.: Understanding the complexity of electronic government: Implications from the digital divide literature. Government Information Quarterly 26(1), 89–97 (2009)

5. Yildiz, M.: E-government research: Reviewing the literature, limitations, and ways forward. Government Information Quarterly 24(3), 646–665 (2007)
6. Castells, M.: The Rise of the Network Society. In: The Information Age - Economy, Society and Culture, vol. 1. Blackwell, Oxford (1996)
7. Day, C.L.: Grassroots involvement in interest group decision making. American Politics Quarterly 27(2), 216–235 (1999)
8. Habermas, J.: Between facts and norms: contributions to a discourse theory of law and democracy. In: Studies in contemporary German social thought, vol. XLIII, p. 631. MIT Press, Cambridge (1996)
9. Dreyfus, H.: On the Internet: Thinking in Action, p. 136. Routledge Press, New York (2001)
10. Dahlberg, L.: The Internet and Democratic Discourse: Exploring The Prospects of Online Deliberative Forums Extending the Public Sphere. Information, Communication & Society 4(4), 615–633 (2001)
11. Koch, A.: Cyber Citizen or Cyborg Citizen: Baudrillard, Political Agency, and the Commons in Virtual Politics. Journal of Mass Media Ethics 20(2/3), 159–175 (2005)
12. Hagemann, C.: Participation in and contents of two Dutch political party discussion lists on the Internet. Javnost-The Public 9(2), 61–76 (2002)
13. Castells, M.: The Internet Galaxy - Reflections on the Internet, Business and Society. Oxford University Press, Oxford (2001)
14. OECD, Participative Web and User-Created Content: Web 2.0, Wikis and Social Networking. OECD, p. 124 (2007)
15. Tapscott, D., Williams, A.D.: Wikinomics how mass collaboration changes everything, p. 324. Portfolio, New York (2006)
16. Medaglia, R., et al.: Characteristics of Social Networking Services. Forthcoming
17. ICT4 Democracy on Facebook (2007),
    http://www.facebook.com/group.php?gid=6299328523
    (cited 2007 10.11)
18. Juris, J.S.: The new digital media and activist networking within anti-corporate globalization movements. Annals of the American Academy of Political and Social Science 597, 189–208 (2005)
19. Hampton, K.N.: Grieving for a lost network: Collective action in a wired suburb. Information Society 19(5), 417–428 (2003)
20. Longan, M.W.: Visions of community and mobility: the community networking movement in the USA. Social & Cultural Geography 6(6), 849–864 (2005)
21. Parameswaran, M., Whinston, A.B.: Social Computing: an Overview. Communications of the AIS 19, 762–780 (2007)
22. Päivärinta, T., Sæbø, Ø.: Models of E-Democracy. Communications of the Association for Information Systems 17, 818–840 (2006)

eParticipation for Political Education:
Challenges and Opportunities

Ursula Maier-Rabler and Christina Neumayer

ICT&S Center, University of Salzburg
Sigmund-Haffner-Gasse 18, 5020 Salzburg, Austria
{ursula.maier-rabler,christina.neumayer2}@sbg.ac.at

Abstract. This paper argues, that the incorporation of eParticipation into political education at schools will broaden the chances of young people for political
and societal engagement and strengthen civil society of a country or state. Frustration with traditional party politics especially of the younger generation is increasing in contemporary society. Since the voting age in Austria was lowered
to 16, new ways of learning for political education by utilizing information and
communication technologies (ICTs) that have the potential to increase participation of young people are considered. However, Austrian young people are not
yet educated in developing and expressing political perspectives and therefore
not prepared for actively taking part in politics. Exemplified on the project Pol-
ipedia.at, a collaborative online textbook on political education, this paper aims
to give recommendations from a social science perspective for integration of
ICTs into political education in order to enhance political participation of youth.

Keywords: Information and Communication Technologies (ICTs), School,
New Media, Political Participation, Youth, Information Cultures.

1 Introduction

Engagement of young people in socio-political decisions by engaging them through
the use of information and communication technologies (ICTs) is a major objective in
current politics. Especially the emergence of social software and a new perception of
the participative potential of the Internet promise to enable decentralized actions,
possibilities to share and exchange information open and free of charge, to collaborate, to foster political and societal participation. The empowerment of people by
ICTs to be able to integrate in bottom-up decision-making process, to make informed
decisions, and the development of social and political responsibility are tasks of eParticipation [1, p.36]. Macintosh describes eParticipation as "efforts to broaden and
deepen political participation by enabling: citizens to connect with one another and
with their elected representatives and governments using Information and Communication Technologies (ICT)" [2]. Hence, the Internet is used for participation by both,
political institutions, e.g. government agencies and political parties, and political
organization and interaction from the grassroots [3, p.3].

Apart from technological skills, that youth usually adopt fast, participatory culture
is a precondition for "purposeful, repetitive, programmable sequences of exchange

A. Macintosh and E. Tambouris (Eds.): ePart 2009, LNCS 5694, pp. 56–66, 2009.
© Springer-Verlag Berlin Heidelberg 2009

and interaction between physically disjointed positions held by social actors in the economic, political and symbolic structures of society" [4, p.412]. Equal access to resources, being open for particular issues, and a public network of participants are characteristics of a critical public sphere [5, p.25]. To become part of the public sphere or engage into participatory culture requires skills that are not part of educational curricula at school. Fuchs et. al [1, pp.14f.] describe different levels of participation. The first levels – interest in political and societal issues and forming an opinion – are preconditions for real participation. Distribution of information, discussion, support of projects and initiatives and provoking changes in society are levels of real participation.

Although the Internet is still at an early stage and values of civic engagement and deliberative communication have to be developed it provides the potential for being a political forum [3, p.5]. Especially for information gathering, but also from a participative point of view the "Internet appears especially well suited to the citizen role" [6, p.351]. There is already a more lively and active presence of young people in Internet politics in certain parts of the world, but these levels have to be sustained to achieve active political interest in the future [7, p.175]. Especially the age of adolescence is important for young people to develop attachment to ideologies, political activities and social movements [8, p.125]. Considering this, eParticipation has to be integrated into political education to foster political engagement of young people.

As Coleman argues "[c]ontemporary democracies suffer from what might be called a deliberative deficit: an absence of spaces or occasions for the public to engage in open and critical discussion in which opinions can be exchanged and reviewed and policy decisions influenced" [9, p.370]. Consequently, it has to be a major target of ePolicies, to establish this space for participation of young people within the curricula of formal education. However, these new opportunities for eParticipation applied for political education at school, challenge equally the education system in general, teachers, schools, students, and the policy-makers themselves. "[P]olicy does not always translate into practice in straightforward or easily controllable ways: it may be resisted, and its always interpreted and negotiated in the light of the everyday realities of schools and classrooms" [10, p.29].

The different outcomes of certain ePolicies must also be analyzed in the context of the political system and political culture. What has been said so far is predominately based on the analysis of Anglo-American literature. The notion of political participation and eParticipation shaped by an Anglo-American perspective of democracy differs considerably from other perceptions of democracies, e.g. the central European. Empowerment of the individual, sharing information, decentralization, collaboration, and participation are differently perceived and estimated in different democratic cultures and consequently differently promoted and mediated throughout society. These differences are embedded in deeply rooted information cultures [11], a concept that is based on prevailing ethical-religious traditions, the dominating political system, and the legal system. Democracies, which have developed within a strong protestant environment, favor individual engagement, community commitment and accountability of the single political representative, and differ weather they put the state or the individual in the centre of their politics. This for example, explains the difference between Anglo-American and northern European democracies. Anglo-American democracies show an information-friendly information culture, favoring access to information for all as a constitutive element of democracy. On the other side, we find democracies, which have developed from catholic-absolutistic traditions and are more hierarchically organized with a representative democracy where the single representative is responsible to the political party and not to the single voter. According to that the predominating information culture has to be described as information-restrictive. Although, none of these information cultures exist in their pure mode, there are remains from the past, which explain current adoption processes of ICTs and of eParticipation tendencies.

Therefore, the same political strategies in order to enhance political participation by the means of ICTs, most probably will show different results according to the predominance of a certain information culture, especially when it is in the context of the education system. This paper draws on experiences from a project in Austria, aiming for introduction of social software technologies for political education at school. Polipedia.at is a wiki-based tool for collaborative production of an online textbook for political education in Austria by pupils, teachers, and interested outsiders alike. By relating practical experience from this participative online project within the information-restrictive culture of the Austrian education system, we aim to develop more general postulations and recommendations for the successful implementation of eParticipation within political education.

2   eParticipation for Political Education: Polipedia.at

Polipedia.at is an example for using social software for political education. The project aims to strengthen participative skills, create space for user generated content, enhance the availability of information about politics, and to foster collaborative knowledge production and political online participation. Polipedia.at is a wiki-based online-textbook that enables youth to exchange and produce knowledge about politics in a collaborative process. Within the classroom, but also independent from school, students (and others) can add and edit content about political topics and suggest further topics that should be discussed [12]. The project fosters an intensive level of participation and can be considered as preparation for real participation outside school. Polipedia.at is still at its initial phase. Although there is principal excitement about the project, when it comes to the concrete content production, there are problems resulting from lacking skills in written expression, the absence of even basic awareness of concepts like copyright and privacy, and lacking acceptance by technophobe teachers, to name a few. Besides the assumption, that the difficulties we face are related to the predominating information-restrictive information culture, we will discuss the observed phenomena in relation to existing studies and assumptions from literature in order to identify challenges and opportunities, which will form the basis for further developments and recommendations.

An important fact is that youth is not used to work with participative, interactive elements at school, especially within the Austrian school system, where top-down structures, hierarchies and ex-cathedra teaching are still predominant. As Rheingold argues "[e]ducation – the means by which young people learn the skills necessary to succeed in their place and time – is diverging from schooling. Media-literacy-wise, education is happening now after school and on weekends and when the teacher isn't looking, in the SMS messages, MySpace pages, blog posts, podcasts, videoblogs that technology-equipped digital natives exchange among themselves" [13]. Asking good questions, critical thinking, using and understanding search engines, assess the validity of information and use it for problem solving are new media skills in terms of eParticipation [7, p.182]. There is an ambivalence that is difficult to handle for teachers and students likewise. Children can already be experts in utilizing the technological means of the information age compared to their teachers, and at the same time adults are worried about a lack in traditional skills, competences and values [14, p.153]. Here the shortcomings of the traditional Austrian school system become visible. Critical thinking, the preference of a good question compared to the right answer, rhetoric and defending different viewpoints, have never been elements of Austrian education. In an information-restrictive environment, information flows mostly top-down and is no subject to critical inquiry [11]. This situation constitutes a severe obstacle for the implementation of participative elements into the school system, because of their tendency to question existing power relationships.

In the context of Polipedia.at students show high skills compared to their teachers in using technologies, especially concerning audiovisual content, and they learn from their peers. At the same time teachers are worried about the missing abilities of students for quoting references, plagiarism, copy-paste content production and the netiquette in general. Mutual distrust between students and teachers foster the continuation of the traditional power relationship, instead of creating the aspired balanced space for collaboration. "In the final analysis it may be the human barriers to creating an ideal public space that are far more formidable than the technological ones" [15, p.138]. Considering this we follow Livingstone who argues that "technological literacy is only the beginning of the story, and the more exciting challenges lie in the realms of inquiry-based or student-centered teaching and learning, of creativity and of critical literacy" [16, p.221].

It is the dominance of a skills-orientated approach, which can hinder open and participative learning environments. Existing ePolicies, independently in which field, still focus too much on the technology-biased aspects of access and skills. It is suggested to put the individual and not the technology in the centre and "therefore ensuring that cognitive, cultural, and social factors become the determining elements of a new ePolicy" [17, p.53]. In the context of strengthening eParticipation, students and teachers should focus on why participation is important in society and practice it by the means of technology. Within such a setting, students and teachers can contribute their knowledge to a collaborative learning environment and follow a common goal rather than competing with each other.

Teachers do not only feel insecure about their lack in technical skills compared to their students, but there is an insecurity of the outcome of the collaboratively produced online content as well. "Taken together, individual biases influencing news use and political discussion, media agenda setting and framing effects, and new forms of media and political consulting, all suggest that while political knowledge is a consistent predictor of political participation, political learning and participation are highly contingent processes, both online and offline" [18, p.149]. In the context of Polipedia.at a so-called power group of senior students was implemented to monitor the content of Polipedia.at in collaboration with the leading project team in order to avoid plagiarism, but also maintaining the netiquette. If everybody is able to participate, add, edit and delete content, there is still a certain amount of control necessary. The "potential freedom from editorial filter and controls" [19, p.158] is an advantage of Internet compared to mass media, but it also has its limitations, especially within the school context. We assume, that students within the school system in information-restrictive cultures are less prepared to exploit this potential freedom, than students in information-friendly systems. This assumption still has to be proofed in future comparative studies.

The advantages of integrating participative elements of the Internet into political education are the basic availability of in-depth information about a particular topic both, historically and current, the principal possibility of quick feedback, the comparison of different political viewpoints, and the discussion of one's own views with others. These possibilities collide with certain opinions about the goals of political education at schools in general. Should political education create a "homo politicus", a critically thinking, tolerant and politically interested person, or should political education explain the existing political and administrative system, the political history, but stay basically out of current politics? Besides information cultures, political history and experience in certain countries influence current practices. In Austria, the abuse of the school system by teachers who were politically agitating in favor of the Nazi regime is still present in the memory of many people. There are still a serious amount of voices saying that politics has to stay completely out of the classroom.

At Polipedia.at students are able to discuss and produce content independently or with assistance of teachers and peers. Learning from peers and discuss political issues with peers is an important aspect of political participation. Regarding the intensiveness of involvement, as well as the basic technological skills, inequalities become visible. "[T]hose people with the least well-developed cognitive schema are the least likely to attend to information at all, but the most likely to be influenced by the ways that the news media and other elites frame information" [18, p.148]. Still, young people will only be enabled for civic participation if they are encouraged by their institutional structures such as school, family and peers [20, p.121]. If school does not integrate participative elements into political education the political information and participation gap is supposed to widen. As Boyd argues by "prohibiting teens from engaging in networked publics, we create a participation divide, both between adults and teens and between teens who have access and those who do not" [21, p.137]. Although many young people are not ready for societal or political participation because of "lack in civic interest, family support, [and] educational opportunities" [22, p.31] and political education at schools is not able to overcome all these disparities, it can balance the chances to develop a political identity.

There are two contrary opinions about identity formation in relation to participation. Some claim that by the anonymity of the Internet "exclusionary tendencies that come with recognition of class, race, gender and even accent are marginalized in the electronic forum" [3, p.4]. At the same time political participation still requires civil skills that are unevenly distributed. Good vocabulary, personal efficiency, the cognitive ability to revert to existing knowledge about a certain topic or the ability to speak, to write, take pictures or videos well, [18, p.147] are examples of these civic skills. This underlines the necessity of introducing civic skills by integrating eParticipation in political education.

Polipedia.at can be seen as a platform that can prepare youth for political participation and provide them with necessary skills. By including participative elements at schools, a counterpart to passive consumption, which is still predominant in the Austrian school system, can be created. Participatory democracy should not only be seen as something different from everyday life, hence school has to play an important role. By engaging youth into innovative methods of political participation they will get nearer to the concept of participatory democracy. Since participatory democracy and deliberative democracy are the two constitutive concepts of democracy underlying Polipedia.at, the project itself is a challenge to the predominating political system. Participation and deliberation are favored principles in many Austrian ePolicies, but there are invisible obstacles that are shaped by the information-restrictive culture.

By combining media literacy with political literacy Polipedia.at enhances the potential for political participation of Austria's youth, but challenges at the same time their experience with online media. Representation, language, information search and filtering are key competences in digital media literacy [10, pp.155f]. The Internet in general and social software in particular is strengthening the role of the users who "generate content by aggregating, mashing-up, (re-)interpreting and distributing information" [23]. Birdsall describes a development from "build it and they will come" to "they will come and build it" focusing on the changing role of content consumption to content production by the user [24]. These possibilities are closely related to the targets of eParticipation, which basically aim for empowerment of students for political engagement.

Drawing from experiences with the project Polipedia.at at schools, we observe multiple ambivalences and contradictions. There is technologically advanced youth who lacks in awareness and knowledge about plagiarism, copyright or privacy issues. Teachers often lack in basic technological skills and are unsure and undecided about overcoming traditional teaching methods in favor of a more participative educational paradigm. Information is a precondition for participation hence participative online projects will not replace traditional political education, but are rather supplementary. Many of these ambivalences and contradictions are on the one hand result of a techno-deterministic perception of integrating information and communication technologies at schools and on the other hand the result of different notions and evaluations of political education at school due to different dominating information cultures.

3 Challenges and Opportunities

Considering politics from a deliberative theory of democracy perspective participation, especially participation of youth, is an important element of politics. The Internet in general, and social software in particular, has the potential to enhance participative engagement of youth. Young people are "disaffected from formal political institutions, processes and actors" [25, p.20] and avoid traditional party politics and politicians who do not address their concerns. Social software applications can build a channel for young people for agenda setting and become a supplement to traditional political education. Pateman differentiates between half or partial participation and full participation where every individual is able to be part of the decision making body and has equal power to influence decision-making processes [26, p.71]. The platform Polipedia.at is based on an intensive form of eParticipation, which is influenced by an Anglo-American understanding of participatory or deliberative democracy. The outcome of participative online projects is not predictable and especially within information-restrictive cultures we expect challenges and opportunities.

The strong acceptance of the Internet by youth and their disinterest for online political participation are closely related to commercialization of the Web and at the same time the lack of interest in these new technological developments from traditional institutions such as schools and political organization. "The growth of participatory online platforms has, in many ways, eclipsed some of the early Web-based efforts to engage youth and provide 'Digital Democracy'. The popularity of YouTube, MySpace, and other user-generated content sites suggests that the emerging digital media culture is expanding the opportunities for young people to connect, engage, and create" [27, p.27]. Youth culture is closely related to youth market and commercialization of the Internet. The youth market is an important business sector and has reached economic and cultural significance [28, p.218]. Hence, participative online projects have to compete with commercial Internet platforms that have focused on youth and new media with high financial investment for a long time. This can limit privacy of youth by commercial interests as in the same way the fear of political participation or surveillance of online activities by teachers can limit the free space youth have conquered. Privacy and surveillance are closely related to eParticipation, hence using participative online projects does not only integrate traditional political themes, but also contemporary problems, that effect youth' everyday life-worlds. "[W]ithout extending existing definitions of media literacies [...] the presumably co-creative and collaborative potential of the new digital and networked media ecology will be an exclusive playground for political and commercial institutions rather than a platform for individual cultural entrepreneurs" [29, p.27].

Besides the economic and entertainment determined space in the Internet, there is a political, educational, and cultural space. To avoid the domination of political and educational spheres by entertainment and business alternatives have to be developed, that integrate usability and functionality of current developments in the online world. The gap between young people who actively participate in political and societal issues and politically disinterested youth will become broader, if political education does not integrate strategies to reduce these disparities. Political information resources in general, as well as participative political online platforms are rather used by people who are politically interested and have a high socioeconomic status. eParticipation requires civil skills that are unevenly distributed. Good vocabulary, personal efficiency, the cognitive ability to revert to existing knowledge about a certain topic or the ability to speak, write, take pictures or videos well, are necessary to engage into political participation online [18, pp.147ff]. This underlines the necessity of bridging this gap by integrating eParticipation in political education.

In addition to societal, political, educational and technological aspects of introducing eParticipation into political education at schools, we tried to point out the dynamics of the underlying information cultures, which could be responsible for success and failure of the same strategies in different educational systems. Jenkins' perception of "participatory culture", is closely related to information-friendly versus information-restrictive cultures and characterized with "relatively low barriers to artistic expression and civic engagement", "strong support for creating and sharing one's creations with others", "some type of informal mentorship whereby what is known by the most experienced is passed along to novices", "members believe that their contributions matter", "members feel some degree of social connection with one another" [30, p.7]. It is more likely to find the characteristics of a participatory culture within information friendly cultures than in hierarchically organized information-restrictive cultures [11].

According to Hasebrink and Paus-Hasebrink the Internet and civic engagement, have the following functions: communication in existing organizations, networking for autonomous projects, a platform for participation and discussion outside of organizational frameworks, and organization and planning of joint actions [31, p.90]. For Macintosh "deliberation entails an individual or group of individuals listening to, understanding and reflecting on an issue and being prepared to change their own point of view based on the arguments of others" [32]. These capabilities are not only difficult to require from young people. Strategies for eParticipation have to integrate a broader societal perspective than simply being integrated into political education. This includes not just involvement by youth, but also by politicians and decision makers who must be ready to listen to the voices of young people in order to change their opinion if necessary. Young people – in the same way as adults – do not feel taken serious if nobody listens or responds and they do not have a real influence on the decisions that are made [20, p.120].

Politics happens in youth' everyday life-worlds. A survey by Maier-Rabler and Hartwig among Austrian youth indicates that young people are ready to participate, but only if it has an effect on their direct environment [33]. Hence, research has to "start from the young people's perspective, from what they understand as politics, from what they actually do with the Internet" [31, p.97]. Political education currently does not sufficiently incorporate youth' interests, their media practices and their perspective on political participation. Young people have already developed their own forms of participation distant from traditional party politics hence these kinds of participation have to be recognized in political education. The "gap between the culture of school and the culture of children's lives outside schools" [10, p.178] can only be closed if the ways youth use new media for independent action are integrated into the educational curricula.

4   Conclusion and Recommendations

The analyses of challenges and limits of eParticipation for political education shows a complex matter which depends on a variety of external factors and shows ambivalences. For integration of eParticipation into the curricula of political education those factors and ambivalences have to be considered. If we agree, that eParticipation has to be incorporated in political education at schools in order to broaden the chances for young people to get involved in political and societal activities and to strengthen civil society of a country, following recommendations both, for further research and for educational policy are suggested:

New policy: ePolicies in general and for eParticipation in particular should aim to implement ICTs for the benefit of all by strategies like equal access and equally distributed chances to obtain the necessary capabilities to decide which digital lifestyle on an individual and institutional level, is aspired. Therefore a clear strategy for the incorporation of eParticipation in political education is required, which focus on the individual and not simply on technology. The leading question within this context is: Which kind of political identity does the Austrian education system want to foster and strengthen?

New cooperation: eParticipation must be conceptualized in cooperation with agents from different disciplines and perspectives, which have not worked together prior in educational questions, i.e. educationalists, technology and software designers, engineers, politicians, social and political scientists, teachers, students, and parents. The integration of various stakeholders from different disciplinary perspectives demands for a new culture of cooperation, which needs to be developed.

New literacy: Integrating eParticipation in political education fosters political literacy and new media literacy at the same time. This requires openness and readiness for learning from both sides - teachers and students. Both have to adjust to different learning environments, which are characterized by the shift from a hierarchical top-down transfer of information to learning within flatter hierarchical structures where teachers and students interact with each other. Teachers have to acknowledge the expert knowledge of their students and youth have to accept the principles of copyright and avoidance of plagiarism and rules such as the basic netiquette. The cooperative production of new content and new methods of learning has to be developed and incorporated in a mutually shaped process.

Participation and equity: eParticipation for political education is a step towards narrowing the digital and participatory divide between young people. Advanced knowledge in Internet usage, especially the new modes of actively using social software, provides the basis for enhancement of the potential for political engagement of youth. Those, who are already capable to articulate themselves for causes, who are interested in politics, and engaged in societal debate, consequently benefit more from the new possibilities of online participation. Integrating eParticipation into the educational curricula can contribute to narrow these disparities and raise the potential for increased involvement of young people.

New cultures: The embedded dynamics of information cultures are supposed to have a major influence on how the development of capabilities for political participation by using ICTs is supported and fostered or neglected. To foster political and societal eParticipation, strengthening of participatory culture could contribute to the creation of an appropriate learning environment. Further comparative research in respect to culture has to be undertaken, in order to enlighten the relationship between educational sector and the prevailing information culture. Policies, which incorporate cultural aspects and translate certain actions into the dominating culture, are more likely to succeed, than policies, which are just copied from other countries or areas of implementation.

School and everyday-life: The conceptualization of eParticipation and political education has to perceive and incorporate youth interests, their perception of politics, and media practices. Besides political education, eParticipation should be a part of everyday life. Ideal democracy is practiced within a familiar field to contribute to bringing together the increasingly drifting apart worlds of school and everyday-life.

References

1. Fuchs, C., Bernhaupt, R., Hartwig, C., Kramer, M.A., Maier-Rabler, U.: Broadening eParticipation: Rethinking ICTs and Participation. ICT&S Research Paper Series 2 (2006)
2. Macintosh, A.: Challenges and barriers of eParticipation in Europe? (2006), http://www.sweden.gov.se/content/1/c6/08/49/42/9d411e53.pdf (cited 08.10.2008)
3. Buckler, S., Dolowitz, D.: Politics on the Internet. Routledge, London (2005)
4. Castells, M.: The Rise of the Network Society: Economy, Society and Culture. Blackwell Publishers, Cambridge (1996)
5. Gimmler, A.: Deliberative democracy, the public sphere and the Internet. Philosophy & Social Criticism 27(4), 21–39 (2001)
6. Olsson, T., Sandström, H., Dahlgren, P.: An Information Society for Everyone? Gazette 65(4-5), 347–363 (2003)
7. Mossberger, K.: Towards digital citizenship. Addressing inequality in the information age. In: Chadwick, A., Howard, P.N. (eds.) Routledge Handbook of Internet Politics, pp. 173–185. Routledge, London (2009)
8. Amadeo, J.A.: Patterns of Internet use and political engagement among youth. In: Dahlgren, P. (ed.) Young Citizens and New Media. Learning from Democratic Participation, pp. 125–148. Routledge, New York (2007)
9. Coleman, S.: E-Democracy: The History and Future of an Idea. In: Avgerou, C., Quah, D., Silverstone, R. (eds.) The Oxford Handbook of Information and Communication Technologies, pp. 362–382. Oxford University Press, Oxford (2007)
10. Buckingham, D.: Beyond Technology. Children's learning in the age of digital culture. Polity (2007)
11. Maier-Rabler, U.: Cultural Aspects and the Digital Divide. Medienjournal 26(3), 14–33 (2002)
12. Diendorfer, G., Banfield-Mumb, A., Mayrhofer, P.: PoliPedia.at Jugendpartizipation im Zeitalter von Web 2.0. In: Proceedings of EDem conference, pp. 201–210 (2008)
13. Rheingold, H.: The Pedagogy of Civic Participation, http://sl.nmc.org/wiki/Rheingold_Presentation (cited 23.02.2009)
14. Livingstone, S.: Agenda Children's Use of the Internet: Reflections on the Emerging Research. New Media & Society 5(2), 147–166 (2003)
15. Davis, R.: Politics Online. Blogs, Chatrooms, and Discussion Groups in American Democracy. Routledge, New York (2005)
16. Livingstone, S.: Young People and New Media, Sage, London, Thousand Oaks, New Delhi (2002)
17. Maier-Rabler, U.: ePolicies in Europe: A Human-Centric and Culturally Biased Approach. In: Ludes, P. (ed.) Convergence and Fragmentation. Changing Media. Changing Europe, Intellect, pp. 47–66 (2008)
18. Brundidge, J., Rice, R.E.: Political engagement online. Do information rich get richer and the like-minded more similar? In: Chadwick, A., Howard, P.N. (eds.) Routledge Handbook of Internet Politics, pp. 144–156. Routledge, London (2009)
19. Oates, S.: Introduction to Media and Politics, Sage, Los Angeles, London, New Delhi, Singapore (2008)
20. Livingstone, S.: Interactivity and participation on the Internet. Young people's response to the civic sphere. In: Dahlgren, P. (ed.) Young Citizens and New Media. Learning from Democratic Participation, pp. 103–124. Routledge, New York (2007)

21. Boyd, D.: Why Youth (Heart) Social Network Sites: The Role of Networked Publics in Teenage Social Life. In: MacArthur Foundation Series on Digital Learning – Youth, Identity, and Digital Media, pp. 119–142. MIT Press, Cambridge (2007)
22. Livingstone, S., Couldry, N., Markham, T.: Youthful steps towards civic participation: does the Internet help? In: Loader, B.D. (ed.) Political engagement, young people and new media, pp. 21–34. Routledge, London (2007)
23. Raffl, C.: Assessing the Impact of Open Content Knowledge Production in Web 2.0. The International Journal of Technology, Knowledge and Society (4) (2008)
24. Birdsall, W.F.: Web 2.0 as a Social Movement. Webology 4(2) (2007)
25. Owen, D.: The Internet and young civic engagement in the United States. In: Oates, S., Owen, D., Gibson, R.K. (eds.) The Internet and Politics, pp. 17–33. Routledge, London (2006)
26. Pateman, C.: Participation and Democratic Theory. Cambridge University Press, Cambridge (1970)
27. Montgomery, K.C.: Youth and Digital Democracy: Intersections of Practice, Policy, and the Marketplace. In: Bennett, L.W. (ed.) Civic Life Online. Learning how the digital media can engage youth, pp. 25–50. MIT Press, Cambridge (2007)
28. Osgerby, B.: Youth Media. Routledge, London (2004)
29. Deuze, M.: Corporate Appropriation of Participatory Culture. In: Carpentier, N., de Cleen, B. (eds.) Participation and Media Production: Critical Reflections on Content Creation, pp. 27–40. Cambridge Scholars Publishing, Cambridge (2008)
30. Jenkins, H.: Confronting the Challenges of Participatory Culture: Media Education for the 21st Century. The MacArthur Foundation, Chicago (2006)
31. Hasebrink, U., Paus-Hasebrink, I.: Young people's identity construction and media use. Democratic participation in Germany and Austria. In: Dahlgren, P. (ed.) Young Citizens and New Media. Learning from Democratic Participation, pp. 81–101. Routledge, New York (2007)
32. Macintosh, A.: eDeliberation: Do we need it? Can we achieve it? (2008), http://www.donau-uni.ac.at/imperia/md/content/department/gpa/verwaltung/egovernmentkonferenz/macinotsh-edeliberation-abstract.pdf (cited 24.02.2009)
33. Maier-Rabler, U., Hartwig, C.: eParticipation – "Jugend aktiv". Das aktive IKT Nutzerverhalten von Salzburger Jugendlichen mit besonderer Berücksichtigung von (politisch) partizipativen Formen von Internet und mobiler technischer Kommunikation. Forschungsbericht, Universität Salzburg (2007)

Evaluating eParticipation Sophistication of Regional Authorities Websites: The Case of Greece and Spain

Eleni Panopoulou, Efthimios Tambouris, Maria Zotou,
and Konstantinos Tarabanis

University of Macedonia, Egnatia 156,
54006, Thessaloniki, Greece
{epanopou,tambouris,mzotou,kat}@uom.gr

Abstract. eParticipation is becoming a political priority in Europe mainly as an essential ingredient of eGovernment policies. In this paper, we evaluate eParticipation sophistication of the websites of all regional public authorities in the two countries using a published evaluation framework. The framework includes three main factors (information, consultation and active participation), each factor measured using suitable metrics. For information we measured the existence of policy documents online; for consultation we checked the existence of electronic consultations; and for active participation the availability of communication tools (chats, blogs, and/or e-forums) and decision-making tools (e-polls), and the ability for citizens to propose topics at e-forums and e-polls as well as for inclusion in the agenda of local representatives' meetings. Overall, the results indicate that although a political priority eParticipation is not yet a common practice in the two countries at least as far as the regional governmental level is concerned.

Keywords: eParticipation, website evaluation, Greece, Spain, regional authority.

1 Introduction

Electronic Participation (eParticipation) is becoming a political priority for many European countries, often perceived as an essential ingredient of eGovernment policies. Strengthening of participation and democratic decision-making, demonstrating by 2010 tools for effective public debate and participation in democratic decision-making, constitutes one of the five priorities adopted by the EU in the i2010 e-Government Action Plan [1]. Also, according to the European Union (EU) *"e-government strategies at all levels should advance trust and confidence in public services and online democratic participation"* [2]. eParticipation emerges as a priority also at a global level. United Nations suggest a three-step plan for enhancing e-participation [3], namely: (a) increasing e-information to citizens for decision making; (b) enhancing e-consultation for deliberative and participatory processes; and (c) supporting e-decision making by increasing the input of citizens in decision making.

At the same time, a recent survey revealed what we perceive as a relatively small number of current eParticipation European cases [4]. A result of that survey was that

A. Macintosh and E. Tambouris (Eds.): ePart 2009, LNCS 5694, pp. 67–77, 2009.
© Springer-Verlag Berlin Heidelberg 2009

most cases were at the local and regional level than national, international and transnational.

In this work we are interested to evaluate the extent to which the official public authorities at regional level offer eParticipation initiatives through their websites. More specifically, we target Greece and Spain for our survey.

In the literature there are extensive references to assessing websites in general. It is therefore well known that sophistication of websites is related to a number of characteristics, such as status visibility, user control and freedom, consistency and patterns, error prevention, aesthetics, etc. [5]. Methods and tools have been also proposed to facilitate the process e.g. [6] [7]. In the case of electronic government (eGovernment) initial work has commenced on benchmarking (e.g. [8]) however, at the same time, there is considerable discussion and criticism as to how eGovernment performance is measured [9].

A few attempts have been made to propose and use specific metrics for assessing the websites of public authorities. For example, it has been proposed that the websites of public authorities should be assessed by considering accessibility, interoperability, security and privacy, information reliability, service agility and transparency. This approach has been used to evaluate 127 PA websites in Brazil [10]. It has been further proposed that criteria can be divided into two groups: information content criteria (namely orientation to website, content, currency, metadata, services, accuracy, privacy, and external recognition) and ease of use criteria (namely links, feedback mechanisms, accessibility, design, and navigability). This approach was used to evaluate 5 websites of New Zealand government entities [11]. Furthermore, an E-Governance Performance Index, containing 98 measures, was used to evaluate the municipal websites around that world [12]. However, citizens' online participation is the less evaluated concept of government websites; only two methods include this in terms of availability of bulletin boards, online surveys and polls [12] [13] and utilization of chats, discussion forums, e-meetings and online decision-making mechanisms [12].

All aforementioned approaches focus on measuring the supply side of PA websites. Although it has been suggested that the demand side should be equally evaluated [9], in this paper we restrict our focus on measuring online sophistication of websites by employing measures that are independent of client involvement hence do not utilise metrics such as citizens' take-up, improvement of PAs efficiency, etc.

The main objective of this paper is to evaluate the eParticipation online sophistication of regional authorities' websites in Greece and Spain to determine how is eParticipation progressing at the regional level. For this purpose, we endorse a published evaluation framework for measuring online sophistication of public authorities' websites [14].

The rest of this paper is organised as follows. In Section 2 we present the methodology followed in this work, including information on the two countries and their administrative division, on the selected evaluation framework and the specific factors and metrics used, on the scoring and weighting scheme, and on the limitations. Then, in section 3 the results of the survey are presented, firstly in Greece, then in Spain, and finally a comparison of the results between the two countries is made. The paper concludes in section 4 with a discussion of the research and future work.

2 Methodology

2.1 Countries and Administrative Division

Spain and Greece display a similar population density, around 86 inhabitants per km^2 [15], and they are both Mediterranean countries implying some similarities in mentality and culture.

At the regional level Greece is divided into Peripheries (Regions) and Prefectures. Specifically, the official regional administrative divisions of Greece are the 13 Regions [16] and the 57 Prefectures [17]. General Secretaries of Regions are not directly elected by the people but appointed by the Greek government; however, prefectural representatives are elected by the citizens every four years.

Similarly, Spain is divided into Autonomous Communities (Regions) and Provinces at the regional level. Each of the 17 Regions [18] consists of one or more of the 50 Provinces [19]. Provincial representatives in Spain are elected by the citizens every four years as in Greece; however, each Region in Spain has its own president, government, and Supreme Court [20] holding thus more power than the corresponding regional authorities in Greece.

The priorities regarding ICT development in Greece have been set out in the "Digital Strategy 2006-2013" document [21], and although different aspects of eGovernment are included, for example e-procurement and provision of electronic services to citizens, it does not include any concepts relevant to eParticipation or eDemocracy. Notably enough, an older governmental white paper on the development of the Information Society in Greece [22], refers to strengthening of the democratic processes through ICT and includes "*encouraging greater participation of citizens in matters of common interest*" as one of its goals. Specifically, in this paper each regional authority is invited to prepare its own plan for the Information Society aimed among others at "*increasing public awareness and active participation in public matters*".

Similarly, the priorities set out for the development of the Information Society in Spain [23] and for the modernisation of the Spanish Administration [24] focus more on issues such as provision of qualitative services to citizens and improvement of public administration processes than on promoting eParticipation. However, the latter also provides for measures aiming among others to the establishment of an online area dedicated to public eConsulting on normative projects or government decisions. Additionally, eParticipation concerns are also mentioned as challenges to be faced by the Spanish Public administration [25].

2.2 Evaluation Framework

For evaluating the eParticipation capabilities of websites of regional public authorities we have applied the framework proposed by Panopoulou et al [14], and in specific the eParticipation axis of the framework. The eParticipation axis is structured based on the OECD levels of participation and includes three factors, namely *information*, *consultation* and *active participation* (Table 1) [26]. According to OECD, Information is a one-way channel that informs citizens about a variety of available resources; Consultation is a limited two-way channel; while Active Participation is a more enhanced two-way channel where citizens have more power over policy formulation.

Table 1. Factors, metrics and weights for evaluating eParticipation

Factors	Metrics evaluating	Factor weight
Information	Online policy documents.	30%
Consultation	Electronic consultations.	30%
Active participation	Communication and decision-making tools, issues proposed by citizens.	40%

For assessing the information factor we employ a metric measuring the availability of online policy documents and the policy level these documents refer to. For assessing the consultation factor we employ a metric measuring the availability of electronic consultations on the website. Finally, for assessing the active participation factor we employ four different metrics. These refer to the availability of communication tools (chats, blogs, and/or e-forums) and decision-making tools (e-polls), and to the ability for citizens to propose a topic at e-forums and e-polls as well as for inclusion in the agenda of the local representatives' meeting. The exact questionnaire used is provided in Table 2. Most of the questionnaire items are dichotomous and 2 items utilise nominal scales (one of them, metric 3, allowing multiple selection).

Table 2. Questionnaire used and weighting of questions

Metric number	Question and possible answers	Metric weight
	Information factor	
Metric 1	Are policy documents available online? *No / Yes, basic documents / Yes, medium level documents / Yes, high level documents*	100%
	Consultation factor	
Metric 2	Are consultations on important local issues organised online (e-consultations)? *No / Yes*	100%
	Active Participation factor	
Metric 3	Is it possible for citizens to communicate through: *Chats / Blogs / eForums*	25%
Metric 4	Are polls organised online that refer to issues of local/regional interest and that are also incorporated into the decision process? *No / Yes*	25%
Metric 5	In the case that a discussion forum is available, is it possible for a citizen to initiate a new discussion topic? *No / Yes*	25%
Metric 6	Is it possible for citizens to provide a new agenda topic for discussion on the PA council meeting? *No / Yes*	25%

2.3 Scoring and Weighting Scheme

With regard to items scoring we award between 0 and 10 points for each question. Thus, dichotomous items are awarded with 0 or 10 points, and items measured in nominal scales may be awarded with different values between 0 and 10 depending on the answer. For developing an overall score for each website a weighting scheme for factors and metrics is employed. For Information and Consultation factors we use a 100% weight as each of them consists of only one metric. For the Active Participation factor we use 25% weight for each of the four metrics so that each metric contributes equally to the factor's result. However, each factor does not contribute equally to the overall result; Information and Consultation contribute 30% each, while Active Participation contributes 40%. This is a decision made by the authors in order to reflect the notion that active participation is the third and most advanced level of participation [20]. The weighting scheme is also displayed in the last columns of Table 1 and Table 2.

The actual evaluation took place in two stages. Firstly, the evaluation of the websites of the Greek Regions and Prefectures was made in September – October 2008. Secondly, the evaluation of the websites of the Spanish Regions and Provinces took place in December 2008 – January 2009. A different yet experienced evaluator has been involved in each evaluation stage. Finally, it should be noted that the websites were evaluated at the following official languages: Greek for all Greek websites and Spanish for all Spanish websites.

2.4 Limitations

It should be acknowledged that the evaluation presented in this paper addresses only the supply side of eParticipation by the regional authorities. For a more holistic evaluation one should also include a measurement of the demand side, namely the actual participation and engagement of citizens through these websites. This constitutes one of the next tasks that authors consider undertaking.

A second limitation refers to the evaluation method employed. More specifically, all websites in this survey have been visited and evaluated from the perspective of the guest user. This means that the evaluators did not register on any of these websites for checking their full functionality for registered users. This decision was made in order to ensure fair consideration of all websites. For example, some websites in Spain contain a private area for registered users which offer discussion possibilities with representatives of the authorities. However, the credentials for accessing this private area are provided by the city councils to inhabitants. This suggests that it was not able for the evaluators to access this area; nevertheless, there was available information to the guest user on the discussion capabilities within the private area so these websites were considered in the results.

3 Evaluation Results

3.1 Greece

In overall, the websites of 12 Regions and 46 Prefectures have been evaluated and the results are presented below. The rest websites (1 Region and 11 Prefectures) are not included in the results (and in the tables/figures provided) because they were either under construction or not in operation.

The overall results for regional authorities' websites in Greece are provided in Table 3. Greek Regions do not offer policy documents online or any features that promote the active participation of citizens. The reason might be that Regions in Greece do not have any significant legislative power. Indeed, the general secretary of regions is not directly elected but rather is appointed by the government. With regards to e-consultation, only one fourth of regions offer relevant online facilities, indicating their intention to engage citizens into discussion on regional matters.

Table 3. Overall results for regional authorities' websites in Greece

Overall Results	Regions	Prefectures	Total
Information	0.00%	15.76%	12.50%
Consultation	25.00%	15.22%	17.24%
Active Participation	0.00%	8.26%	6.55%
Total	7.50%	12.60%	11.54%

On the other hand, Greek Prefectures offer information, consultation and active participation possibilities to citizens. However, not all of them utilise all these opportunities at the same degree. As presented in Fig. 1, most Prefectures gathered low scoring in all participation levels. Nevertheless, around 30% of them seem to offer adequate information and active consultation opportunities, while 15% offer e-consultation features.

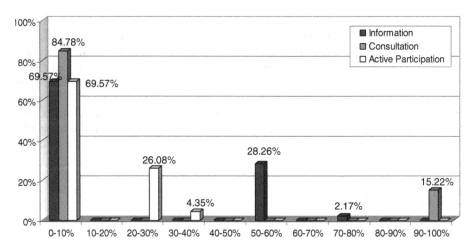

Fig. 1. Score frequencies for Prefectures in Greece

3.2 Spain

In overall, the websites of 17 Regions and 46 Provinces have been evaluated and the results are presented below. The rest websites (4 Provinces) are not included in the results (and in the tables/figures provided) because they were either not in operation or non-existent.

The overall results for regional authorities' websites in Spain are provided in Table 4. Contrary to Greece, most of Spain's regional authorities have adopted a specific template for offering and organising content on their websites. This is the reason for the high similarity between the scores of Regions and Provinces in Table 4.

Table 4. Overall results for regional authorities' websites in Spain

Overall Results	*Regions*	*Provinces*	*Total*
Information	73.53%	73.37%	73.41%
Consultation	17.65%	17.39%	17.46%
Active Participation	1.76%	1.41%	1.51%
Total	28.06%	27.79%	27.87%

At the information level nearly all websites in Spain gathered a very good score, as they provide online policy documents for citizens. At the consultation level only 17.5% of the websites provide e-consultation facilities, and finally at the active participation level nearly all websites score close to 0%, with the exception of a limited amount of websites that offer blogs, e-forums and e-polls. Due to the aforementioned similarity of findings for Regions and Provinces, we provide the score frequencies for all websites in Spain in one figure (Fig. 2).

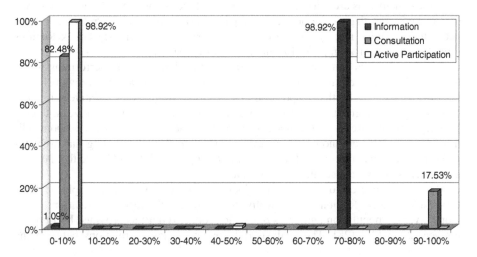

Fig. 2. Score frequencies for Regions and Provinces in Spain

3.3 Comparison and Discussion

A comparison of the overall results for Greece and Spain is provided in Fig. 3. At the information level, Spain has a very big advantage over Greece scoring in average 60% more. On the contrary, at the active participation level and although both countries display low scores, Greece has a clear advantage over Spain. Nonetheless, both countries' regional authorities seem to place a similar emphasis at e-consultation facilities, scoring both around 17%.

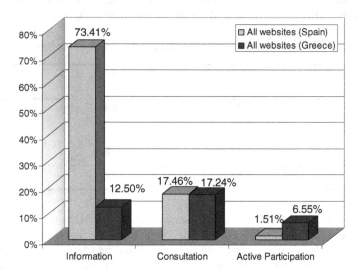

Fig. 3. Scores for all websites in Greece and Spain

When comparing the results per Regions or Prefectures/Provinces in the two countries, the conclusions are fairly the same (Fig. 4). There is only one additional observation to be made, that at the active participation level only Greek Prefectures score better than Spanish Regions and Provinces; as explained previously Greek Regions scored 0% at information provision and active participation.

Additionally, it is worth noting that in overall Greek regions are performing worse than all other regional authorities in the two countries. As mentioned previously, the reason for this may be that responsibilities of Greek Regions are relatively limited; they do not have legislative power and are not elected directly by the citizens. On the contrary, Spanish Regions are much more autonomous and hold many responsibilities. However, this autonomy makes even more interesting the finding that websites of Spanish regional authorities follow a similar template, while in Greece that no such autonomy is observed a similar approach has not been adopted.

Moreover, we tried to relate the results of this survey with demographic data of Greek and Spanish Regions. Specifically, we examined the results in relation to Regions' average population and gross domestic product (GDP) as provided by Eurostat for year 2006 [27] [28]. The analysis did not reveal any correlations between the

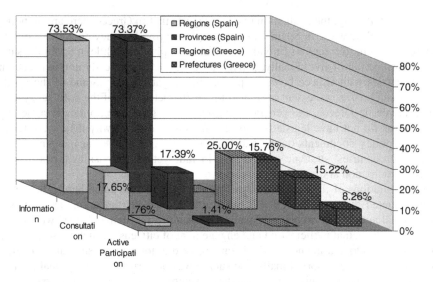

Fig. 4. Comparison of Greek and Spanish Regions and Prefectures/Provinces

results of this survey and the demographics, so the hypotheses that eParticipation sophistication is higher in more populated Regions or in Regions with higher GDP cannot be supported.

In overall, it could be concluded from this survey that neither country's regional authorities are adequately advanced in eParticipation. Of course, Spain performs very good as far as information provision, namely availability of policy documents, is concerned. However, when it comes to more engaging participatory features such as e-consultations, e-forums, e-polls, chats, etc. only a few regional authorities in Greece and Spain offer such opportunities. Especially at the active participation level results are discouraging; not only aren't there many opportunities for the citizens to actively participate but also nearly no evidence have been found that such participation could be "heard" by the regional authorities. These poor results could be partially attributed to the lack of governmental strategic planning for adopting such eParticipation opportunities. As explained previously, both countries' strategic and policy documents on the Information Society do not include specific goals or measures for eParticipation especially when it comes to its adoption at the regional or even local level. It is evident that both countries have a long way ahead in order to be able to fully exploit the advantages of eParticipation.

4   Conclusion

In this paper we have surveyed the eParticipation initiatives at regional level in two European member states, namely Greece and Spain. This was performed through evaluating all available official websites of regional public authorities in the two countries. For evaluation purposes, a published methodology was used [14].

Overall, the results suggest that eParticipation initiatives are not yet in large supply in both countries. This indicates that the benefits of eParticipation are not yet fully exploited in the two countries.

More specifically, the evaluation results suggests that in Greece there are no policy documents online while in Spain 3 out of 4 regions provide policy documents online. In Greece one in four regions provide e-consultation platform while in Spain the same is true for one out of five. Finally, active participation is practically non-existence in both countries with Greece however performing slightly better. Some of the results however can be to some extent attributed to the characteristics of the political system. For example, in Greece, the general secretariats of regions are politically appointed and regions do not have legislative power; this might explain why their websites do not offer policy documents online and the possibility for online engagement. Moreover, both countries' strategic goals do not include yet any provisions for promoting online participation at the regional level.

The limitations of the survey methodology should also be noted here. The survey only evaluated the "supply side" i.e. the availability of eParticipation capabilities at the regional authorities' websites. Equally important is the "demand side" which aims to evaluate the actual participation and engagement of citizens through these websites. However, the adopted methodological framework did not care for such an evaluation which is left as future work. Finally, the survey was performed in all regional authorities' websites however only as far as the guest visitor's perspective is concerned.

Acknowledgments

Authors would like to acknowledge that the work presented in this paper has been partially funded by the EU through the "WAVE: Welcoming Argument Visualisation to Europe" project (EP-08-01-002, www.wave-project.eu).

References

1. European Communication: i2010 e-Government Action Plan: Accelerating e-Government in Europe for the Benefit of all. 173 final, COM (2006)
2. European Communication: The Role of e-Government for Europe's Future. 567 final, COM (2003)
3. United Nations: e-Government Readiness Knowledge Base (2007)
4. Panopoulou, E., Tambouris, E., Tarabanis, K.: eParticipation initiatives: How is Europe progressing? European Journal of ePractice (7) (March 2009)
5. Nielsen, J.: Designing WEB Usability: The Practice of Simplicity. New Riders Publishing (2000)
6. Bauer, C., Scharl, A.: Quantitive evaluation of Web site content and structure. Internet Research: Electronic Networking Applications and Policy 10(1), 31–43 (2000)
7. Wang, L., Bretschneider, S., Gant, J.: Evaluating Web-based e-government services with a citizen-centric approach. In: Proceedings of the 38th Hawaii International Conference on System Sciences (2005)
8. European Commission: Benchmarking Framework, i2010 High Level Group (2006)
9. Janssen, D.: Mine's bigger than yours: Assessing international egovernment benchmarking. In: Bannister, F., Remenyi, D. (eds.) 3rd European Conference on eGovernment. Reading: MCIL, pp. 209–218 (2003)

10. Garcia, A.C.B., Maciel, C., Pinto, F.B.: A quality inspection method to evaluate E-government sites. In: Wimmer, M.A., Traunmüller, R., Grönlund, Å., Andersen, K.V. (eds.) EGOV 2005. LNCS, vol. 3591, pp. 198–209. Springer, Heidelberg (2005)
11. Smith, A.G.: Applying evaluation criteria to New Zealand government websites. International Journal of Information Management 21, 137–149 (2001)
12. Holzer, M., Kim, S.-T.: Digital Governance in Municipalities Worldwide. In: A Longitudinal Assessment of Municipal Websites Throughout the World. The E-Governance Institute, National Center for Public Productivity, Rutgers, the State University of New Jersey, Campus at Newark (2005)
13. Henriksson, A., Yi, Y., Frost, B., Middleton, M.: Evaluation instrument for e-government web sites. In: Proceedings Internet Research 7.0: Internet Convergences, Brisbane, Australia (2006)
14. Panopoulou, E., Tambouris, E., Tarabanis, K.: A framework for evaluating web sites of public authorities. Aslib Proceedings: New Information Perspectives 60(5), 517–546 (2008)
15. Eurostat: Population density,
    http://epp.eurostat.ec.europa.eu/tgm/table.do?tab=table&init=1&language=en&pcode=tgs00024&plugin=1
16. Wikipedia: Peripheries of Greece,
    http://en.wikipedia.org/wiki/Peripheries_of_Greece
17. Wikipedia: Prefectures of Greece,
    http://en.wikipedia.org/wiki/Prefectures_of_Greece
18. Wikipedia: Autonomous Communities of Spain,
    http://en.wikipedia.org/wiki/Autonomous_communities_of_Spain
19. Wikipedia: Provinces of Spain,
    http://en.wikipedia.org/wiki/Provinces_of_Spain
20. Ministerio de Administraciones Públicas: Constitución,
    http://www.map.es/documentacion/legislacion/constitucion.html
21. Ministry of Economy and Finance: Digital Strategy 2006-2013 (2005)
22. Greece in the Information Society: Strategy and Actions (2002)
23. Ministerio de Industria, Turismo y Comercio: Plan Avanza 2006-2010 (2005)
24. Ministerio de Administraciones Públicas: Plan Moderniza 2006-2008
25. Ministry of Public Administration: White Paper on the Improvement of Public Services, 2nd edn (2000)
26. OECD, Citizens as Partners: OECD Handbook on Information, Consultation, and Public Participation in Policy-Making (2001)
27. Eurostat: Total average population by NUTS 2 regions,
    http://epp.eurostat.ec.europa.eu/tgm/table.do?tab=table&init=1&language=en&pcode=tgs00001&plugin=1
28. Eurostat: Regional gross domestic product (PPS per inhabitant) by NUTS 2 regions,
    http://epp.eurostat.ec.europa.eu/tgm/table.do?tab=table&init=1&language=en&pcode=tgs00005&plugin=1

Enacting e-Participation Tools: Assemblages in the Stream of Life

Andrea Resca

Luiss "Guido Carli" University, Centre of Research in Information Systems (CeRSI),
Via G. Alberoni 7, 00198 Rome, Italy
aresca@luiss.it

Abstract. This study on e-participation is based on a project led by the Emilia Romagna region in collaboration with other Italian public administrations. This project has been investigated turning to a twofold perspective: the e-participation kit enhancement and its actual implementation. A temporary collaboration of involved public administrations and the putting together of already existing technological devices provided by implicated administrations have composed this ad hoc technological solution (an assemblage). The analysis of the kit implementation gives way to an understanding of reality based on sense of 'content' (objects, people, physical and temporal circumstances etc.), sense of 'relation' (network of meanings and references among objects, people, physical and temporal circumstances etc.) and sense of 'actualisation' (how sense of 'content' and sense of 'relation' have been enacted and made active) representing a tentative attempt to introduce also factors such as existential disposition and mood in the study of this e-participation kit implementation.

Keywords: e-participation, assemblage, ontology, sense-making.

1 Introduction

In simple terms, government can be seen as the sum of public bodies in charge of: 1) providing services to citizens and companies; 2) planning and policy implementation and 3) organizing procedures and human resources in order to put into practice points 1) and 2) (Ciborra, 1993). However, this definition does not take into consideration the fact that new actors are involved in the management of public goods. The term governance (Kooiman, 1999; UNDP, 1997) is used to represent a situation whereby both planning and policy implementation, on the one hand, and service provision, on the other hand, pursue an active role in non-public actors. The so-called public-private partnerships serve as examples in this proposal. The concept of "good governance" (UNDP, 1997) further contributes to this aspect emphasizing the role played by an environment in which that of society shares the social, political and economic priorities to a large extent.

Information and communication technology (ICT) is an additional factor of this scenario. E-government is the general term that defines the alliance between government and ICT. The large majority of interventions in this field concerns the above-mentioned points 1) and points 3). The so-called front office (point 1), and the back

A. Macintosh and E. Tambouris (Eds.): ePart 2009, LNCS 5694, pp. 78–89, 2009.
© Springer-Verlag Berlin Heidelberg 2009

office (point 3) have been objects of significant investment and a large number of applications have been introduced on the basis of an efficiency rationale. This managerial perspective has significantly contributed to the introduction of ICT in the sphere of public administration. Nevertheless, focusing on "good governance" implies a diverse approach for developing e-government. Factors such as legitimacy, accountability, justice and participation integrate the efficiency rationale introducing a wider perspective to put ICT in the public sector.

E-participation initiatives are seen in this perspective. ICT is seen as an instrument for improving citizens' social and political participation and therefore that of "good governance" replaces the managerial rationale. At least in Italy, the context of the present study, e-participation is moving its first steps and a series of experiments have been put into place. One of them is the focus of this research study. It is denominated Partecipa.Net and it consists in the assembly of an e-participation kit from the Emilia Romagna region in collaboration with other Italian public administrations.

Two parts compose the present work even though they are connected to each other. The first part consists in a study of the process that led to the creation of this e-participation kit whereas the second one consists in a study of the actual implementation of this kit in two specific cases. The reason of this twofold point of view is due to the possibility to outline the nature of the techno-institutional context in which Partecipa.Net is emerged and the passage from this context to its actual use in two situations in which citizens have been called on to express their opinions on specific issues.

The development of the Partecipa.Net kit has been investigated from the concept of assemblage (Lanzara, 2009). This concept is beneficial due to the characteristics inherent in the institutional and technological aspects of the project. The kit emerges through a temporary collaboration between a series of public administrations, on the one hand, and existing technological devices provided by the administrations concerned, on the other. Therefore, both technological and institutional components have been composed in an ad hoc solution that is appropriately represented by a concept like assemblage.

The study of the Partecipa.Net kit applications involved a varied itinerary. Here, Heidegger's work on the phenomenology of religious life (2004) has been taken as point of reference outlining an understanding of reality based on sense of 'content' (objects, people, physical and temporal circumstances etc.), sense of 'relation' (network of meanings and references among objects, people, physical and temporal circumstances etc.) and sense of 'actualisation' or 'enactment' (how sense of 'content' and sense of 'relation' have been acted out and made active). In this proposal, the applications of the e-participation kit have been investigated focusing 1) on the style of mediation adopted by facilitators in charge of the kit and its highly functioning usages 2) on the characteristics and dynamics that took place in the participation activity, and 3) on the atmosphere experienced by the users (participants in the study). All of these perspectives have been studied from the perspective of sense of 'content', sense of 'relation' and sense of 'actualisation' or 'enactment'. Aspects such as existential disposition, mood, affectedness and emotion were then tentatively introduced into the research activity.

2 The Partecipa.Net

In Italy, the diffusion of e-democracy is strictly related to a public advice of the Italian Ministry for Technological Innovation that co-funded 56 projects in this field all over Italy. E-participation, here, is considered an aspect of e-democracy and represents the whole of technological and methodological instruments turned to provide a further factor for rendering possible citizens' participation. In this regard, the Internet and other innovative channels constitute a possibility for transforming institutional and political communication. In fact, two-way communication becomes possible in order to support decision-making processes and inquire about public life, for instance.

Partecipa.net is a direct result of this initiative of the Italian government. It is an e-participation kit envisaged by a consortium led by the Emilia Romagna Region in order to spread e-participation practices on its territory. It comes to light in 2005 because of the above-mentioned funds and of the Ministry of Innovation, the coordination and evaluation role played by Cnipa (National Centre for ICT in the Public Administrations) and the support of 21 local governments and 9 social associations. At the basis of this e-participation kit there are two software applications: UNOX1 and Demos. UNOX1, a communication multi-channel system, has been developed by the Municipality of Modena whereas Demos, an electronic discussion forum, by the Municipality of Bologna. These two main applications are integrated by methods and guidelines for enabling citizens' participation.

To investigate further in detail Partecipa.net kit, it is useful to subdivide it into electronic identification, back office and front office (Rossi, 2007). Partecipa.Base is the software module dedicated to the system access and username and password are required to login. So, every user has to register his/her name (also a nickname is allowed) to the Partecipa.net portal indicating also an email address in order to complete the registration procedure. Once this procedure is terminated, access to Partecipa.net functionalities is available.

These functionalities are based on back office technologies and a database of users' profiles constitutes an important element among them as it enables the provision of services according to users' selected options. The FAQ (Frequently Asked Questions) engine is another back office element and a CMS (Content Management System) makes possible the organization of contents of a variety of formats (doc, txt, pdf, ppt, jpg etc.) both by back end and front end users. A GPL (General Public License) characterizes all Partecipa.Net kit software programs in order to allow code reuse to other public administrations.

Borders between electronic identification, front office, and back office are becoming continuously more uncertain. Partecipa.Base for example, managing users' profiles, makes possible the organization of thematic newsletters. Newsletters of interest selected during the registration phase are then forwarded regularly to subscribers. The FAQ function goes over back office borders as well. Users have at disposal instrument in order to inquire contents available and Partecipa.Ask is the module dedicated to this function. It consists in the possibility to submit specific questions to experts in a specific field. Partecipa.Poll is a further module. It is a system devised to do survey about issues at stake supporting a sort of e-voting procedure. The Partecipa.Forum module enables electronic forum and open debate activities. This module allows moderator' interventions and content full-text researches other than interactions and discussion among enrolled citizens. In order to facilitate discussion activities, a virtual multimedia library is available. Partecipa.Biblio is the module dedicated to this function. To sum up, Partecipa.Base, Partecipa.Ask, Partecipa.Poll, Partecipa.Forum and Partecipa.Biblio compose the Partecipa.net kit.

The Partecipa.net kit is the final result of a project that had at its basis funds available from the public advice of the Italian Ministry for Technological Innovation. This is the spark that puts into motion the entire process. At this point, the Emilia Romagna Region summons up local governments (municipalities and provinces) that could be interested in the e-democracy field. At first, the Regional Assembly, three municipalities, an association of municipalities and two provinces answered yes (only later the number of local governments reached 21). The reasons that lead these institutions to be part of the Partecipa.Net project are diverse. In some cases there is the motivation to upgrade software applications already available; in other cases the spur came from the provision of a regional law that calls upon a wider involvement of citizenship in democratic processes or personal interests of local governors to experiment e-democracy solutions, for example. All these actors gathered in a working group that developed the project. The constitution of this group has been considered a success not only because it succeeded to accomplish the Partecipa.Net project deliverables and requirements but also because it transformed itself in a platform for developing other projects. In other words, the division of labour established among different actors involved, the nature of their relationships and the characteristics of knowledge shared led to an entity ready to be used in other similar projects.

3   Partecipa.Net: An Assemblage?

The first part of this work focuses on the modalities through which Partecipa.Net has taken shape. In other words, may a concept represent the series of events that lead to the establishment of Partecipa.Net? Is it possible to describe, in detail, the characteristics of this e-participation kit and also its possible evolution? The notion of assemblage is considered useful in this proposal. Even though it has been introduced by several authors (Cooper, 1998; Ong and Collier, 2005), Lanzara's definition (2009) is taken into account. "Assemblages result from the encounter and the multiple mediations between large ICT systems and the existing institutional frameworks and codes of the society. They are made up of heterogeneous components displaying multiple logics which cannot be easily reduced to one another. Hence, assemblages are not 'hybrid' entities, but rather 'composites' – collection of components, which tend to maintain their specificities (Lanzara, 2009 pp. 13-14). It is supposed that these few lines succeed to illustrate rather well what effectively happened in the Partecipat.Net project. UNOX1 and Demos are the two ICT systems at the basis of this project, the Ministry for Technological Innovation, CNIPA, the Emilia Romagna Region, and other local governments represents the institutional framework and the necessity to improve the quality of social and political participation can be seen an aspect in the code of the society. What is emphasized by the concept of assemblage is that all these elements do not transform themselves into a new entity. On the contrary, UNOX1 and Demos are still there as other public bodies involved in the project. Therefore, assemblages are loosely structured and its components, even though evolve continuously, maintain their autonomy in a situation in which boundaries and linkages tend to shift and drift. This means that assemblages are always ad hoc and changes continuously. Changes take place at different speed according to the different elements involved given that each component has its own time of evolution. Therefore, in these conditions, equilibriums are always unstable.

Lanzara (2009) identifies a series of features that characterize assemblages: 1) The presence of multiple actors and authority structures of which none of them exercises full control on the project whereas each is in charge only of a part of it (i.e. CNIPA, Emilia Romagna Region and other local governments); 2) institutional sponsors and project champions emerge. That is, some actors acquire a leading role promoting innovation and taking responsibility of coordination (i.e. Emilia Romagna Region); 3) episodes, discontinuous activities and situated interventions are seen as further characteristics of assemblages. In other words, activities are not regular (the business as usual of the different components has to go on) but based on specific agreements among actors involved in a specific commitment (i.e. in Partecipa.Net, working groups were autonomous and slightly coordinated by the Emilia Romagna Region); 4) adapting, repairing and redesign available components consist of the fact that design activities tends to be focused on components already in place that need to be tailored to a new context. At the basis of this way of doing, there are the following questions: what is possible to do with what is already available? What functionalities can be added to present systems in order to pursue our objectives? What kind of simplifications can be introduced in order to streamline existing procedures? (i.e. UNOX1 and Demos experienced this type of handling); 5) converting, linking and plumbing. They are related to the conversion and the following connection of components at place in order to build a more complex assemblage (i.e. UNOX1 and Demos have been re-adapted and connected each other); 6) redesigning administrative routines, interfaces and jurisdictions are enabled by the different systems that now are connected to each other. Procedures involved in separated domains are now linked leading to new way of doing things (i.e. the combination of UNOX1 (a system for informing citizens about social and institutional life of the Municipality of Modena) and Demos (an electronic forum) as basis of participation activities electronically supported); 7) characteristics of the installed based (pre-existing technical and institutional materials) can be more or less obtrusive or enabling. The possibility to introduce gateways, the level of re-combinability and the degree of modularity contribute to the taking shape to new assemblages (i.e. UNOX1 faces technical problems in its adoption and Demos functionalities support a specific decision making process that can be in contrast with normal procedures in off line situations).

To conclude, Lanzara (2009) suggests that assemblages can be evaluated according to three main perspectives: technical compatibility, functional compatibility and institutional compatibility. Technical compatibility refers to standards, modularity, interfaces, protocols etc. At present, Partecipa.Net technical compatibility is still at stake. Several pilot projects have already been put into practice and two of them will be taken into consideration in the following sections. Nevertheless, Partecipa.Forum is considered too rigid and outdated from a technical point of view, interoperability issues have continued to emerge among the different components and security standards of Partecipa.Net do not match Emilia Romagna Region requirements, for example. Concerning functional compatibility, the question related to the consonance between technological components and social and institutional components (i.e. does Partecipa.Net effectively support social-political participation?) has been raised as well. Is Partecipa.Forum exactly the more appropriate tool as it is based on a specific method of participation named Delphi that is considered too complex to be implemented? Only institutional compatibility (satisfactory forms of collaborations among agencies and organizations involved in assemblages due to a shared language, mutual understanding and accountability) does not seem to be put into question. All of this means that the future of Partecipa.Net is uncertain and it is not excluded that it will be discharged even though, most probably, as an assemblage, it will continue to transform itself taking other shapes.

4 Sense of 'Content', Sense of 'Relation' and Sense of 'Actualization' or 'Enactment': A Way to Emphasize Ontology in e-Participation Research?

Research activity, at least in the realm of social science, tends to concentrate on epistemology (how we know what we know and how knowledge can be acquired on the entities being examined) rather than ontology (the study of being, of what exists and of what is thinkable). Every research paper dedicates a portion of it to epistemology. Conversely, ontology is often neglected or considered tacitly. Among the objectives of this work, there is that one to focus on ontology. That is, to emphasise the range of what is the object of investigation trying, at the same time, to take into consideration further aspects of reality. An opportunity in this respect is provided by Heidegger's work on the phenomenology of religious life (2004). Here, he suggests a comprehension and an investigation of reality (ontology) based on sense of 'content', sense of 'relation' and sense of 'actualization' or 'enactment'.

Sense of 'content' refers to entities present in a situation: objects, people, physical and temporal circumstances etc. It delineates a facet of existence or reality that emphasizes the objectivity and materiality of entities and also what is experienced. It highlights the objective aspect and the characteristics of the 'content' under examination. Even the concept of assemblage can be seen according to the lenses proposed by sense of 'content'. ICT systems, the existing institutional frameworks and codes of the society that are the main components of assemblages can be considered factors of such sense.

Sense of 'relation' refers to the network of meanings and references among entities of the same situation. It answers to the 'how' question rather than the 'what' question that typifies sense of 'content'. Therefore, how is 'content' connected? That is, how are its components related to each other? In addition, how these connections are experienced? To answer to these issues means to investigate relationships and references established within the sphere of 'content'. In this case as well, the concept of assemblage is helpful for investigating sense of 'relation'. The fact that assemblages are made up of heterogeneous components displaying multiple logics, which cannot be easily reduced to one another, emphasizes this sense. Here, the range of analysis is not only restricted to objective aspects of phenomena, here, meanings and references due to interactions among these aspects are investigated as well. This is to say that a dual perspective connotes concepts such as assemblage due to the possibility to throw light both to objective aspects and relational and dynamic aspects of phenomena.

Nevertheless, this kind of concepts shows its limits when at stake there is the stream of life in which phenomena are embedded. As far as it concerns objectifying descriptions and meanings related to phenomena, these instruments of analysis are considered appropriate but fall short if existential terms are taken into consideration. Sense of 'actualization' or enactment is the answer in the respect of the ontological issue posed at the beginning of this paragraph. Here, the focus moves towards how 'content' and 'relation' have been enacted and made active. Precisely, the point is to grasp attitudes and the ways in which existence informs 'content' and 'relation' as sense is created through life's practices. However, to highlight life enactment prevents us in placing excessive importance on the objectification of 'content' and 'relation' which casts a shadow on their actualization and how existence is carried out through the senses of 'content' and 'relation'.

The ontological perspective proposed in this work is also emphasized by the analysis of term enactment proposed by Weick's important works (1977 among others). According to Weick's point of view, enactment acquires a diverse meaning in comparison with what has been proposed by Heidegger's work. Using Piaget (1962) as point of reference, the cognitive aspect rather than the existential one is at the centre of the discourse. Here the individual is seen as an entity that punctuates and activates the flow of experience, which is then transformed "in a network of causal sequences or causal map" (Weick, 1977 pp.275). In both perspectives the process of "sense making" is crucial, nevertheless, in the latter, it is intended as the final result of a mental process in which local circumstances are detected and elaborated (based on inputs acquired in the context of which actions are taking place). Heidegger's perspective is far from emphasizing causal sequences as the engine of the sense-making process. Rather, it is the consequence of existential disposition, mood, affectedness and emotion. The sense making process can only be represented in this way.

Sense of 'content', sense of 'relation' and sense of 'actualization' or 'enactment' add existential aspects to our comprehension of phenomena. Institutional and historical circumstances, for instance, continue to be fundamental to the understanding or the interpretation, nevertheless existential aspects, to some degree, add colour to the phenomena under investigation.

Furthermore, Heidegger's approach questions an instrument of research as theories. Sutton and Staw conceive them as "stories about why acts, events, structure, and thoughts occur" (1995 quoted in Yin, 2003 pp. 29). But, for this reason, they are seen as obstacles in order to investigate reality and the sense-making process if, at the centre of this argument lies factual life experience (Heidegger, 2004). Factual life experience is intended as something more than a cognitive experience and may not be interpreted through epistemological perspectives. Objects are transformed into a "world" so that what the self-experiences and what is actually experienced are no longer separated. It is the how individuals stand in relation to events in everyday life that is important. In factual life, subjects do not experience themselves in a series of acts and procedures. Rather, what the individual experiences is related to human emotions such as hurt, pain, happiness and joy.

5 e-Participation and Sense Making

The point now is to examine the introduction of the Partecipa.Net kit in two specific contexts: "gli orari della città" and "per via Gallucci". In the "gli orari della città" case, the objective was that one to involve citizens of the Municipality of Modena in order to reorganize opening hours of bars, shops, public offices and also public transportations timetables and, in this way, to render more welcoming the city. "per via Gallucci" represents an attempt to put under control conflicts aroused between via Gallucci residents, on the one hand, and customers and barkeepers of the same street, on the other hand, as Via Gallucci is one of the more famous streets for its night spots in Modena.

The methodology used to investigate these two e-participation projects is in the circle of the case study research (Yin, 2003). The research question at stake here is related to the meanings and the interpretations of participation emerged in the two cases under examination. In order to follow this objective, Partecipa.Net facilitators have been interviewed. In fact, the functioning of this e-participation tool requires a figure in charge both of possible technical problems occurred to users and of possible misunderstandings and conflicts aroused among participants in the use of Partecipa.Forum.

Study propositions or issue sub-questions are helpful in order to enrich the research question at stake enlightening more in detail the directions that this study pursued. Three sub-questions seem to be significant in this regard: the style of mediation or facilitation, the characteristics of participation and the atmosphere experienced by users.

Units of analysis represent a further step in this research design. Units of analysis in this case are "gli orari della città" and "per via Gallucci" facilitators. As it has been mentioned above, it is through their role that the research question and, of course, even sub-questions, have been examined. However, this role has been interpreted turning to the three "worlds" proposed by Heidegger (2004): the 'surrounding world' (milieu), the 'communal world' and the 'self world'. Actually, the units of analysis are based on the overlapping of these three "worlds".

The final step concerns the interpretation of findings and then modalities that lead to meanings and understandings related to participation in "gli orari della città" and "per via Gallucci". Even in this case, Heidegger's perspective proposed above has been taken as point of reference. This means that the investigation of sense of 'content', sense of 'relation' and sense of 'actualization' or 'enactment' constitute the main factors to examine the "rationale" (verbum internum) of the introduction of Partecipa.Net kit in these two cases. Case similarities (users coming from the same context, a same technological kit and similar subject of application) lead us to study them altogether rather than in their singularities.

5.1 The Style of Mediation: Meanings and Interpretations

The mission of the facilitator was not that one to be directly involved in what was going on in the forum or in other activities that supported participation. Rather, it was in his/her responsibility to supervise activities in a detached way without influencing the substance of what was object of discussion. Nevertheless, it was fundamental to play an active role leading debates and exchanges of ideas in what was considered relevant for the issues at stake. This was the reason why facilitators were trained, even though not in an exhaustive way, both in order to avoid problems of etiquette in the forum conduct and to guide discussions to support the creation of the so-called collective intelligence as it has been emphasized by one of the facilitators. Collective intelligence consists in identifying viable solutions in order to deal with issues at stake and all of this requires a series of activities related not only to the management of interactions but also to the support of appropriate information, contents, statistical data etc. All these considerations emphasize sense of 'content' of mediation.

Sense of 'content' refers to entities present in a situation as objects, people, technology, values and cultures. Differently, sense of 'relation' refers to the network of meanings and references emerged from relationships established by these entities. Therefore, the point now is to analyse the nature of connections that took place at the level of mediation. Technical problems, substantially, did not occur. In some cases, it has been necessary to support users at the authentication stage but this was all. A more active role played by mediators was required when discussions turned to be useless, not creative or not containing a proposal. This was mainly the case when objects of debate were not closed to participants' needs. In those situations, it was necessary to revitalise interactions even though, sometimes, the role of leadership put at stake by facilitators was not considered sufficient. Probably, it would have been necessary to be more incisive in order to bring into question relevant issues that could not get into the debate only relying upon forum users' interventions.

The objective, at this point, is to examine sense of 'actualisation' or 'enactment' experienced in the course of mediation. That is, the wonder is how 'content' and 'relation' have been made active and in the stream of life by facilitators. The role of the facilitator has been lived in a rather distant and aloof way. The professional character prevailed rather than an approach more closed to existing debates. Users considered facilitators as a sort of gatekeeper that supervised forum activities and a gentlemen agreement imposed itself in the course of forum activities. Partecipa.Net was provided by the Municipality of Modena and this was not neutral on the characteristics of interactions. The institutional role played by this local government brought about a kind of fear and also suspicious to users influencing the nature of debates. Besides, it was not clear if, once specific results will be reached, they would be taken into consideration for the policymaking.

5.2 The Characteristics of Participation: Meanings and Interpretations

Even in this case, the analysis of the features of participation begins from the sense of 'content'. In this proposal, the themes object of debate in the electronic forum have been considered important. The level of interactions risks being sterile, fruitless and unable to attract a considerable number of participants in case they were not really closed to citizens. The point that themes have been decided by the Municipality and not by citizens themselves has been considered an aspect that, in some way, influenced negatively the development of "gli orari della città" and "per via Gallucci" projects. A further factor that outlines the what of participation is related to its size and taken measures in order to allure a large number of citizens. A traditional advertising campaign for explaining in detail the terms of the issues at stake to be faced through deliberative procedures was considered fundamental. Besides, information spread across existing electronic means as the Municipality mailing lists or to the UNOX1 services was used as well. In this regard, it is not an easy task to inform citizens about the possibility to participate actively in a decision making process through the Internet. Municipality attitude in respect of Partecipa.Net tool was not completely supportive, all potentialities of such a tool have not been taken into consideration and also their planning stage was not considered sufficient.

Concerning sense of 'relation', in both cases under examination it was possible to detect a learning process. That is, the modalities and also the quality of discussions improved considerably as time passed by. Users developed a reciprocal understanding, evaluations on the objects of debate became continuously more accurate and constructive proposals emerged deeming the several aspects of the discussions in course. Nevertheless, it was not possible to say that at the end of the process a sort of community took shape. Or, better, an interesting phenomenon happened at least in one project. Members of a local council, represented of specific interests, decided to join the forum. However, even though their activities contributed significantly to enrich the level of discussions, their specific position was over represented biasing the terms of the debate. This is one of the negative side effects enabled by e-participation tools.

Sense of 'actualisation' or 'enactment' is investigated focusing both on Municipality and citizens' attitudes in respect of "gli orari della città" and "per via Gallucci" projects. Citizens who decided to be involved in these two projects saw e-participation as a further instrument to have a say in the city government. Frustrations and also hostility toward the Municipality were perceptible due mainly to problems aroused in Via Gallucci. Dissatisfactions that usually had no chance to be expressed in the public sphere founded a new way to be channelled. The wonder was if this new opportunity allowed a more incisive protest and also the possibility to make some proposals. Actually, some results have been reached and suggestions determined in the forum have been taken into consideration. Besides, as time passed by, the hostile attitude reduced significantly and the level of discussion turned to be more fruitful. The Municipality of Modena is not alien to this situation. Tools like Partecipa.Net were seen as something new, a little strange, and marginal and not as a solution to be prioritised. Therefore, there has been the impression that the decision to adopt these tools was to pretend to be innovative and up to date. Nevertheless, it was not available sufficient knowledge of these instruments and this led to a perceived risk of politicians to not be in control of the situation. This means that traditional ways to stimulate participation like local assemblies seemed still preferred.

5.3 The Atmosphere Experienced by Users: Meanings and Interpretations

In order to take into consideration sense of 'content' related to users, let's start from their features. There were not only young people. On the contrary, the majority was between the 30 and 50 years old. The language style used suggested that many of them were professionals or highly educated and with a significant computer literacy. This means that the young and the old range of the population were not importantly represented. In addition, participation was not anonymous. As it has been already mentioned users' registration was required, even though it was possible to use a nickname rather than the real one.

Concerning sense of 'relation', it has to be mentioned that discussions have also reached high levels of significance. So, we are not in the range of chatting. Rather, there has been the impression that participants have been motivated and committed to their own points of view. It could be possible to perceive a shared awareness about the importance and the value of activities in course. Tits for tats have not been missed. Nevertheless, they did not compromise the entire discourse. At least in one of the two cases, two categories of participants could be detected. On the one hand, those ones connected to the local council mentioned above and the rest. The former tended to focus only on the subject of direct interest whereas the latter touched a far larger range of issues.

These two categories influenced also sense of 'actualization' or 'enactment'. A sense of solidarity emerged in the local council group. The proverb "united we stand, divided we fall" well represents the atmosphere shared by this group of people. The rest of the participants expressed a different attitude. The attitude of gentlemen/gentlewomen that cordially even though firmly exchanges ideas on subjects at stake.

6 Conclusions

In some sense, this can be considered a longitudinal study as it has been followed the development of an e-participation kit from its planning to its actual implementation. This is the reason why it has been necessary to pursue a dual perspective based on the concept of assemblage (Lanzara, 2009), in order to investigate Partecipa.Net enhancement, and on Heidegger's work on the phenomenology of religious life (2004), in order to investigate its use in two specific contexts. Turning to this dual perspective has given also the opportunity to focus on ontology. In particular, sense of 'content', sense of 'relation' and sense of 'actualisation' have introduced existential terms in the analysis of a phenomenon like the implementation of an e-participation kit. Terms that are absent in the perspective proposed by the concept of assemblage, for example. The consequences of the introduction of the stream of life in the analysis of social phenomena according to the perspective proposed lead to a reconsideration of the role of theory in social research. Here, sense making is not intended as a chain of events or as an established and rigorous order of entities. On the contrary, this "rationale" is strictly connected to specific historical conditions rather than to a predefined order. It is in this view that the introduction of Partecipa.Net has been examined. The objective has been that one to converge sense of 'content', sense of 'relation' and sense of 'actualisation' in order to move from an object-historical understanding to an enactment-historical one. In other words, the purpose has not been that one to generalize specific results obtained following a specific theoretical approach but to have a live picture of e-participation tools in action.

References

1. Ciborra, C.: Teams, Markets, and Systems: Business Innovation and Information Technology. Cambridge University Press, Cambridge (1993)
2. Ciborra, C.: Note Fenomenologiche su Milano e le Reti. In: Magatti, M. (ed.) Milano, Nodo Della Rete Globale: Un Itinerario Di Analisi e Proposte. Mondadori, Milano (2005)

3. Cooper, R.: Assemblage notes. In: Chia, R.C.H. (ed.) Organized Worlds: Essays in Technology and Organization with Robert Cooper. Routledge, London (1998)
4. Heidegger, M.: The Phenomenology of Religious Life. Indiana University Press, Bloomington (2004)
5. Kooiman, J.: Social-Political Governance. Public Management Review 1(1), 67–92 (1999)
6. Lanzara, G.F.: Building Digital Institutions: ICT and the rise of assemblages in government. In: Contini, F., Lanzara, G. (eds.) ICT and Innovation in the public sector. Palgrave Macmillan, Houndmills (2009)
7. Ong, A., Collier, S.: Global Assemblages, Anthropological Problems. In: Ong, A., Collier, S. (eds.) Global Assemblages: Technology, Politics, and Ethics as Anthropological Problems. Blackwell Publishing, Oxford (2005)
8. Piaget, J.: Play, Dreams and Imitation in Childhood. Routledge and Kegan Paul, London (1962)
9. Rossi, L.: Un caso di e-democracy nel Comune di Ferrara: il progetto 'Partecipa FERRARA'. University of Ferrara (2007)
10. Sutton, R., Staw, B.: What Theory Is Not. Administrative Science Quarterly 40, 371–384 (1995)
11. UNDP: Governance for Sustainable Human Development (1997),
    http://www.magnet.undp.org/policy
12. Weick, K.: Enactment Processes in Organizations. In: Staw, B.M., Salancik, G.R. (eds.) New Directions in Organizational Behavior. St. Claire Press, Chicago (1982)
13. Yin, R.K.: Case Study Research: Design and Methods. Sage Publications, Thousands Oaks (2003)

DoIT Right: Measuring Effectiveness of Different eConsultation Designs

Åke Grönlund and Joachim Åström

Örebro University, 701 82 Örebro, Sweden
ake.gronlund@oru.se, joachim.astrom@oru.se

Abstract. eConsultations have been used in many countries over many years, yet most research in the field is case descriptions and there is so far little systematic evidence as to the effectiveness of consultations as a tool for enhancing democracy. Using a case survey method we investigate what factors make a consultation succeed or fail based on data from 57 cases reported in the literature. Success is measured as high participation, deliberative mode of discussion, and impact on policy. We test three hypotheses from the literature claiming, respectively, that institutional design, democratic intent, and quality of research are the most important factors behind the reported success. We find support for all hypotheses. Using consultation at the analysis/decision making stage, mixing online and offline methods and active strategic recruiting are institutional factors positively contributing. Democratic intent and content analysis research both have positive influence.

Keywords: consultation, e-consultation, online consultation, case survey.

1 Introduction

Online consultations[1] are an important ingredient in eParticipation[2]/eDemocracy efforts. While consultations can take place at any level of government local government

---

[1] A consultation is in this context "ICT [Information and Communication Technologies, authrs' remark] in official initiatives by public or private agencies to allow stakeholders to contribute their opinion, either privately or publicly, on a specific issue" (Demo_net, 2006). The OECD (2001) points out that a consultation is a two-way relationship in which citizens provide feedback to government where governments define the issues for consultation, set the questions and manage the process, while citizens are invited to contribute their views and opinions. This means government has a leading role. Following these definitions, an online consultation, or an e-consultation, is in this paper a consultation using some ICT application(s) designed for consultations which allow a stakeholder to provide information on an issue and others to answer specific questions and/or submit open comments.

[2] eParticipation is here defined as "the use of information and communication technologies to broaden and deepen political participation by enabling citizens to connect with one another and with their elected representatives" (Macintosh, 2006). The term e-democracy was used in a similar meaning around the turn of the century (Grönlund, 2003) but as it later became increasingly used to mean specifically e-voting the concept of eParticipation became commonly used to refer to the full spectrum of voter-representative communication means. eParticipation is also the name of an EU Preparatory Action funding a number of projects designed to create awareness and citizen involvement in the legislation process. This EU Action is not in any way related to the research presented in this paper.

A. Macintosh and E. Tambouris (Eds.): ePart 2009, LNCS 5694, pp. 90–100, 2009.
© Springer-Verlag Berlin Heidelberg 2009

is at the focus of this study for two important reasons. First, this is where most consultations take place. Second, this is where the democratic aspects are most highlighted and of most immediate concern because of the closeness between the stakeholders involved and the immediacy of the issues. While consultations at EU level tend to focus on long-term general issues, such as "how should democracy be improved?", local level consultations tend to be about issues of the day directly influencing people's lives; "how should we redesign the city square?" While there are many case descriptions there is so far little systematic evidence to the effectiveness of consultations as a tool for enhancing democracy. Some reasons for that are that research is often done by people involved in action research style, research takes place in different countries and at different times making it hard to synchronize research over multiple cases, and that cases often focus on specific local and technological conditions uses making findings hard to compare to other cases. Using a case survey method this paper investigates what factors make a consultation succeed or fail based on data from 57 consultation cases found in the literture. Success is measured in terms of improved participation. This paper hence makes both a practical and a theoretical contribution to the field of eParticipation. Practically, by systematically comparing data from 57 cases and finding success factors, and relations among these, pertaining to consultation design that are important to understand for practitioners. Theoretically, because testing hypotheses on multiple cases is new in this field which is dominated by case studies and little systematic research.

There is a widespread concern that somehow local democracy is not what it once was or, at least, is not what it should be. This is a reflection of a concern about the subsiding interest for traditional forms of participation, that citizens disengage themselves from the political parties and show an increasing distrust against local politicians (Norris, 1999). Along with these problems there are worries about a social capital in decline (Putnam, 2000), democratic exclusion and marginalization of minorities and culturally distinct groups, and so on. Despite the fact that local democracies differ in many ways – there are variations in local autonomy, state traditions, political and governance set-up etc. – similar complaints about democratic deficits are taken as a starting point for reforms in many places, which show remarkable similarities in quite different systems (Daemen & Schaap, 2000). One of the latest fashions, or perhaps hopes, is e-consultations. Many local governments have embarked upon a wave of e-consultation policies, in Europe encouraged by EU policies, and many experiments with new interactive arrangements such as issue forums and online surveys, e-panels and juries, are developing on the ground. What chances of deepening democracy these various avenues in fact have is vigorously debated, but sparsely researched. Currently, there is a range of studies in the format of quantitative analyses of web pages, enabling a rough outline of the policy development and an identification of the values that are being emphasized by local governments in different contextual settings. There are also many single case studies, providing in-depth insights to processes, challenges and outcomes in specific situations. However, these approaches do not in themselves enhance understanding of what works, when and why (Demo-net 2006). To satisfactorily answer these types of questions, research must move from mapping exercises and descriptions of isolated projects towards comparative evaluation.

While there are several ways of dealing with this gap in the literature, this article uses the case-survey method as a means to aggregate the collective judgments of previous researchers regarding the impact of e-consultations on local democratic practices. The *aim* is to *evaluate how successful cases have been in meeting different goals* – participation, deliberation and policy impact – *and to identify the contextual and procedural attributes of the cases that relate to success and failure,* here operationalized as institutional design, democratic intent, and research quality.

The literature is replete with suggestions concerning the success and failure of consultations, but there are few if any studies across many cases investigating results in a structured way. In this paper 57 European and United States case studies are used to test three specific claims. The first claim, made by Archon Fung (2003), argues that the success of consultations and their consequences for democratic governance depend upon 'the details of their institutional construction'. In his view the methods for how participants are selected, the timing of consultations, the mode(s) of communication used etc., set the decisive context of participant interaction. The second claim is presented by Ricardo Blaug (2003) who argues that democracy is an ongoing process of struggle and contestation rather than the adoption of a standard recipe of institutional designs. Successful consultations will therefore only occur if deliberative changes are made in the structures of political power. The third claim is suggested by Ann Macintosh (2006). According to her the reported successes and failures of consultations are not necessarily the result of either designs or power struggles, but depend rather upon the quality of research; there is simply no yardstick so success and failure can be claimed for many different reasons and with little if any comparison with other cases.

The paper is designed as follows. Section 2 presents our research model and discusses the advantages and limitations of the case-survey method in this context. Section 3 presents the results and Section 4 concludes by a brief discussion.

2 Method

Because of the situation where there are a lot of case studies but little research across cases, we conducted a case survey as a way of taking a systematic look at the development so far. This method applies a structured investigation protocol to a number of case studies for the purpose of applying statistical methods for analysis. This is particularly useful in a situation where the existing research is mainly comprised of case studies and where it is difficult to do structured primary research across cases. For practical reasons it would be virtually impossible to approach all the cases in this study directly, as they span many years in time, different countries and languages, etc. The case survey method offers some other advantages as well, such as the ability to assess a great number of cases and observe patterns among them, generalizability, reliability and the possibility to test theories more conclusively than in single-case or few-case studies. Because case studies are typically 'information rich', involving many factors and qualitative data, a case survey can also benefit from being able to address many more factors than can typically be included in a survey. However, it is important to bear in mind that the quality of the data in any case survey is only as good as the quality of the case studies from which the data comes. Since the original case studies are done by different researchers and for different purposes they also tend to leave gaps in the data.

Another challenge concerns the selection of cases. Cross-case comparisons are in general concerned with the analysis of differences and similarities in order to understand and explain different phenomena. Isolating similarities and common tendencies across cases, as well as the specificities of particular cases, improve our understanding of the processes under investigation and how they operate in different contexts. In this study we originally aimed for 50 European and 50 US case-studies to make a comparison between different democratic systems possible. These were searched for in traditional channels such as online libraries, Google scholar and other web search tools, conference proceedings etc. We also surveyed the network of scholars in the eParticipation field for cases. Somewhat surprisingly, however, we found much fewer case studies in the United States than in Europe. Considering the sizeable community of Internet users in the US, there should be incentives for local governments to provide new means of participation (Peart & Diaz, 2007). This turned out to not be the case. A possible reason for the lack of initiatives in the US might be the society-centred approach to understanding politics. In this approach, the state and the specific nature of government institutions is played down and the debate is more about the distribution and exercise of power among different groups, with governments and public institutions being treated just as one group among others (Loughlin, 2001:6). The final selection included 50 European and only 7 US cases[3]. It should be noted that there is no way of knowing the "whole population" of eParticipation cases. A natural limitation is *reported* cases – many local trials go unreported because they do not attract researchers' attention – but even so there may obviously be cases reported in other languages than English, or cases we simply did not find using the traditional methods for searching.

There are basically two ideal-type strategies for choosing cases for comparison: the first is to choose cases that are as similar as possible (in terms of their contextual characteristics) and to analyse the differences in outcomes and isolate the factors that explain these differences; the second is to chose cases as different as possible and analyze their commonalities, i.e. what are the common explanatory variables of otherwise diverse cases that explain similar outcomes (Seawright & Gerring, 2008; Yin, 1994). We have used the most different strategy, in order to test the three claims mentioned above. We strived at including cases from different countries, cases that use different methods both for the actual implementation and for the research on them, and cases that are done on different scales; some are very small and some quite large. All in all this would increase the probability that the relationships and similarities we find are generalizable, and not due to particular circumstances or unmeasured variables.

To make sure not to compare apples to oranges we only included cases where some online activity spanning physical distances was included (which excluded many US cases where a large number of people meet physically to sit at computers at special local events, earlier often called "electronic town hall meetings"), where there was a sufficiently comprehensive and well reported study so data could be extracted from it,

---

[3] For lack of space the list of papers reviewed is not included; it occupies 4 pages. It can be retrieved from the authors on request.

and where there was proximity in time. While we could not impose a strict time limit as some cases stretch over several years, we focused on cases after year 2000 because we wanted to exclude apparently old technology which is not in use anymore (such as used in cases from the 1980s) and because we wanted to focus on the contemporary situation in general, where for example it is common to have a computer at home and where everybody at least knows how to use one.

The coding scheme[4] was based on literature in the field. It consisted of three categories of variables: (i) background; (ii) case description; and; (iii) critical factors inhibiting or contributing to success. Each case was coded by one of two PhD students, or by both. To ensure consistent coding we conducted an inter-coder reliability test in which both researchers initially read and coded the same sub-set of case studies independently after which the agreement percentage was mesured and differences in coding discussed. The process was repeated until the reliability test showed greater than 80 percent coder agreement (which only took two cycles), a level of reliability regarded as satisfactory in the literature (Larsson, 1993).

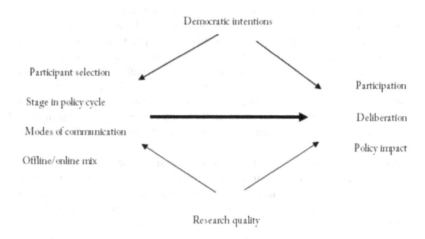

Fig. 1. Research model

Three dependent variables were used to measure the authors' judgments concerning the success and failure of e-consultations: (1) quantity of participation; (2) quality of deliberation and; (3) impact on policy. The measures from the papers surveyed were categorized by using a scale that included the alternatives low, medium, high and not measured. Absolute numbers could not be used as projects were so different, including very differently sized cities as well as different types of consultations. Figure 1 summarizes our research model hypothesizing direct influence on participation, deliberation and policy impact from four institutional factors and both direct and indirect influence from democratic intent and research quality.

---

[4] For reasons of space the full research instrument is not included here; including all alternatives for responses it occupies 8 pages. It can be retrieved from the authors on request.

The independent variables were democratic intent, institutional design, and research quality. These were investigated independently and in combination. All independent variables were composites. Democratic intent was coded as 'mixed' when the case-authors had identified a weak government commitment, weak engagement of elected representatives, or conflicts between representative democracy and the e-consultation initiative. Otherwise intentions were coded as 'strong and clear'. Institutional design was defined by four variables, the method for participant selection, the stage in the policy cycle where the consultation was used, the mode of communication used (deliberative or not), and the communication channels used (online only or a mix of online and offline activities). Research quality included direct involvement of researchers and research methods used, in particuar if and how citizen perspectives were investigated.

3 Results

A first inspection of the data reveals that the failure rate is rather high in relation to all three criteria; 41 percent for participation, 39 percent for deliberation and 49 percent for impact on policy. Furthermore the case studies show clear similarities, despite the fact that they are taking place in quite different contexts. When comparing the numbers in relation to design choices, democratic intentions and research, systematic patterns are evident. In fact, all three claims are supported by the data. Taken together this encouraged us to find out which factors – when controlling for all other variables – are most important, and how the odds for online consultations might possibly change. Since we are dealing with a relatively limited number of cases the use of more advanced statistical techniques is somewhat precarious. But with the caveat that the results should be interpreted with caution, we undertook a series of logistic regression tests.

In Table 1, the regression coefficients are reported with participation (0=low, 1= high) as dependent variable. The crucial value here is Exp (B), which is an indicator of the change in odds. From these values we find that stage in the policy life cycle is the strongest predictor among the variables.

Table 1. Odds for high number of participants

Model estimates	Coefficient	Significance	Exp(B)
Participant selection	.901	.222	2.462
Stage in policy cycle	2.171	.064	8.768
Offline and online mix	1.071	.150	2.918

In probability terms we can say that the chances for success in participation rate, when controlling for other variables, are almost 9 times higher when implementing the consultation at the analysis or decisional stage. The result is statistically significant at the 0.1level. It is interesting to note that also the ways participants are selected and the mix of online and offline methods changed the odds in the way we would expect, however these results were not statistically significant.

In Table 2 the regression coefficients are reported with deliberation (0=low, 1= high) as dependent variable. The result shows high odds for change for four factors

Table 2. Odds for high quality deliberation

Model estimates	Coefficient	Significance	Exp(B)
Participant selection	1.673	.065	5.329
Modes of communication	2.142	.017	8.519
Democratic intentions	1.730	.053	5.640
Content analysis research	2.034	.038	7.643

and significance (at the 0.05 level) for two of them, "modes of communication" and "content analysis research".

As for democratic intentions the change in odds is considerable, and significant at 0.1 level, but the total effect of this variable is likely more important than what the numbers in Table 2 indicate due to the fact that democratic intent is related to design choices. We found co-variation between democratic intent and institutional design factors. As Table 3 shows, the co-variation is strongest for deliberation and aggregation mechanisms; while 78 % of the cases where "strong and clear intentions" were at hand provided deliberation and/or aggregation mechanisms, only 37 % of those where intentions were "mixed" did.

Taking the analysis of institutional designs one step further we examined the predicted probabilities for an online consultation to achieve successful deliberation when using different modes of communication and actively selecting participants. This analysis showed that online consultations with no particular mechanisms for deliberation or aggregation or selection principle yielded a low 18 % probability for the discussions to be assessed as good. In contrast, active invitation and mechanisms for deliberation and aggregation increases the probability to 91 %.

Table 3. Co-variation between democratic intent and institutional design factors

	Participant selection		Stage in the policy cycle	
Democratic intent	Voluntary	Strategic/ random	Analysis/ Decision	Any other stage
Strong and clear	50 %	50 %	35 %	65 %
Mixed	58 %	42 %	21 %	79 %

	Deliberative mode		Online – offline	
	Express preferences	Deliberate/ aggregate	Online only	Online & offline
Strong and clear	22 %	78 %	39 %	61 %
Mixed	63 %	37 %	58 %	42 %

Table 4 shows that policy impact is more sensitive to input factors than the other dependent variables, which is shown by the Exp(B) values being very high for all factors. The reason that the factor Timing of study (i.e. at what time, during or after the project, the research was done) is so important appears to be the fact that many studies were done at an early stage while policy impact typically can only be measured after some time. Table 4 also shows that three other factors were very important; participant selection, modes of communication, and online/offline mix of channels, each of them increasing the chances of success considerably.

Table 4. Odds for high impact on policy

Model estimates	Coefficient	Significance	Exp(B)
Constant	-6.184	.003	.002
Participant selection	2.792	.031	16.318
Modes of communication	2.908	.019	18.312
Online and offline mix	2.899	.015	18.154
Timing of study	3.854	.003	47.182

Analysis of the predicted probabilities show that the probability for a consultation to succceed in making impact on policy is 22 % using voluntary participant selection, but raises to 83 % using strategic selection. For "modes of communication" the corresponding numbers are 22 % for the case when participants may only express opinions and 84 % when deliberative mechanisms are provided (all other factors kept at average values). When neither strategic participant selection nor deliberative mechanisms are at hand the probability for success is only 6 %. When both factors are at hand, the probability is 95 % in our material.

4 Discussion and Conclusion

This research has surveyed 57 e-consultation projects, as reported in the scientific literature, by three hypotheses investigation what influences the outcome; (1) institutional design, (2) democratic intent, and (3) research quality, which might affect the reporting of the results but also possibly the oactome because of better consultation design. Success was operationalized by three dependent variables, high participation, deliberation and policy impact. We found support for all hypotheses, and we also found that they were interrelated; however, not all factors are equally important for all success factors.

Our data show that to achieve high participation consultations should be applied at the analysis or decision making stage in the policy process, i.e. the later stages in the process. To achieve deliberation, mode of communication is the most important factor with content analysis a runner-up. Achieving impact on policy is more sensitive to input factors than the other dependent variables. Three factors, strategic participant selection, deliberative modes of communication, and providing a mix of online and offline channels, all have very high odds for making a difference.

We found it interesting that some institutional design features had a positive effect regardless of whether or not there was democratic intent, e.g. stage in policy cycle. This is in contrast to a common stance in the debate where it is often claimed that unless there is democratic intent there is no point in arranging a consultation. Our research suggests that even if the intent is mixed there are chances for positive outcomes. This is interesting because it means that even if democracy is in fact a struggle (as the second hypothesis claims) consultations can indeed be used as a tool for change. This finding supports a less dichotomized view on both democracy and consultations; change can come both from above and from below.

While there is still a lot of uncertain ground to cover as to the usefulness of consultations, the results from this case survey clearly indicate that it is possible to succeed, and that success is related to a few design criteria and to democratic intentions. The flip side of this is that without adhering to these factors, e-consultation is not of much use. Important design criteria include applying consultations at the decision making stage, mixing online and offline activities and allowing deliberation or aggregation. Against these findings it is easy to suggest improvements to existing practice as most initiatives do not follow these designs. A majority of case studies are describing initiatives that are at the agenda setting stage, that are online only, and that do not make much use of deliberative or aggregative mechanisms.

Considering that experimentation is taking place in very different contexts, the results show considerable similarities. All general claims find quite strong support. There may be several reasons for these similarities. First of all, the differences between countries may not be as huge as often supposed. Local democracies in all the countries we have studied share a theoretical foundation; they are first and above representative democracies. The most challenging task in relation to e-consultations is therefore to find a new balance between participatory and representative forms of democracy.

In conclusion, this paper contributes to practice by identifying critical factors for consultation success. It contributes to theory by testing hypotheses across a large number of cases modelling the causal relationship among factors affecting success. By this we provide a first step towards systematic knowledge building in the field of eParticipation.

References

Albrecht, S.: Whose Voice is Heard in Online Deliberation? A Study of Participation and Representation in Political Debates on the Internet. Information, Communication & Society 9(1), 62–82 (February 2006),
http://www.informaworld.com/smpp/title%7Econtent=t713699183%7
Edb=all%7Etab=issueslist%7Ebranches=9#v9,
http://www.informaworld.com/smpp/
title%7Econtent=g741434872%7Edb=all
Beierle, T., Konisky, D.M.: Values, Conflict, and Trust in Participatory Environmental Planning. Journal of Policy Analysis and Management 19(4), 587–602 (2000)
Blaug, R.: Engineering democracy. Political Studies 50, 102–116 (2002)
Daemen, H.H.F.M., Schaap, L. (eds.): Citizen and City: Developments in Fifteen Local Democracies. Delft, The Netherlands (2000)
Danielson, M., Grönlund, Å., Ekenberg, L., Larsson, A.: Public Decision Support - Using a DSS to Increase Democratic Transparency. International Journal of Public Information Systems 1(1) (2005), Electronic journal, http://www.ijpis.net/
DEMO_net Demo_net D5.1: Report on current ICTs to enable participation (2006),
http://www.demo-net.org (retrieved December 16, 2008),
DEMO_net /eParticipation Evaluation and Impact. /DEMO-net D13.3./ (2006b),
http://www.demo-net.org (retrieved December 16, 2008),
DEMO_net Analytical report on eParticipation research from an Administrative and Political Perspective./ DEMO_net D14.1(2008) (retrieved December 16, 2008),
http://www.demo-net.org
Dunn, W.N.: Public Policy Analysis. Prentice Hall, Englewood Cliffs (1994)

Hayward, C.: Introducing e-enabled citizens panels. The Local e-Democracy National Project (2005), http://www.e-democracy.gov.uk

Fung, A.: Recipes for Public Spheres: Eight Institutional Design Choices and their Consequences. The journal of Political Philosophy 11(3), 338–367 (2003)

Fung, A.: Varieties of Participation in Complex Governance. Public Administration Review (December 2006); Special issue

Grönlund, Å.: Emerging Electronic Infrastructures - Exploring Democratic Components. Social Science Computer Review 21(1), 55–72 (spring 2003)

Jankowski, N.W., Van Os, R.: Internet-based Political Discourse: A Case Study of Electronic Democracy in Hoogeveen. Paper presented at the Conference Prospects for Electronic Democracy, Pittsburgh, PA, September 20-21 (2002)

Jensen, J.L.: Virtual Democratic Dialogue? Bringing together Citizens and Politicians. Information Polity 8(1) (2003)

John, P.: Methodologies and Research Methods in Urban Political Science. In: Baldersheim, H., Wollman, H. (eds.) The Comparative Study of Local Government and Politics: Overview and Synthesis. Barbara Budrich Publishers, Opladen (2006)

Polat, K., Rabia: The Internet and democratic local governance: the context of Britain. The International Information & Library Review 37, 87–97 (2005)

Larsson, R.: Case survey methodology: Quantitative analysis of patterns across case studies. Academy of Management Journal 36(6), 1515–1546 (1993)

Loughlin, J.: Subnational Democracy in the European Union. Challenges and Opportunities. Oxford University Press, Oxford (2001)

Lucas, W.: The case survey method of aggregating case experience. Rand, Santa Monica (1974)

Macintosh, A.: eParticipation in policy-making: the research and the challenges. In: Exploiting the Knowledge Economy: Issues, Applications, Case Studies. IOS Press, Amsterdam (2006)

Macintosh, A., Whyte, A.: Evaluating how eParticipation Changes Local Democracy. In: eGovernment Workshop 2006 (eGOV 2006), September 11, 2006. Brunel University, West London, UB8 3PH (2006)

Morrison, J., Newman, R.: On-line Citizenship: Consultation and Participation in New Labour's Britain and Beyond. International Review of Law Computers & Technology 15(2), 171–194 (2001)

Märker, O., Morgenstern, B., Hagedorn, H., Trénel, M.: Integrating Public Knowledge into Decision Making. Use Case: Internet Public Hearing in the City of Esslingen. In: Wimmer, M. (ed.) Knowledge Management in e-Government - KMGov 2002. 3rd International Workshop on Knowledge Management in e-Government, May 23-24, 2002. Trauner Druck, Linz (2002)

Norris, P.: Digital divide? In: Civic engagement, information poverty, and the Internet worldwide. Cambridge University Press, Cambridge (2001)

Peart, M.N., Diaz, J.R.: Comparative Project on Local e-Democracy Initiatives in Europe and North America. University of Geneva, Geneva (2007)

OECD. Citizens as Partners: Information, consultation and public participation in policy-making: OECD, Paris (2001)

Olsson, J., Åström, J. (eds.): Democratic eGovernance: Approaches and Research Directions. Almqvist & Wiksell International, Stockholm (2006)

Phillips, A.: Why does Local Democracy Matter? In: Pratchett, L., Wilson, D. (eds.) Local Democracy and Local Government. MacMillan Press Ltd. London (1996)

Putnam, R.: Bowling Alone. In: The Collaps and Revival of American Community. Free Press, New York (2000)

Rose, J., Saebo, O.: Democracy Squared. Designing On-line Communities to Accommodate Conflicting Interests. Scandinavian Journal of Information Systems 17(2), 133–168 (2005)

Rowe, G., Frewer, L.J.: Evaluating Public-Participation Exercises: A Research Agenda. In: Science, Technology & Human Values, vol. 29(4), pp. 512–556 (2004)

Seawright, J., Gerring, J.: Case Selection Techniques in Case Study Research. A Menu of Qualitative and Quantitative Options. Political Research Quarterly 61(2), 294–308 (2008)

Stewart, K.: Write Rules and Win: Understanding Citizen Participation Game Dynamics. Public Administration Review (November/December 2007)

Yin, R.: Case study research: Design and methods, 2nd edn. Sage Publishing, Beverly Hills (1994)

Åström, J.: Mot en digital demokrati? Teknik, politik och institutionell förändring (Towards a digital democracy? In: Technology, politics, and institutional change). Örebro Studies in Political Science, vol. 9, Örebro University, Orebro (2004)

The Use of Facebook in National Election Campaigns: Politics as Usual?

Kim Normann Andersen and Rony Medaglia

Copenhagen Business School, Center for Applied ICT, Howitzvej 60, DK-2000,
Frederiksberg, Denmark
{andersen,rm.caict}@cbs.dk

Abstract. The uptake of online media in election campaigning is leading
to speculations about the transformation of politics and cyber-democracy. Politicians running for seats in Parliament are increasingly using online media to
disseminate information to potential voters and building dynamic, online communities. Drawing on an online survey of the Facebook networks of the two top
candidates running for seats in the 2007 Danish Parliament election, this study
suggests that the online sphere is primarily populated by users who already
know the candidates through the traditional channels of party organizations, and
that they do not expect to influence the policy of their candidates. Instead, users
view Facebook mainly as an information channel and as a means to gain social
prestige.

Keywords: eParticipation, Social Networking Service, election campaign,
e-democracy.

1 Introduction

The use of digital media in political campaigns in conjunction with the national elections has rapidly been growing worldwide. National elections in the US and the UK,
among others, well exemplify this (e.g., [1], [2]). In other countries with the highest
penetration of Information and Communication Technologies (ICTs) among citizens,
ICT is being applied in national political campaigning. The use of ICT for participatory purposes in general, is seen to be more likely to occur in contexts that are less
affected by the issues of digital divide. Studies on the digital divide highlight the fact
that social groups with a lack of financial resources are less likely to have access to,
and to use ICT, particularly internet-enabled features [3]. Such a constraint on the
demand of ICT-enabled forms of interaction affects the diffusion of the use and adoption of ICT for participatory purposes. However, research on the use of ICT in political campaigning has only just begun to investigate the impact on citizen participation
in political campaigns that the most recent web 2.0 tools, such as RSS feeds, forums,
wiki applications, and social networking services, would have [4].

In this paper we address the Facebook phenomenon and its use in the last Danish
national election campaign (2007). We do so by posing two research questions: What
communication tools and channels do social network users use to interact with
politicians, and what benefits do they expect? Does the political orientation of the

A. Macintosh and E. Tambouris (Eds.): ePart 2009, LNCS 5694, pp. 101–111, 2009.
© Springer-Verlag Berlin Heidelberg 2009

candidate with whom interaction is sought make a difference in the use of social network by users?

Such research questions involve a twofold dimension of the way that ICT is assumed to have an impact on political participation. One is concerned with the potential of ICT-mediated communication to shape the traditional forms of citizen/politician interaction. The other is concerned with the role of political orientation in affecting the outcomes of such potential.

We conducted an online survey on Facebook users, attempting to understand the mechanisms underlying the decision to link with the political candidates by social networks platform users. We thus address the issue of which tools are actually used, and which benefits are expected from the engagement in different forms of interaction with the political actors through virtual social network.

The aim is to better understand the impact of social network interaction on eParticipation processes. We refer to the definition of eParticipation as "the use of information and communication technologies to broaden and deepen political participation by enabling citizens to connect with one another and with their elected representatives" [5]. Although there is a variety of current definitions of eParticipation, we acknowledge this one as being concerned not just with top-down government initiatives to engage with citizens, but rather to include all stakeholders in democratic participatory decision-making.

The paper is organized as follows. The next section draws on existing research on the issues of eParticipation processes as bottom-up processes that take place in virtual environments, and discusses how different existing models of political democratic engagement interact with different technological platforms. Section 3 presents the methodology of the study, carried out through an online survey of Facebook users during the 2007 Danish national election campaign. In Section 4 and 5, the findings from the survey will be illustrated and discussed, referring to the research questions formulated in the introduction. The conclusion sums up findings from the study, assessing the actual impact of Facebook on the modes of political participation, and provides a first suggestion on the hypothesis of participatory processes enabled by social networking services as "politics as usual."

2   Background and Prior Research

The swift development of the internet has inspired claims that large scale transformations in the structure of political influence in the US, the UK and the EU are under way: the populist claim that the internet will erode the influence of organized groups and political elites, and the community-building claim that the internet will cause a restructuring of the nature of community and the foundations of social order. These claims are significant because they address not only the currently fashionable subject of the internet but also fundamental questions about the causal role of communication in public life [6], [7], [8], [9].

The political scientist Robert Dahl [10] suggested with his book on pluralism that politics would progress to diversity and multifaceted communication channels and content. From this angle, eParticipation and the use of Facebook is yet another facet of democracy and could potentially add pluralism only. Transformation of politics or the interaction between politicians and citizens would not be likely to occur. At best, the online network technologies, such as Facebook, would be expected to lead to "accelerated pluralism," with fragmentation of the present system of interest-based group politics and a shift toward a more fluid, issue-based group politics with less institutional coherence [11]. This would be supported by the work by Danziger et al. [12] that argues that the uptake of new technologies in politics would reinforce existing imbalances in power and would not be able to shift any balance between the dominant coalition and the opposition. The ones in order would actively use digital media that could help reinforce their position and structural and cognitive power, resulting in an actual enforcement of ICT-mediated political communication as "politics as usual" [13].

In line with this, although voice and audio technologies are evolving, text-based participation applications have dominated the spectra of applications. Thus, governments lag behind in the uptake of media that support involvement based on audiovisual media and synchronous dialogue, such as chat. Also, most of the applications designed for involvement are done half-heartedly, in the sense that critical parameters, such as scalability, logs, and software transparency/ updates, are left unattended at the time of the first round of implementation of the application. Moreover, most applications for involvement seem to be top-down driven, supporting formal communication following the traditional administrative-bureaucratic procedures and standards, where institutional values are applied as measures. As depicted in Figure 1, representing the different direction of flows in bottom-up and top-down approaches, few applications are situated on the left hand side of the involvement flow.

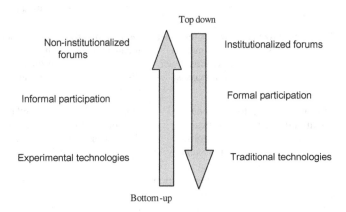

Fig. 1. Top-down and bottom-up approaches to eParticipation [14]

Different types of involvement enabled by ICT are thus assumed to have an impact on the type of interaction between citizens and governments in democratic systems. As a result, a range of models of democracy has been drawn in research focusing on the relationship between ICT and transformations in democratic systems. Hoff et al. [15] suggest four modes of ICT-enabled and supported democratic participation: the consumer, the demo-elitist model, the neo-republican model, and the cyber-democratic model. These modes are breaking new grounds for how to perceive the

Table 1. Emerging modes of democracy for the information age (Hoff et al. [15], adapted by Sæbø and Rose [16])

Characteristics	Consumer	Demo-Elitist	Neo-Republican	Cyber-Democratic
Dominant democratic value	Freedom of choice	Effectiveness	Deliberation and participation	Community, acceptance of diversity
Citizen's role	Voting for representatives (less active between elections)	Voting for representatives (less active between elections)	Active citizens as opinion formers	Active citizens as decision makers
Central form of political participation	Choice of public services	Consensus creation, lobbying	Public debate, associations	Virtual debate, virtual and real actions
Political nexus	Producer/consumer relation	Expert discourse	Public sphere, media	Electronic discussion (Internet)
Main political intermediary	Service declarations, consumption data	Negotiation and campaign institutions	Meetings, hearings (real and virtual)	Electronic networks, electronic communities
Typical ICT application	Websites, citizens cards, databases	Websites, mail, information systems, voter compasses	Geographically located and moderated discussion groups	Self-organised discussion groups (virtual communities)
Main objectives for the use of ICT	Disseminating high quality information to citizens	Supporting vertical relations, transparency	Quality of discussion and bi-directional information	Strengthening the essential network
Dominant political issues	Data security, privacy, service delivery	Re-legitimation and re-orientation of governance	Increasing participation, improving the quality of discussions	Increasing political reflexivity competences and autonomy

relations between the government administration and their citizens. Table 1 illustrates the four modes of eParticipation.

The four modes of involvement demonstrate that, depending on which model guides government, there are different levels of involvement and different means of interaction. The *Consumer* model focuses on the value of freedom of choice by citizens as consumers of public services, and leaves the normative view on the role of institutions – such as parliament, elections and the party system – unaltered. The *Demo-Elitist* model of democracy enabled by ICT also leaves the role of representative institutions unquestioned, while stressing the need to delegate management powers to an elite group of experts who ensure efficiency and effectiveness of public decision-making. The *Neo-Republican* model assumes citizens to be active and take part in deliberation processes within a public sphere, especially at the local level; politicians and citizens alike are thus brought together in ICT-enabled shared spaces to engage in debate and confrontation, leading to decision-making to be subsequently implemented by professional policy executors. Finally, Hoff et al. [15] draw a model representing radical change enabled by ICT, the *Cyber-Democratic*, in which traditional institutions completely leave space to network-based groups and self-organised communities interconnected by ICT means. Political discourse gets scattered across networks, while decision-making powers are decentralised from institutions and put in the hands of citizens.

Concerning the role of political orientation of the actors involved in ICT-mediated interaction – raised by our second research question: "Does the political orientation of the candidate with whom interaction is sought make a difference in the use of social network by users?" – we have to take into account the argument that the political views endorsed by decision-makers on policy-making, and specifically on the relationship between citizens and government in a political context, can have an influence on the ways eParticipation is adopted as a means of involving citizens in the public sphere process. Involving citizens in the public decision-making process is a much debated policy issue that is obviously heavily linked to underlying views about the role that both the politicians in charge and the citizens should play in governmental activities, reflected in the above discussed models.

The relevance of technological innovation in shaping the structure of the relationship between citizens and governmental bodies – that is, the political public sphere – has been highlighted and investigated since the work of Jürgen Habermas on the structural transformation of the public sphere [17]. The diffusion of printing technology in Europe in the course of the XVII century is argued to have enabled the emergence of a public discourse transcending face-to-face communication and has shaped the agenda of confrontation on political matters.

The development of different democracy models related to different views on the role of ICT in the relationship between citizens and governments arose from classic modelling of democratic regimes, as in David Held [18], or Carole Pateman [19]. In particular, Held's distinction between historical ideal-types of democracy (Classical Athenian, Republicanism, Liberal and Direct Marxism) and contemporary models (Competitive Elitist, Pluralist Legal and Participatory) has influenced the development of models of democracy as enabled by the introduction of ICT.

However, on the empirical side, the research literature has thus far produced very little formal theory or evidence linking political ideology to choice of ICT for participation [20], [21], [22]. Guthrie et al. [23] have argued that local political culture shapes the use of technology within an urban context, in that more liberal cities with inclusive politics will be more likely to use information technology to improve citizen participation. The relative importance traditionally attributed to political values, such as social inclusion and participation in the political community by left-wing oriented parties and political actors, can thus be argued to match the adoption of ICT for participatory purposes [24].

Although there is a poor empirical basis supporting such an argument – when not explicitly bringing evidence against it [25], [26], [27], [28] – it is still found prudent not to overlook the role of the actors' political stance in tackling a sensitive issue concerning the relationship between citizens and governments, such as the one involved in eParticipation forms of interaction.

Musso et al. [28] interestingly suggest that one might expect that members of "third parties" on both ends of the ideological spectrum would voice more demand for information technology because members of third parties are more likely to feel dissatisfied with the status quo, and thus may have more interest in having an alternative, possibly ICT-enabled, forum for expressing their concerns. Moreover, members of third parties may have few opportunities to see their views publicised in the "mainstream" media, and also in "off-line" traditional channels.

Even if this latter argument can raise some interest, it is found prudent to hypothesise a higher likelihood of adopting eParticipation features by social democratic parties, as opposed to liberal ones. Centre-left political actors traditionally tend to argue in favour of administrative reforms to support improved citizen participation, more than centre-right ones which, on the other hand, tend to stress the need for a reduction in administrative costs by improving management efficiency and, thus, are more likely to endorse Schumpeterian models of democracy [18] that do not contemplate the bottom-up involvement of citizens [24].

3 Methodology

The two top candidates running for the seat of Prime Minister in the 2007 Danish National Election (held on November 13, 2007), Ms. Helle Thorning-Schmidt and Mr. Anders Fogh Rasmussen, have used Facebook as part of their campaign, with Anders Fogh Rasmussen having 2,367 registered "friends" and Helle Thorning-Schmidt having 2,134 "friends" (figures captured November 6, 2007). From the online list of their friends, we selected the subgroup "Denmark" to ensure they presumed interest in the national election, and then we selected one in every ten persons listed until reaching the sample of 210 persons for each candidate.

An online survey was prepared and sent as a link in an email to each of the sample members. The online survey software SurveyMonkey™ was used to collect and analyse the data.

We asked each candidate three sets of questions:

- What is your relation to/ knowledge of the candidate?
- Which digital communication do you have with the candidate?
- Which benefit do you expect to get from linking with the candidate?

A reminder was sent to non-respondents in the first round. The final response rate of the survey was 69.7%.

4 Findings

The substance of the survey was to understand the motivation of Facebook users for being "friends" with the two politicians, to find out what type of digital communication they had with the candidates, and to understand whether, and what, they had gained from the virtual link they had established.

The following table shows findings concerning the type of relation between the Facebook users and the candidates.

Table 2. Knowledge/ relation to the candidate, distributed on the candidate linked

	Sum		Social democratic candidate		Liberal candidate	
What is your relation to/ knowledge of the candidate?	*N*	*%*	*N*	*%*	*N*	*%*
We are friends (personal)	2	2%	2	2%	0	0%
We are colleagues (work)	4	3%	3	4%	1	2%
I know him/her through the party	72	54%	47	56%	25	51%
I know him/her through Facebook only	53	40%	31	37%	22	45%
We are family related	2	2%	1	1%	1	2%
Total	133	100%	84	100%	49	100%

Data shows that the overwhelming majority of the respondents have an indirect knowledge of the candidates, either through the party (54%) or through Facebook only (40%). While there are no relevant differences in percentages between the social democratic and the liberal candidate, it is striking to see that the number of Facebook users claiming to know the candidates through the party are relevantly higher than the number that claim to know them through Facebook. This clearly suggests that, in the case of Facebook, the impact of the presence of the candidates on the social network of the virtual platform is relevant, but yet to a lower extent than that of traditional communication channels, i.e., the party organization.

The following table illustrates the array of different tools of interaction that respondents use to communicate with the candidates, also distinguishing between users linked to the social democratic and the liberal candidate.

Table 3. Digital communication with candidates, distributed on the candidate linked

	Sum		Social democratic candidate		Liberal candidate	
Which digital communication do you have with the candidate?	*N*	*%*	*N*	*%*	*N*	*%*
Through Facebook	81	57%	49	57%	32	57%
Mail	9	6%	8	9%	1	2%
Chat through other programs such as MSN and Skype	10	7%	6	7%	4	7%
None	42	30%	23	27%	19	34%
Total	142	100%	86	100%	56	100%

Figures show that the majority of the respondents use the Facebook platform itself to communicate with the candidates, while only 13% use other means to establish an interaction, such as mail or chat services. It is interesting to see how almost one out of three social network users do not use any of the digital tools to communicate with the politicians that they are "friends" with. This could be interpreted as a share of users that approach virtual social network contact with political actors in a passive, non-interactive fashion. Such a relevant share of users appears to be made more of virtual "spectators" of what goes on in the political arena – in a way that is similar to processes occurring within the traditional political communication of broadcast media – rather than to seek active engagement in political activity by digital means.

The last table shows data concerning the benefits expected by social network users from linking with the political candidates, also distinguishing between users linked to the social democratic candidate and the liberal one.

Table 4. Benefits expected from linking with the candidate, distributed on the candidate linked

	Sum		Social democratic candidate		Liberal candidate	
Which benefit do you expect to get from linking with the candidate?	N	%	N	%	N	%
Increased knowledge about their policy	53	45%	32	46%	21	45%
Influence on their policy	11	9%	6	9%	5	11%
Visibility on the internet	34	29%	24	34%	10	21%
Social prestige	19	16%	8	11%	11	23%
Total	117	100%	70	100%	47	100%

Data show that, overall, the majority of the motivators for linking by virtual means with the candidates are concerned with the opportunity to increase knowledge about the candidates' policy (45%), and to obtain visibility on the internet (29%). Similarly to the other questions, there is no relevant difference in this issue between users that link with the social democratic candidate and those that link with the liberal one, except for the fact that the latter seem to identify social prestige as a motivator to link to a slightly greater extent, while users that link with the social democratic candidate appear to be more motivated by visibility, compared to those linking with the other candidate.

Most interestingly, figures show that the least cited motivation for linking with the candidates is the possibility of influencing their policy. This finding strikingly suggests that users appear not to gain benefit from the social network platform in terms of the participatory use of it – that is, to "have a say" in the political process. Only less than one out of ten respondents claim to use Facebook to affect the politicians' activity. In this case, the use of social network clearly seems not to be intended by users as a channel of eParticipation.

5 Discussion

The findings enable us to provide some initial answers to the research questions, even though the overall empirical basis of the data is still not particularly robust, and thus findings should be regarded as being suggestive, rather than as statistically based considerations.

As far as the type of knowledge that social network users have of the political candidates is concerned, the study suggests that social network platforms seem not to have any revolutionary impact on the traditional means of knowledge and communication between politicians and the electorate. Social network users that link to candidates most frequently do so while already being in contact with them through the party organizations. The impact of Facebook, therefore, seems not to be relevant in this case, in the sense that the creation of a virtual "friendship" on the social network platform does little more than reproducing the existing channels of contact with the politicians, as in the "off-line" world.

When investigating the array of digital tools that Facebook users adopt to interact with their "friend" candidates, we observe that there is poor integration between communication occurring within the social network and other digital tools available for the citizen-politician relationship. In other words, the average Facebook user uses only Facebook itself to interact with the candidates, without seeking any other digital means. It has to be specified, however, that this applies only to social network users who do interact somehow with the candidates that they link with. It is to be noted that a striking around 30% of social network users do not engage in any ICT-enabled interaction at all. This rather relevant share of users appears to look at social network contact as an occasion for being passive spectators in the candidates' arena only, without seeking any form of interaction or active engagement.

The scenario is summed up by looking at the last research question, that is, the benefits expected by Facebook users in linking to the candidates. The social network platform is mainly seen as a means to obtain information, that is, establishing a one-way relation in which information is retrieved from policy-makers for use by citizens. Such a relation established with the sole objective of obtaining information is described as the lowest level of eParticipation enabled in the citizen-politician relations by ICT means [29], [30]. Moreover, no significant difference on this question, as in the others, is related to the political orientation of the candidates that users link with: users that link with the social democratic party candidate do not seek to influence the candidates' policy more than those linked with the liberal party candidate do.

Summarizing, the findings, overall, clearly suggest arguments against a significant impact of the social network type of interaction on the way that political processes, such as a national election, work. If we refer to the models of ICT-enabled democratic relations discussed in section 2, it is to be acknowledged that a clear-cut move toward a Cyber-democratic mode of ICT-enabled participation is definitely not occurring by the means of the existing social networking platform. On the contrary, the case of Facebook users in the Danish National Election is arguably to be encompassed within modes of ICT-enabled democratic relations that give citizens a more passive role – such as the Consumer mode or the Demo-elitist mode. In this sense, findings suggest that the citizen-politician interaction within the Facebook environment does not introduce significant changes in the way politics traditionally works. In other words, Facebook politics, at least thus far, is "politics as usual."

6 Conclusion

In this paper we addressed the Facebook phenomenon and its use in the Danish national election campaign. We did so by posing two research questions: what communication tools and channels do social network users use to interact with politicians, and what benefits do they expect? Does the political orientation of the candidate with whom interaction is sought make a difference in the use of social network by users? On the substantive dimension, the paper proposes that Facebook politics appears to be "politics as usual," in the sense that the Facebook users who decide to link with the two candidates are already connected with them through the traditional, off-line channels, such as previous employment or membership of the political party. Moreover, their expectation to obtain information on politics through social networking can be attributed to the previous knowledge and network, rather than to the expectations of the impacts of the Facebook connection per se. Thus, social network users do not expect to gain increased influence on politics.

At this stage, there is clearly a need to investigate the underlying motivations of the propositions suggested in this paper. This particularly applies to the observation that social network involvement is clearly not seen as a means to actively participate in the political process by influencing the politicians' proposed policies. In this perspective we need to understand, for instance, whether this phenomenon occurs because Facebook network users, as such, are not interested in actively engaging in the political sphere – even if the possibility were to be given – or whether the phenomenon occurs because the social network platform per se is not perceived as being apt to enable eParticipation in a relevant way.

References

1. Gibson, R.K., Margolis, M., Resnick, D., Ward, S.J.: Election Campaigning on the WWW in the USA and UK: A Comparative Analysis. Party Politics 9(1), 47–75 (2003)
2. Coleman, S. (ed.): Cyberspace Odyssey: the Internet in the UK Election. The Hansard Society, London (2001)
3. Norris, P.: Digital Divide: Civic Engagement, Information Poverty, and the Internet Worldwide. Cambridge University Press, New York (2001)
4. Kampitaki, D., Tambouris, E., Tarabanis, K.: eElectioneering: Current research trends. In: Wimmer, M.A., Scholl, H.J., Ferro, E. (eds.) EGOV 2008. LNCS, vol. 5184, pp. 184–194. Springer, Heidelberg (2008)
5. Macintosh, A.: eParticipation in Policy-making: the research and the challenges. In: Cunningham, P., Cunningham, M. (eds.) Exploiting the Knowledge Economy: Issues, Applications and Case Studies, p. 1. IOS press, Amsterdam (2006)
6. Coleman, S., Ward, S. (eds.): Spinning the Web: Online Campaigning during the 2005 General Election. Hansard Society, London (2005)
7. Gibson, R.K., Römmele, A.: Truth and Consequence in Web Campaigning: Is there an Academic Digital Divide? European Political Science 4(3), 273–287 (2005)
8. Lusoli, W.: The Internet and the European Parliament Elections: Theoretical Perspectives, Empirical Investigations and Proposals for Research. Information Polity 10(3/4), 153–163 (2005)

9. Lusoli, W., Ward, S., Gibson, R.K. (Re)connecting Politics? Parliament, the Public and the Internet. Parliamentary Affairs 59(1), 24–42 (2006)
10. Dahl, R.: Who Governs?: Democracy and Power in an American City. Yale University Press, New Haven (1982)
11. Bimber, B.: The Internet and Political Transformation: Populism, Community, and Accelerated Pluralism. Polity 31(1), 133–160 (1998)
12. Danziger, J.N., Dutton, W.H., Kling, R., Kraemer, K.L.: Computers and Politics: High Technology in American Local Governments. Columbia University Press, New York (1982)
13. Margolis, M., Resnick, D.: Politics as Usual: The Cyberspace Revolution. Sage, Thousand Oaks (2000)
14. Andersen, K.V., Henriksen, H.Z., Medaglia, R., Secher, C.: Costs of eParticipation: the Management Challenges. Transforming Government: People, Process & Policy 1(1), 29–43 (2007)
15. Hoff, J., Horrocks, I., Tops, P.: Democratic Governance and New Technology: Technologically Mediated Innovations in Political Practice in Western Europe. Routledge, London (2000)
16. Sæbø, Ø., Rose, J.: Democracy squared. Scandinavian Journal of Information Systems 17(2), 133–167 (2005)
17. Habermas, J.: The Structural Transformation of the Public Sphere: An Inquiry into a Category of Bourgeois Society. MIT Press, Cambridge (1991)
18. Held, D.: Models of Democracy. Blackwell, Oxford (1996)
19. Pateman, C.: Participation and Democratic Theory. Cambridge University Press, Cambridge (1970)
20. Medaglia, R.: The challenged identity of a field: The state of the art of eParticipation research. Information Polity: The International Journal of Government & Democracy in the Information Age 12(3), 169–181 (2007)
21. Rose, J., Sanford, C.: Mapping eParticipation Research: Four Central Challenges. The Communications of the Association for Information Systems 20(55), 909–943 (2007)
22. Sæbø, Ø., Rose, J., Skiftenes Flak, L.: The shape of eParticipation: Characterizing an emerging research area. Government Information Quarterly 25(3), 400–428 (2008)
23. Guthrie, K.K., Dutton, W.H.: The politics of citizen access technology: The development of public information utilities in four cities. Policy Studies Journal 20(4), 574–597 (1992)
24. Kearns, I.: Digital change and centre-left values: Getting beyond e-democracy. New Economy 8(3), 183–185 (2001)
25. Hoff, J., Lofgren, K., Torpe, L.: The state we are in: E-democracy in Denmark. Information Polity 8, 49–66 (2003)
26. van der Graft, P., Svensson, J.: Explaining eDemocracy development: A quantitative empirical study. Information Polity 11(2), 123–134 (2006)
27. Medaglia, R.: Measuring the diffusion of eParticipation: A survey on Italian local government. Information Polity: The International Journal of Government & Democracy in the Information Age 12(4), 265–280 (2007)
28. Musso, J., Hale, M., Weare, C.: Electronic Democracy and the Diffusion of Municipal Web Pages in California. Administration and Society 31(1), 3–27 (1999)
29. Macintosh, A.: Characterizing E-Participation in Policy-Making. In: Proceedings of the 37th Hawaii International Conference on System Sciences (2004)
30. OECD: Promises and problems of e-democracy: Challenges of citizen on-line engagement. OECD, Paris (2003)

Fostering e-Participation at the Urban Level: Outcomes from a Large Field Experiment

Fiorella De Cindio and Cristian Peraboni

DICo – Dept. of Informatics and Communication
Università degli Studi di Milano, Via Comelico, 39, Italy
{fiorella.decindio,cristian.peraboni}@unimi.it

Abstract. e-participation software environments, more than other web applications, are "very early social machines" that need to "evolve through trial, use and refinement" with a twofold goal: learning from the field experience success and failure lessons and tuning the e-participation technologies. The paper presents the main outcomes of a large field experiment involving ten cities of the Lombardy region. . After presenting the project and sketching the main characteristics of the ten municipalities, the paper explores the outcomes emerged from these experiences drawing some lessons about what can foster e-participation at the urban level and reduce the impact of the hindrances that may hamper it.

Keywords: eParticipation, online deliberation, social machine.

1 Introduction

Since the pioneers' age of Internet, many people cherish the dream and the thought that Internet could be a platform able to give voice to citizens and to increase democracy [1], [2], [3], [4]. In the '80 and '90 Free Nets, Community and Civic Networks represented a significant effort to involve citizens in public affaires. They were grassroots initiatives, basically based on BBS technologies, which succeeded in fostering citizens' participation as public squares able to collect civic intelligence useful for addressing local problems collaboratively [5], [6]. Community networks flourished in U.S., Canada as well as in Europe, and often disappeared, as described in [7] In particular in Italy two pioneering experiences took place in Milan (www.retecivica.milano.it) and in Bologna (www.comune.bologna.it) paving the way for several other initiatives, including OnDe and RecSando which will be considered in the sequel. As suggested by the often quoted [8], years after those early efforts, the so called web 2.0 can be viewed in this perspective as a platform enforcing a shift of paradigm from publishing to participation. This "new" vision of the web rediscovers the participatory and social dimension of the net in vogue before the advent of the web (Fidonet, Internet newsgroups, community networks, among the others).

Actually, Tim Berners-Lee, since its very beginning, points out the relevance of this social dimension of the web. Recently, in the paper *Web Science: An Interdisciplinary Approach to Understanding the Web* [9] that he co-authored with four

A. Macintosh and E. Tambouris (Eds.): ePart 2009, LNCS 5694, pp. 112–124, 2009.
© Springer-Verlag Berlin Heidelberg 2009

colleagues, they state that "today's interactive [web] applications are very early social machines" and "the ability to engineer successful [web] applications requires a better understanding of the features and functions of the social aspects of the systems". They also claim that "an important aspect of research exploring the influence of the Web on society involves online societies using Web infrastructure to support dynamic human interaction. This work – seen in trout.cpsr.org [now hosted at www.publicsphereproject.org] and other such efforts – explores how the Web can encourage more human engagement in the political sphere. Combining it with the emerging study of the Web and the coevolution of technology and social needs is an important focus of designing the future Web."

There is the need to carry on such efforts combining the development of interactive web applications and their field experiments and trials. Web applications, indeed, "are unlikely to be developed through a single deliberate effort in a single project or site; rather, technology is needed to allow user communities to construct, share, and adapt social machines so successful models evolve through trial, use, and refinement" [9].

The work presented in this paper can be placed in this stream of research. It concerns the development of an integrated set of web applications supporting participation (mainly, but not necessarily only, at the local level) and their field trial. The experience done with a first prototype [10], [11] provided inputs for a larger development in the framework of a national programme for promoting e-participation. While [12] was focused on the design and on the functionalities of the software tools, here the focus is on the outcomes of the field experiments of their application in ten different sites. Even if these outcomes have been probably not up to expectations, it is worth sharing and analyzing them with the objective to understand which lessons can be learned in order to foster e-participation at the urban level and to reduce the impact of the hindrances that hamper it.

The paper is organized as follows: section 2 introduces the project under which the e-participation experiments took place, section 3 presents the outcomes from the field experiments and section 4 draws some conclusion and direction for future work.

2 The Field Experiments

The "Call for Selecting Projects to Promote Digital Citizenship (e-Democracy)" issued in 2004 by Italy's Ministry for Reforms and Innovation in Public Administration within the second phase of the e-government programme provided the umbrella for developing a large field experiment involving ten different municipalities in the Lombardy region, in the North of Italy. The role of promoter and scientific leader of the project was undertaken by an association – AIReC – set up in 1996 by the Lombardy region and by the University of Milan to promote civic informatics. It has been responsible of the main choices in designing and managing the project, while the managerial responsibility of the project was upon one of the municipalities member of the consortium.

The definition of the consortium was driven by a variety of considerations:

- the requirement of including both larger and smaller cities;
- the requirement of including municipalities with (resp., without) earlier experience in participation and in e-participation;

- the requirement of including municipalities administrated by a left-oriented government coalition as well as municipalities administrated by a right-oriented government coalition.

Regarding the administration disposition toward citizen's involvement, the short time range of the project (two years), suggested to include municipalities with (at least) some previous commitment in this direction. The network of municipalities which had already signed the Aalborg chart sounded worthy of consideration since they were already committed by a formal act (either of the city council or of the city government) to pursuing the Kyoto Protocol by involving citizens in sustainable development projects and activities, managed according to the local Agenda 21 participatory approach.

The project staff decided to involve only municipalities in the Lombardy region: on the one end, because it has a good and homogeneous rate of penetration of the Internet in all its territory, while it would have been too difficult to consider the differences among the North, the Center, and South of Italy; on the other hand, for testing one of the tools by using the authentication card distributed by the Lombardy government to all its citizens (even though, finally, this test did not take place). The consortium of cities which entered as partners in the project consists, after all, of the following municipalities:

- Mantua has been selected as project leader mainly because of its managerial experience as leader of the *People* project, funded in the first phase of the abovementioned e-government programme. Mantua had also extensive experience in Agenda 21 processes and a long-dated interest — even though with no actual experience — in community networking;
- Mantua brought in the project three municipalities (Brescia, Sesto San Giovanni, and Vigevano) which had been partners in *People* project. Their focus and goal in joining the new project was initially more technology-oriented then participation-oriented;
- two municipalities (Lecco and Pavia) had strong previous experience in Agenda 21 projects. Namely, Lecco was the leader of the Lombardy association of the municipalities engaged in Agenda 21;
- two municipalities (Desenzano sul Garda and San Donato Milanese) had previous strong experience in community networking. Desenzano s.G. administration promoted the ONDE (ONline DEsenzano) community network in 1995, leaving quite a large autonomy in managing the activities to a group of young computer professionals. RecSando is the community network active in San Donato M.se since 1996, promoted and managed by a group of (mainly young) volunteers under the umbrella of a left-oriented cultural association. It is worth mentioning that RecSando never succeeded to establish stable relationships with the town government, even when leaded by a left-oriented coalition;
- Vimercate was quite well-known for its engagement in one of the first experiments in Italy of participatory budget;
- Como was included into the consortium to have another (besides Lecco and Vigevano) influential municipality administrated by a right-oriented coalition.

After the consortium was set up, during the first six months of the project three main activities took place:

- the analysis of the participatory processes running in the partner municipalities and the identification of possible participatory processes to run within the project. Each municipality was required to define the 'participatory contract' with the citizenry, by personalizing a pattern of contract provided by the project staff;

- the definition of the software key features and functionalities as well as the development priorities. This work was based of a preparatory research and of a prototypal implementation and trials of the e-participation tools, already presented in [13]. For sake of consistency of this paper, it is worth recalling that the e-participation software consists of three interrelated spaces: the *community space*, aimed at facilitating the rise of mutual trust between participants through free discussions; the *deliberation space* to foster the creation of a shared position among the participants, i.e., to finalize a deliberative process which has to produce a well defined outcome. An *information space* (aimed at facilitating the collection and sharing of information provided by citizens to support group activities) is integrated in both the others two spaces.

    The explicit request coming from the municipalities suggested the idea of introducing the so-called CityMap, as the main tool of the community space, for attracting citizens before involving them in participatory processes. It allows people to "tag" places of a territory with discussions and documents related to them. After the CityMap, in chronological order, the *Informed Discussion*, the *Certified Citizens Consultation* and the *Deliberative Meeting* [12] have been implemented as tools of the deliberative space;

- the definition of a communication strategy for promoting the project and its e-participation activities. It has been put into action in each of the partner Municipalities, through a multiplicity of communication channels: local media (newspapers, radio, and the like) as well as community "points", e.g. libraries and schools.

3 Outcomes from the Field Experiments

Ten different instances of the openDCN software environment, one for each municipality partner of the e21 consortium, were created and put online: the first ones have been Como and Sesto s.G. (late April 2007) – as they wanted to publish the website, even in an early stage, before the forthcoming municipal elections scheduled for late May 2007 – followed by Vimercate, Brescia, Mantua and Pavia (May 2007), Lecco and Vigevano (June 30, 2006), Desenzano s.G. (August 31, 2007) and San Donato M.se (December 6, 2007). The Co.Ri. consortium published its website in June 2007, when it was not yet part of the e21 consortium; however we keep this as the starting date of the online activities. Co.Ri. became part of the e21 consortium in November 2007, in place of Sesto s.G. whose new local government, elected in May 2007, decided to leave the e21 project. In the following paragraphs, we therefore consider ten e21 websites, including Co.Ri. and excluding Sesto s.G. We firstly provide figures

(Fig. 1, 2 and 3) which present some basic participation indicators of the activity in the ten websites plotting their e-participation trends. The figures respectively present:

- the monthly page views (Fig.1);
- the number of registered participants (Fig.2);
- the number of messages sent in the CityMap (Fig.3).

It is worth noting that the data plotted in the figures mainly come from the CityMap, since, as we shall discuss later on (cf. § 3.3), the activities in the deliberative space have been in essence void in every site.

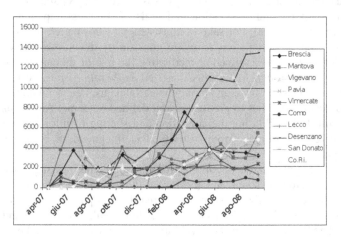

Fig. 1. Monthly Page Views

In the next paragraphs we draw qualitative consideration for interpreting these data.

3.1 Degrees of e-Participation

The indicators plotted in the figures lead to group the ten sites[1] in three classes:

- the first one consists of the two most active sites – Vigevano and Desenzano s.G.; they primarily emerge in Fig. 1, and are confirmed by Fig. 2 and 3, especially if one remembers that Desenzano s.G. came online only by the end of August 2007;
- the second one consists of the sites – Como, Lecco and Co.Ri – which, although online for a significant lapse of time, actually never took off;
- the third one consists of the remaining sites: Brescia, Pavia, San Donato M.se, Mantua and Vimercate. Good potentialities and serious difficulties, peak moments and quick flops: a variety of reasons that we will discuss in the sequel left e-participation, in all these sites, in an *aurea mediocritas* state, neither alive nor really dead.

---

[1] Here and in the sequel, we use *sites* to refer to the e21 websites coupled with the related activities occurring in the city. It is in fact impossible to study e-participation in itself, forgetting what happens in the physical world. The online and offline dimensions of participation are inherently coupled.

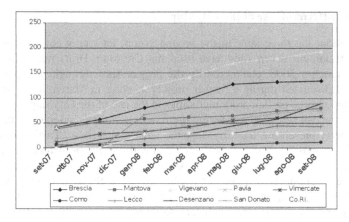

Fig. 2. Number of registered participants

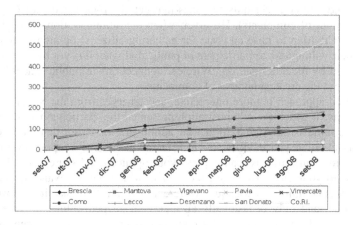

Fig. 3. Number of messages

Before disregarding the three sites in the second group (the dead ones), it is worth discussing what caused their failure. In Lecco the alderman, who was the leading actor of the local Agenda 21, fell ill just before the starting of the e21 activities and his successor was not at all interested in promoting participatory processes. Como story is somehow similar to Sesto s.G.: after the municipal elections in May 2007, even though the alderman in charge of the e21 project was re-elected, the dislocation of power and interests in the new administration were such that the e21 project was *de facto* canceled. Co.Ri. website has been published in June 2007 to support a participatory process for waste management. However, at that stage citizens' involvement in offline activities was already ahead, it continued basically in presence and the website was seen as a space for distributing and accessing information resulting from the offline forum. This explains the relatively high number of page views with respect a quasi null number of registrations and messages by citizens.

3.2   Three Patterns of Use of the CityMap

Forgetting about the three sites in the second group, let's now consider the way in which the remaining seven sites have used the CityMap. Hints raised in a project meeting in January 2008, elaborated by the project staff through in-depth contents analysis, and discussed during a further project meeting in March 2008, support the identification of three participatory modalities in the use of the CityMap.

The first one can be called a *listening approach*. It has been adopted in the Mantua website, where, presenting the CityMap, the alderman writes: "Participants will be able to make proposals, confront each other and with the Public Administration about topics and issues they consider relevant. At the same time, the Public Administration will promote discussions on issues of public interest with the goal of gathering the citizens' opinions". This approach sees the CityMap as a space where citizens are the main actors and the administration listens to their voices. In the meeting in March 2008, the Mantua alderman more explicitly claimed that the CityMap is a *free space* made available to citizens to discuss any topics they wish. The administration takes the commitment to consider only the ones that get significant audience (typically in terms of number of comments). However, when the administration pursued the idea of using the CityMap to raise an issue for gathering citizens' opinion, they promptly manifest their willingness to participate in public dialogue: it is not by chance that the thread opened by the alderman on "Wireless connections in public spaces" has been the one that got the greatest number of comments.

The second approach is more interactive, and emerges from the Vigevano experience. The way in which the administration presented the 'participatory contract' was basically the same as in Mantua. In fact the administration writes that it conceives the CityMap as an online space "dedicated to listening to citizens' proposals for the city", a space where "you [citizens] can express your opinions and share your ideas on issues related to your city". However, the way in which the Vigevano administration interpreted this commitment was quite different. While in Mantua citizens were actually left alone, and only occasionally an alderman peeped online, in Vigevano the administration delegated to the public relation officer, who readily accepted, the responsibility of promoting the online discussions. He also involved other employees. As soon as one of them see something relevant (because of the topics; to explain the administration position upon a critique; or to answer some explicit questions concerning public interest, rather than personal, issues), he posts a comment. Although it is clear to everybody that they belong to the city administration, they have adopted a peer-to-peer communication style. The CityMap thus became a dialogue space between citizens and with the administration. During the above mentioned project meeting in March 2008, this approach has been explicitly acknowledged as *the online extension of the municipal public relations office*.

The third approach has been undertaken in Brescia. The 'participatory contract' explains that the CityMap is aimed to "define policies for improving the urban quality and make the city more livable together with the citizenry". It is therefore much more explicitly *oriented to provide the breeding ground for policy-making participatory processes*. It says the strong commitment of the alderman in charge of traffic issues. Indeed, he personally opened discussions to listen to citizens' opinion in the perspective of involving them in a decision-making process. In one case he wrote: "What do you think about allowing bicycles to circulate in two-way in the one-way streets of the old town "30km/h area"?" He got 26 comments, some pro and some contra, all pertinent and fair, also when in disagreement. Of course, this promising approach gained the attention of the citizens, and by consequence, Brescia was, in the first months of the project, in the group of the most successful sites. Unfortunately, as the Spring 2008 municipal elections began to draw near, in a very difficult political situation for the administration in office, the alderman seemed to shy from direct, open contact with the electorate. As a result, the liveliness of the website immediately bore the brunt, as can be seen in Fig. 1. In May the elections yield a change of administration, and this interesting experience definitively ended (typically, almost no more citizen register since then).

The fact that CityMap supports different participatory approaches is important to dynamically allow an evolution from one to the other, from the less demanding (just listening) to a more continuous and ambitious level of participation. This happened in Vigevano that started by declaring a mere listening contract, but than adopted a much more interactive approach which is the basis of its success. According to [14], we can say that the CityMap acts as a facilitator of ideas and changes.

3.3 Continuity and Discontinuity in e-Participation

The overall trend of the participation indicators deserves attention. On the one hand, Fig. 2 and 3 show a slow although continuous increment of registered users and messages; on the other hand, ups and downs characterize page views (Fig. 1). In the following we analyze continuity and discontinuity aspects within this e-participation experience for better understanding the relation existing among them.

The (Positive) Role of Preexisting Community Networks. To discuss the importance of continuity in promoting e-participation it is worth considering, within the e21 sites, the cases of Desenzano s.G. and San Donato M.se. Their e21 websites have been delayed with respect to the others because of the municipal elections held in May 2008.

San Donato M.se e21 website went online in January 2008 and in one month it became the third most successful one. We believe that this can be explained only by considering that in San Donato M.se the RecSando (http://www.recsando.it) community network was running since 1996 (cf. §2). The relationship between RecSando and the city government saw ups and downs over the years (more downs than ups, we should say). Nevertheless, RecSando has managed to nurture a culture and practice of civic knowledge sharing and engagement through the net. As soon as the e21 site was up, several members of the RecSando community mobilized to exploit the new online environment for opening a dialogue (not free of controversy) with the newly elected city administration (cf. the peak in Fig.1 around February 2008). However, as they did not find reliable interlocutors, their attention on the initiative quick decreased and the San Donato M.se website fell into the 'aurea mediocritas' class.

The Desenzano s.G. website became operative September 2007. Also in the Desenzano s.G. the OnDe (http://www.onde.net) community network was running since 1995. We believe that the fact that Desenzano s.G. is now one of the two still alive e21 website depends on the breeding ground created by OnDe as well as from the capability of the current administration to profit of this background, despite some conflict with the OnDe staff. Recently, the local government has decided to promote a participatory process with the objective of involving citizens in the drafting the regulation of the municipal public media library, an historical place for the OnDe community.

These examples validate the claim that e-participation requires time, resolution and perseverance by all the involved social actors to set up an online trusted public space devoted to discuss public affaires [2]. These two examples also confirm that a community can provide the suitable continuity of participation activities which leads to a well-established participation habit.

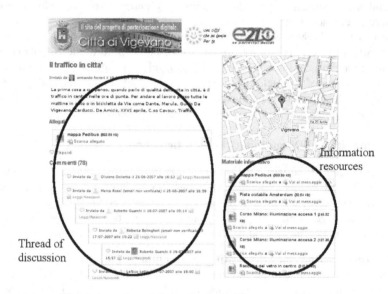

Fig. 4. A portion of discussion in the Vigevano website

Building an Online Community. The in-depth analysis of the seven CityMaps reports the increasing quality of the discussions through the participants' growing ability to carry on fair, rational and interactive discussions [15]. This trend is more evident in the Vigevano and Desenzano s.G. websites. Citizens as well as public officers learn to reply each other in a well focused way and to profit from the facilities provided by the tool to collect informative resources for illustrating their position (cf. the right-hand frame in Fig. 4 from the Vigevano website). The increasing quality of participation over time is endorsed by Fig. 5: it shows, again in the case of Vigevano, the percentage of messages sent by using the three different authentication modes: as registered users; as users who confirm the post with an email; as users who don't leave an email to guarantee for their post[2]. Fig. 5 shows a decreasing number of messages posted with this last mode: at the end of the period only the 15% of them has been sent using such a weak authentication. A similar result can be observed in the

---

[2] It is worth pointing out that in any case, the first and family names must be provided. What changes is the chance that a fake identity is used. Only registered users can open a new thread of discussion, while everybody can post a comment.

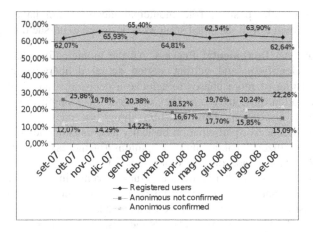

Fig. 5. Vigevano trend of messages per user

case of Desenzano s.G. These two remarks indicate that *civic online communities* are rising in the two more promising websites (Vigevano and Desenzano s.G.) creating the proper conditions for establishing the participation to higher levels. Tools of the community space can enable the creation of a shared and trusted online environment which supplies the suitable substrate upon which peaks moments can occur and increase participation. The Vigevano experiment indicates that, where an online community doesn't exist, it is important to create the conditions for moving toward its creation.

A Peak (Negative?) Moment: The Municipal Elections. A typical peak moment occurs in the occasion of the municipal elections. For instance, the peak of page views for the Brescia website in March 2008 is due to propaganda activities at the opening of the electoral campaign.

We already mentioned the almost always negative consequences of the municipal elections in Como, Sesto s.G. and Brescia. In Desenzano s.G. and San Donato M.se the elections stopped the project for a long period and this is the reason why they arrived so late to publish the e21 website. In Mantua and Vimercate the (negative) effect of the elections arose in between the submission of the project (in 2004) and its actual beginning (in 2006): in both cases, although the left-oriented coalition was re-elected, the members of the government and their agenda changed, so that the initial strong commitment in the e21 project (and, more in general, in citizens participation) seriously decreased. In order to reduce the negative effects of the political changes, e-participation should be as far as possible released from the fortune of the government that promotes it, by engaging members of the municipal administration.

However, as the above mentioned peak moment in Brescia shows, the electoral campaign could also be considered as a moment that enhance participation. At election time, politicians are particularly willing to meet voters and listen to their problems, complaints, and suggestions. Citizens as well display a participation potential as they feel the possibility of receiving consideration by the candidates. In [11] we widely discuss the positive role municipal elections can have for enforcing e-participation, when a well-designed strategy is designed to pursue this opportunity.

e-Participation: An Incremental Process. All the municipalities have had serious difficulties in identifying and getting started actual deliberative processes, i.e., processes consisting of more phases to achieve a decision. Candidate participatory processes were often quite trivial, as they consisted of a single step managed by a simple informed discussion. This situation shows on one hand that municipal governments still conceive participation basically as a listening activity to be carried out by gathering citizens' comments and opinions (in the case under consideration through the CityMap) and, on the other hand, that it is difficult to undertake participatory processes which require the actual citizens' involvement in decision-making if the information and listening levels of participation (making reference to the OECD classification [16].) are not well-established. The three levels are to some extent incremental and every level provides the basis for the next one. This implies that, in order to run deliberative processes, it is necessary to create the proper conditions, by creating a participatory space characterized by fair exchange of ideas among the participants – citizens, public officers and administrators –, sharing of experiences, information and knowledge., i.e., ultimately, a basis of mutual trust among them. The opportunity of starting an e-participation initiative directly from the deliberative level should not be ruled out. However, experiments are needed to give evidence to this possibility.

Therefore e-participation looks like as an incremental process during which the various social actors meet each other – online and/or offline – and learn to carry on fair public dialogue on civic issues. It requires to be supported by software tools modular and flexible enough to be dynamically configurable for matching the changing participatory scenario.

4 Conclusion

The above described field experience provides advices at two different levels: on one hand, it is worth relating its outcomes to the issues considered at the beginning of the project for setting up the consortium; on the other hand, it is worth thinking over e-participation in a more general way.

From the project point of view the size of the cities (in terms of number of inhabitants) didn't play a relevant role: in the range of the considered cities (which do not include any metropolis), both smaller and bigger cities have encountered similar difficulties. It is worth noting that, even if the two most successful sites are in middle-sized cities (Vigevano e Desenzano s.G.), till April 2008 Brescia (the second largest city of the Lombardy region, with its 187,000 inhabitants) was the most successful site and only the municipal elections sounded the death knell for the initiative. Analogously, there is no significant difference amongst municipalities administrated by left-oriented vs right-oriented government coalitions. As argued in §3.3, the political elections have been the only political aspect of relevance for the project.

The results in term of participation within the e21 project websites say that previous experience in *offline* participation processes is neither necessary nor sufficient for guarantee a good level of e-participation. All the municipalities with a strong preexisting participation experience (Mantua, Lecco, Pavia, Vimercate and 'Co.Ri.), indeed, belong to the two less active website classes identified in §3.1. Things are different regarding, the significantly high positive impact of earlier *online* participation initiatives. In §3.3 we have widely discussed the positive impact of the preexisting community networks in Desenzano s.G. and in San Donato M.se.

A last remark is due about technology, since one of the goals of such a large project was carrying on the design and development of the e-participation software environment used to manage the websites and tuning it through use in real contexts. On the one hand, the initial phase of the project provided helpful input regarding the set of tools to be provided and their priorities. The CityMap was conceived for answering a need expressed by the public officers and administrators, and it resulted to be successful for involving citizens in a public dialogue (even though the more successful use of the CityMap is not within the e21 project). On the contrary, the tool for online brainstorming has been considered not relevant, and its development postponed (cancelled within the e21 project). On the other hand, during the actual use of the (implemented) tools, participants, through their questions and help requests, provided feedbacks on their usability which have been considered for improvements now under implementation. However, in no situation usability, or any other technology problem, looked as critical to affect or inhibit citizens' participation, while some features expressly introduced to support participation have been explicitly appreciated. Moreover, the large field experiment run using the same software environment in ten different e-participation experiences clearly indicates that software tools must be modular and flexible enough to be dynamically configurable for matching changing participatory scenarios.

From a more general perspective, the main lesson from the project is that e-participation needs time for creating the proper conditions so that citizens, public officers and administrators become acquainted to the use of online spaces for carrying on civic dialogue and deliberation. It is important to stress that it is less and less matter of technology skills, but rather matter of getting knowledge through experience of how using ICTs for enhancing participation. Moreover, field experiments in Lecco, Como, Sesto s.G., Desenzano s.G., San Donato M.se and Brescia are evident symptoms of the relevant influence of politics over the course of the e-participation projects. In these cases, the decreasing politicians' engagement gave rise to the failure or the (temporary) stop of the initiative. Once more, the experience confirms what Coleman [17] states: "the key question for research is not whether new media are capable of capturing, moderating and summarizing the voice of the public, but whether political institutions are able and willing to enter into a dialogical relationship with the public". However, the positive role played, within the project, by the preexisting community networks suggests that grassroots open-ended initiatives, able to establish a public dialogue space, can help to overcome this problem.

Acknowledgments. This work has been partly funded by the research project PRIN # 2006148797_002 "Soluzioni informatiche a supporto della cittadinanza digitale, della accountability democratica e dei processi deliberativi." We wish to thank the e21 staff: without their tireless work, this paper would have never been possible.

References

1. Rheingold, H.: Electronic democracy; the great equalizer. Whole Earth Review, 4–8 (Summer 1991)
2. Blumler, J.G., Coleman, S.: Realising Democracy Online: A Civic Commons in Cyberspace. IPPR, London (2001)
3. Mossberger, K., Tolbert, C.J., McNeal, R.S.: Digital Citizenship - The Internet, Society and Participation. The MIT Press, Cambridge (2008)
4. Schuler, D.: Liberating Voices: a pattern language for communication revolution. MIT Press, Cambridge (2008)
5. Schuler, D.: New Community Networks – Wired for Change. Addison-Wesley, Reading (1996)
6. Venkatesh, M. (ed.): Special Issue on ICTs and Community Networking. The Information Society Journal 19(5) (2003)
7. Schuler, D.: Community Networks and the Evolution of Civic Intelligence. AI and Society Journal (to appear)
8. O'Reilly, T.: What is Web2.0: Design Patterns and Business Models for the Next Generation of Software (2005),
   http://www.oreillynet.com/pub/a/oreilly/tim/news/2005/09/30/what-is-web-20.html
9. Handler, J., Shadbolt, N., Hall, W., Berners-Lee, T., Weitzner, D.: Web Science: An interdisciplinary approach to understanding the web. Communications of the ACM 51(7), 60–69 (2008)
10. De Cindio, F., De Marco, A., Ripamonti, L.A.: Enriching Community Networks by supporting deliberation. In: Steinfield, C., Pentland, B.T., Ackerman, M., Contractor, N. (eds.) Communities & Technology 2007. Springer, Heidelberg (2007)
11. De Cindio, F., Di Loreto, I., Peraboni, C.: Moments and modes for triggering civic participation at the urban level. In: Foth, M. (ed.) Handbook of Research on Urban Informatics: The Practice and Promise of the Real-Time City, Information Science Reference, IGI Global, Hershey (2008)
12. De Cindio, F., Di Loreto, I., Peraboni, C.: Outlining an e-participation environment. In: Ferro, E., Jochen Scholl, H., Wimmer, M.A. (eds.) Electronic Government: Proceedings of ongoing research and projects of EGOV 2008. 7th International Conference, EGOV 2008, Trauner Druck, Linz, pp. 81–88 (2008)
13. De Cindio, F., De Marco, A., Grew, P.: Deliberative community networks for local governance. International Journal of Technology, Policy and Management 7(2) (2007)
14. Riley, T.B.: E-platform for citizens' engagement: A three-tier approach. In: International Conference on Engaging Communities, Workshop on Platform for e-Participation, Brisbane, Queensland (2005)
15. Winkler, R.: Online deliberation: Towards a research framework for the assessment of online debates. In: Avdic, A., Hedström, K., Rose, J., Grönlund, A. (eds.) Understanding eParticipation. Contemporary PhD eParticipation Studies in Europe, pp. 183–201. University Library, Örebrö (2007)
16. OECD: Citizens as Partners: Information, Consultation and Public Participation in Policy-Making. OECD Publishing (2001)
17. Coleman, S.: E-democracy: the history and future of an idea. In: Quah, D., Silverstone, R., Mansell, R., Avgerou, C. (eds.) The Oxford Handbook of Information and Communication Technologies. Oxford University Press, Oxford (2007)

Using Argument Visualization to Enhance e-Participation in the Legislation Formation Process

Euripidis Loukis[1], Alexandros Xenakis[2], and Nektaria Tseperli[3]

[1] University of the Aegean, Samos, Greece
eloukis@aegean.gr
[2] Panteion University, Athens, Greece
a.xenakis@panteion.gr
[3] NTUA, Athens, Greece
nektariatseperli@yahoo.gr

Abstract. Most public policy problems are 'wicked', being characterised by high complexity, many heterogeneous views and conflicts among various stakeholders. Therefore citizens interested to participate in such debates in order to be sufficiently informed should study large amounts of relevant material, such as reports, laws, committees' minutes, etc., which are in legalistic or in other specialist languages, or very often their substance is hidden in political rhetoric, putting barriers to a meaningful participation. In this paper we present the results of the research we have conducted for addressing this problem through the use of 'Computer Supported Argument Visualization' (CSAV) methods for supporting and enhancing e-participation in the legislation formation process. This approach has been implemented in a pilot e-participation project and then evaluated using both quantitative and qualitative methods based on the 'Technology Acceptance Model' (TAM), with positive results. Based on the conclusions of this evaluation an enrichment of the IBIS framework has been developed for improving the visualization of legal documents.

Keywords: e-participation evaluation, argument visualization, legislation formation process, public policy debate.

1 Introduction

Many countries all over the world attempt to extend citizens' participation in public policies formulation and politics in general through the use of Information and Communication Technologies (ICT) at three levels: for supporting i) the provision of relevant information to the citizens, ii) the consultation with them and also iii) their active participation [1],[2],[3],[4]. It is widely recognized that the above two higher levels of e-participation, aiming at the consultation with the citizens and their active participation, have as basic precondition the first level of sufficient relevant information provision to them. The quality of e-participation, and also of 'off-line' participation and in general of all political debates as well, relies critically on how informed the participating citizens are on the problem under discussion and the opinions that have been previously expressed on it.

A. Macintosh and E. Tambouris (Eds.): ePart 2009, LNCS 5694, pp. 125–138, 2009.
© Springer-Verlag Berlin Heidelberg 2009

However, public policy problems are 'wicked' [5], being characterised by high complexity, many heterogeneous views and conflicts among various stakeholders. Therefore citizens interested to participate in such debates, in order to be sufficiently informed and make a meaningful contribution, should study large amounts of relevant material, such as reports, plans, laws, committees' minutes, etc., which are in legalistic or in other specialist languages, or very often their substance is hidden in political rhetoric. This is putting barriers to public participation (both 'on-line' and 'off-line'), since most citizens today do not have enough time for such extensive study, and also some of them lack the required familiarity and education. The use of Computer Supported Argument Visualisation' (CSAV) [6] may result in a reduction of these barriers to e-participation, however it has been only to a limited extent explored [7], [8], [9], so further research is required in this direction.

The research presented in this paper has been part of the LEX-IS project ('Enabling Participation of the Youth in the Public Debate of Legislation among Parliaments, Citizens and Businesses in the European Union') (www.lex-is.eu) of the 'eParticipation' Preparatory Action of the European Commission [10].

This paper consists of seven sections. In section 2 the background is briefly described, while in section 3 the development of a comprehensive approach to the use of CSAV in the legislation formation process for supporting and enhancing e-participation in it is described. Then in sections 4 and 5 are presented a pilot implementation of this approach and its evaluation. In section 6 is described a proposed enrichment of the IBIS framework for the visualization of legal documents, and some final conclusions are outlined.

2 Background

Computer Supported Argument Visualization (CSAV) is the compact representation in a diagrammatic form of the arguments contained in textual documents or debates, using a set of interconnected nodes of various types. It was introduced by [11] Wingmore, who proposed a 'chart method' for representing in a simplified diagrammatic form the extensive material of legal cases, which assists in gaining a better understanding of the substantial elements and reaching conclusions. Toulmin [12], building on Wingmore's work, developed a model (language) for formulation and analysis of arguments, which was a sound foundation for many subsequent developments and applications. The introduction and penetration of computers gave a boost to argument visualization, leading to the development of the CSAV domain, and also to the expansion of its practical application in various areas, such as education, products design, analysis of environmental impacts, commerce, research, etc. [6]. CSAV can be very useful for solving a class of problems termed by Rittel & Weber [5] as 'wicked', in contrast to the 'tame' problems; wicked problems are characterised by many stakeholders with a different problem views, values and concerns, and also they lack mathematically 'optimal' solutions and pre-defined algorithms for calculating them, having only 'better' and 'worse' solutions, the former having more positive arguments in favour them than the latter. Kunz and Rittel [13] suggest that wicked problems are most effectively countered by argumentation among stakeholders, and propose for this purpose the use of 'Issue Based Information Systems' (IBIS), which aim to *'stimulate a more scrutinized style of reasoning which more explicitly reveals the arguments. It should help identify the proper questions, to develop the scope of positions in response to them, and assist in generating dispute'*. They are based on a simple but powerful framework for the representation of such problems, whose main elements are 'questions' (issues-problems to be addressed), 'ideas' (possible answers-solutions to questions-problems) and 'arguments' (evidence or viewpoints that support or object to ideas) [13],[14],[15].

Most public policy problems belong to this class of wicked problems, being characterised by high complexity, many heterogeneous views and conflicts among various stakeholders; these characteristics, in combination with the legalistic or specialist languages of the relevant government documents (e.g. reports, plans, laws, committees' minutes, etc.), make most public policy problems and the political debates on them difficult to understand by the 'simple citizen'. This has a negative impact on the quantity and quality of the political debates on them, putting barriers to both 'on-line' and 'off-line' public participation. However, limited research has been conducted on how we can use CSAV methods for conveying political information to the citizens concerning the substantial points and arguments of important political debates and documents in an easily and quickly understandable form, and how useful such an approach is for citizens. According to Renton & Macintosh [8] 'The use of argument visualization in a political context is still in its infancy'. Renton [7] investigates the use of CSAV in order to clarify to the public complex political issues, taking the minutes of two debates from the Scottish Parliament (concerning the introduction of the 'Terrestrial Trunk Radio Masts' (TETRA), and the 'Antisocial Behaviour'), converting them into arguments visualizations and then having them evaluated through one structured and two unstructured qualitative interviews. Renton & Macintosh [8] deal with how CSAV can be used to encourage debate and deliberation by citizens on public issues, in a manner that an electronic 'policy memory' can be formed; they demonstrate their approach (consisting of overview maps, dialogue maps and argument maps) through the creation of a set of maps representing the discussion that took place in the Scottish Parliament concerning the 'Smoking in Public Spaces' policy. Ohl [9] describes the application of CSAV for the diagrammatic representation of citizens' submissions in a public discourse on a draft South East Queensland Regional Plan, aiming to promote government transparency and accountability. It should be noted that all these three investigations of the exploitation of CSAV in the area of politics have been based on the abovementioned IBIS framework and used the 'Compendium' tool (http://compendium.open.ac.uk/ institute/). From the above review of relevant literature it is concluded that further research is required for formulating appropriate ways and practices of using CSAV in the area of politics, for evaluating its usefulness in this respect and for identifying advantages, disadvantages and possible improvements of practices and tools.

3 Research Methodology

In order to develop a comprehensive approach to the use of CSAV in the legislation formation process for supporting and enhancing e-participation, and also 'off-line' participation as well, and in general the whole political debate on proposed new legislation, we adopted the following methodology:

- Initially we analyzed the process of legislation formulation in the Greek Parliament, the stages it includes and its main documents.
- Based on this analysis, we designed our approach concerning the documents for which visualizations should be constructed.
- Then we designed our approach concerning the most appropriate framework and tool to be used for these visualizations.
- As a next step we proceeded to a pilot 'real-life' implementation of the above approach for a bill under discussion in the Greek Parliament.
- Then we evaluated this pilot implementation using both quantitative and qualitative methods.
- Finally based on the conclusions of this evaluation we made the required improvements in our approach.

In particular, in order to understand and analyze the process, stages and documents of legislation formation we conducted interviews with three experienced officials of the Greek Parliament. Additionally we studied carefully and analyzed the justification reports and the main content (articles) of five laws from five different Ministries, which have been proposed to us by the above three officials of the Greek Parliament as representative ones; furthermore, we studied carefully and analyzed the minutes of the sessions of the competent Parliamentary committees in which these laws were discussed, and also of the corresponding plenary sessions. As such for each bill under discussion visualizations should be constructed for:

a) The justification report of the bill, representing the main reasons that necessitate the proposed law and the basic directions and solutions it provides,
b) The content of the bill, representing the issues settled by its articles, and the particular settlements provided,
c) The opinions and positions of each of the stakeholders' representatives and the experts invited in the competent Parliamentary committee (as recorder in its minutes), representing the main strengths, weaknesses and suggestions mentioned.
d) The positions of each of the parties' main speakers in the competent Parliamentary committee (as recorder in its minutes), representing the main strengths, weaknesses and suggestions mentioned.

Additionally, it is useful to construct an 'overview map' as well, as a starting point for the user, which includes nodes representing the above visualizations, and also the corresponding textual documents, providing hyperlinks to them.

For these visualizations we decided to use the IBIS framework [14],[15], as implemented by the 'Compendium' tool (http://compendium.open.ac.uk/institute/) as it is mature, having been used extensively in the past for arguments visualization in several different areas, including the area of politics [7],[8],[9], as mentioned in section 2, and it provides a simple but powerful typology of nodes for the representation of wicked problems.

4 A Pilot Implementation

A pilot implementation of the above visualization approach was made, as part of a Greek e-participation pilot of the LEX-IS project (www.lex-is.eu), which involved an e-consultation concerning the bill on the 'Contract of Voluntary Cohabitation', which regulates the matter of the formal voluntary co-habitation of two persons. This law formalizes and regulates an existing social situation: many couples, especially among the younger age groups, are reluctant to proceed directly to marriage, and choose to live together for long periods of times; during that time many of them have children, share living expenses and buy property, just to mention some of their most important common actions, and these need to be regulated. Before the beginning of this e-consultation we constructed the visualizations mentioned in the previous section for this bill on the 'Contract of Voluntary Cohabitation', which were provided to the participants, together with the corresponding textual documents, as basic reference material; from these visualizations some representative ones are shown below.

The initial overview map is shown in Figure 1. It includes four map nodes, representing the visualizations of the bill justification report, the bill content, the experts' opinions and the parties' positions on it (arranged horizontally in chronological order), which are hyperlinked to the corresponding visualizations; also, it includes four reference nodes hyperlinked to the corresponding textual documents.

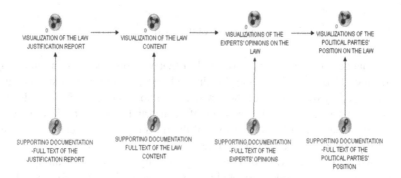

Fig. 1. Overview map

The visualization of the justification report is shown in Figure 2. It includes three of the types of nodes supported by the tool, with an adaptation of their meaning: note/information nodes (adapted as 'clarification' nodes), question nodes (adapted as 'problem-need' nodes) and idea nodes (adapted as 'solution' nodes). It is structured in four layers. The first layer includes (as clarification nodes) the reasons that create the need to legally regulate the voluntary cohabitation, which is modelled through a problem-need node in the second layer. The third layer represents this bill (proposed law) on the 'Contract of Voluntary Cohabitation' as the basic solution for this need, while the fourth layer includes the general directions of the law and the particular solutions it provides (modelled through solution nodes), and also a clarification on it, further elaborated by two more clarifications (all modelled as clarification nodes).

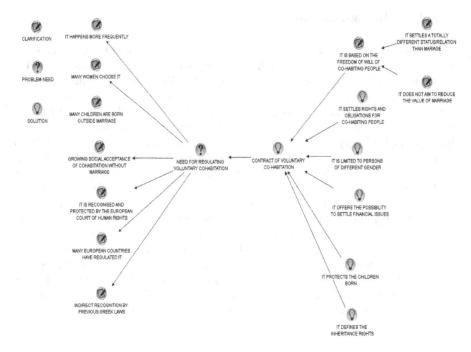

Fig. 2. Visualization of the justification report

The visualization of the content of the bill that we constructed was quite lengthy, so we decided to break it into: i) one high level visualization, which shows the main issues regulated by the articles of the law (as issue nodes) (Figure 3), and also ii) one lower level visualization for the content of each article; since the law includes 13 articles, we constructed 13 visualizations of them (in Figure 4 we can see the visualization of the content of the seventh article). For the visualization of the content of the bill we used four of the types of nodes supported by the tool with an adaptation of their meaning: question nodes (adapted as 'issue' nodes), idea nodes (adapted as 'settlement' nodes), note/information nodes (adapted as 'clarification' nodes) and map nodes (in the high level visualization, for providing hyperlinks to the lower level visualizations of the articles).

The visualization of the opinion of one expert invited by the competent Parliamentary committee is shown in Figure 5. It includes four of the types of nodes supported by the tool, with an adaptation of their meaning: one idea node (adapted as 'settlement' node) representing the whole bill, one contra-argument node (adapted as 'negative point' node), note/information nodes (adapted as 'clarification' nodes), and one question node (adapted as 'issue' node). We can see that this expert mentioned one main weakness of this bill (modelled as a negative point node), elaborating it through three clarifications (modelled as clarification nodes), which poses one basic issue (modelled as an issue node).

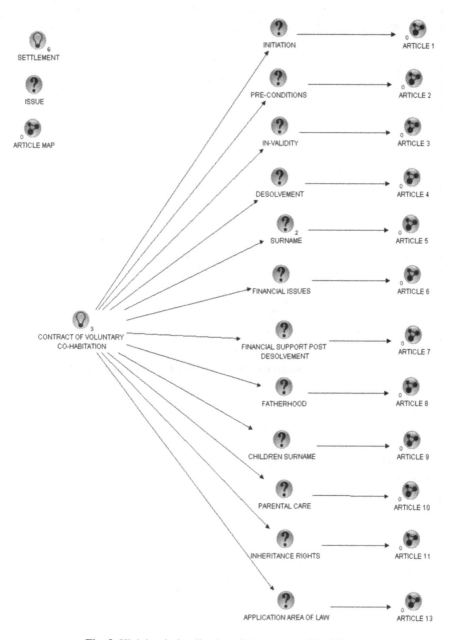

Fig. 3. High level visualization of the content of the bill

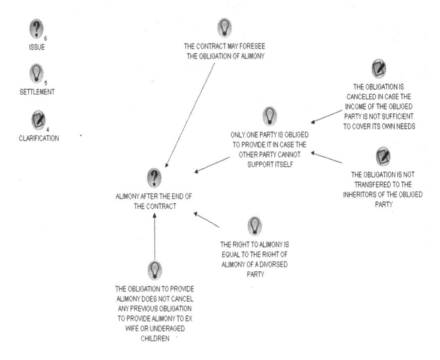

Fig. 4. Lower level visualization of the content of the seventh article of the bill

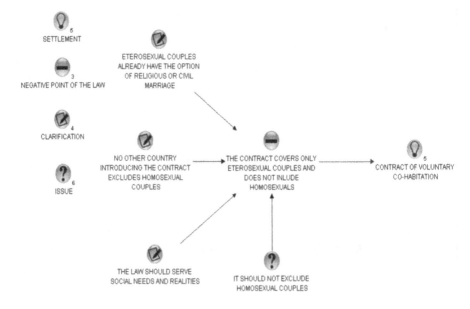

Fig. 5. Visualization of the opinion of an expert

Finally in Figure 6 we can see the visualization of the position on this bill of a political party. It includes four of the types of nodes supported by the tool, with an adaptation of their meaning: one idea node (adapted as 'settlement' node) representing the whole bill, contra-argument nodes (adapted as 'negative point' nodes), note/information nodes (adapted as 'clarification' nodes), and one question node (adapted as 'issue' node). We can see that this political party mentioned four main weaknesses of this bill (modelled as a negative point nodes), and elaborated two of them it through clarifications (modelled as clarification nodes); also they raised one issue (modelled as an issue node) associated with one of the weaknesses.

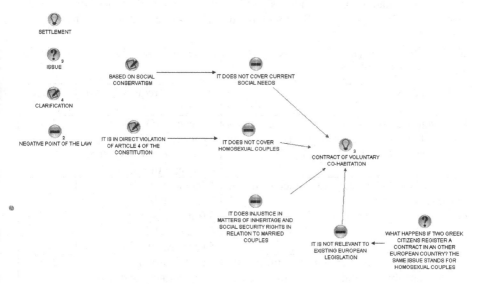

Fig. 6. Visualization of the position of a political party

5 Evaluation

The above pilot implementation of the proposed approach to the use of CSAV in the legislative process has been evaluated using both quantitative and qualitative methods, based on the 'Technology Acceptance Model' (TAM) [16],[17]. According to TAM, the main determinants of the attitude towards using an IS of its potential or real users are:

- its perceived usefulness (PU), defined as the extent to which users believe that using this IS will enhance their performance in a particular task,
- and its perceived ease of use (PEU), defined as the extent to which users believe that using the system will be free of effort.

In this direction in the participants' questionnaire we designed for the quantitative evaluation of this LEX-IS project e-participation pilot we included questions assessing the perceived ease of use and the usefulness of the visualizations. Also, in the in-depth semi-structured discussion we conducted for the qualitative evaluation of the same e-participation pilot one of the topics was the visualizations (with main sub-topics their ease of use, usefulness and proposed improvements).

Quantitative evaluation: The abovementioned quantitative evaluation questionnaire was returned by 27 out of the 79 registered participants in this e-participation pilot (34% response rate). In the following Table 1 we can see for each of the visualiza-tions' evaluation questions the relative frequencies of answers (in the second column) and the average rating of the respondents (in the third column).

The first question concerns the extent of use of the visualizations. We remark that most of the respondents used the visualizations once, probably before the beginning of the e-consultation (52%), while a significant percentage of them used the visualiza-tions more than one (44% = 28% two-three times + 16% several times). The next two

Table 1. Relative frequencies of answers and average ratings of the respondents in visualiza-tions' evaluation questions

QUESTION	Relative frequencies of answers	average rating
Did you use the visualizations of the articles of the law, the expert reports and the party positions, provided in the platform?	1 (never): 4% 2 (once): 52% 3 (two-three times): 28% 4 (several times): 16%	2.56
Was it easy for you to understand the visualizations?	1 (not at all): 4% 2 (a little): 0% 3 (rather easy): 40% 4 (easy): 24% 5 (very easy): 32%	3.80
Were the visualizations sufficiently understandable, or did you feel the need to access the reference text in order to understand them?	1 (not at all): 4% 2 (moderately und.): 76% 3 (very understandable): 20%	2.16
To what extent did the visualization of the justification report of the bill help you to understand its content in a short time frame?	1 (not at all): 4% 2 (a little): 8% 3 (moderately): 44% 4 (much): 28% 5 (very much): 16%	3.44
To what extent did the visualization of the articles of the bill help you to understand their content in a short time frame?	1 (not at all): 4% 2 (a little): 8% 3 (moderately): 44% 4 (much): 16% 5 (very much): 28%	3.56
To what extent did the visualization of experts' opinions and parties' positions on the bill help you to understand their content in a short time frame?	1 (not at all): 4% 2 (a little): 12% 3 (moderately): 24% 4 (much): 20% 5 (very much): 40%	3.80

questions concern the 'ease of use' of the visualizations. We remark that most of the respondents find the visualizations rather easy (40%), easy (24%) or very easy to understand (32%) (with an average rating of 3.80), and also moderately understandable (76%) or very understandable (20%) (closer to the former with an average rating of 2.16). Therefore the respondents believe that the visualizations, though not very easy, can be understood with a reasonable effort. The final three questions concern the 'usefulness' of the visualizations. We remark that the respondents on average find that the visualizations help them to a moderate to large extent to understand the justification report (average rating 3.44), the content (articles) of the bill (average rating 3.56) and also experts' opinions and parties' positions on the bill (average rating 3.80). We can see that the visualizations were more useful for understanding in a short time the opinions of experts and the positions of parties on the bill, than the content (articles) and the justification report of it, since the latter are both in a more legalistic and compact language, so they are more difficult to visualize and understand.

Qualitative evaluation: Additionally, a qualitative in-depth discussion of about four hours duration about this e-participation pilot was held in a focus-group, consisting of four participants in the pilot, a Legal Expert, a Lawyer Assistant to the Member of the Parliament (MP) who was the main speaker of the governing party for the bill, and one Official of the Parliament. The whole discussion was initially tape-recorded, and later transcribed. In this section are summarized the opinions expressed about the visualizations.

All the persons who participated in this discussion accepted that the visualizations were understandable to a rather good extent, after some first learning period of familiarization with the symbols of the nodes. However, it was mentioned that they would be easier to understand if all of them were read in the same direction (e.g. from left to right, harmonized with the direction of reading books), which should be clearly indicated. The visualizations of the opinions of the experts and the positions of the parties were more understandable and useful (since the corresponding textual documents were quite lengthy), than the visualisations of the content (articles) of the bill and its justification report. As main advantages of visualizations are regarded the time efficiencies created for the participants who did not have the time to go through all the lengthy relevant textual documents provided. It was also mentioned that the visualizations of the positions of the parties helped them to 'filter-out' the excessive rhetoric and the irrelevant or generic comments (not directly related to the bill under discussion), which are quite usual in such political speeches, and focus on the main points raised by them and also understand better their stance in the final balloting on the bill. A weakness of the visualizations of the articles of the bill came from the opinion of the Legal Expert involved in this focus-group discussion; in particular, she argued that in the visualization of the articles all the types of settlements included were represented by a single type of node ('settlement node'), though there are different kinds of legal rules, such as prohibitive, imperative, permitting and presumptions [18],[19], which should be represented by different types of nodes. Also, in these visualizations of the articles the sequence of reading these 'settlement' nodes should be indicated, and follow their sequence of the corresponding settlements in the text of the bill, since some of them were associated with previous ones.

6   Improvements and Conclusions

Based on the conclusions of the evaluation we proceeded to an improvement of our approach to the visualization of the bills' articles. In particular, we enriched the typology of nodes provided by the IBIS framework and the Compendium tool, by refining the 'settlement' type, taking into account the classification of rules proposed by jurisprudence [18],[19], into the following five types:

a) Prohibitive Rule: They are rules through which it is imposed to abstain from a particular behavior or exclude the coming of a certain outcome. This prohibition is usually accompanied with ratifications (e.g. invalidity, forfeiture of a right, obligation of reimbursement) in the case of its violation. These rules are usually expressed using the verb "prohibit". For instance, a minor is prohibited, without the consent of his guardian, to acknowledge the obligation or expropriation of his property.
b) Imperative Rule: They are rules which impose a positive behaviour. These rules are usually expressed using the verbs "owes to", or "has to", or "must", etc. For instance, the banks have to report some types of transactions (for which there is a suspicion of association with fraudulent activities) to the Ministry of Finance.
c) Permitting Rule: They are rules which recognize to a person a certain authority or permit to it a certain action. These rules are usually expressed using the verbs "can", or "has a right to", etc. For instance, a minor who has completed his 14th year of age is able to (can) dispose, without the consent of his guardian, everything that he gains from his work or everything that he was given for his own use.
d) Legal Presumption: These are the outcomes which the law defines that should be initially deduced as far as unknown incidents are concerned, from other known ones, in order to facilitate the judge to find out the truth or the untruth of litigants' pleas, for which finding evidence is impossible or very difficult. For instance, a child who took birth during the marriage of his parents is initially presumed that has got for father the man to whom his mother is married to (except evidence for the opposite is presented).
e) Settlement: With this type will be modeled rules defined in bills' articles, which do not belong to any of the above four types.

In Figure 7 we can see the visualization of the content of the seventh article of this bill using the proposed enriched typology of nodes, which has been designed using the 'Visio' tool (its initial visualization appears in Figure 4).

In the previous sections has been described a comprehensive approach to the use of CSAV in the legislative process, aiming to support and enhance e-participation in it, which has been designed based on the analysis of this process, its main stages and documents. Furthermore, a pilot implementation of this approach has been presented, which has been made as part of a pilot e-participation project in the Greek Parliament concerning the bill on the 'Contract of Voluntary Cohabitation'; it has been followed by a quantitative and qualitative evaluation, based on the 'Technology Acceptance Model' (TAM). From this evaluation it has been concluded that such visualizations are understandable to a rather good extent, after some familiarization period required; they can significantly help citizens to understand more easily and quickly the basic documents of the legislative process, enabling them to participate in it in a more meaningful manner. Our findings provide evidence of a high potential of CSAV in the area of politics, which can contribute to higher citizens participation in it, both from

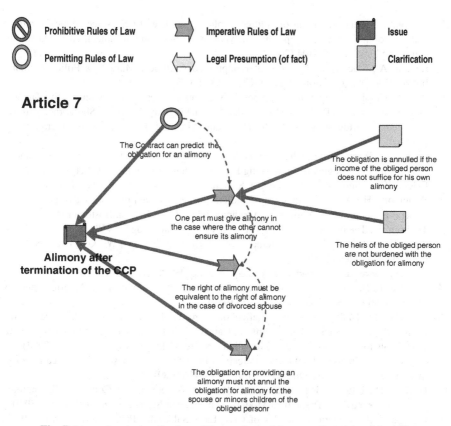

Fig. 7. Lower level visualization of the content of the seventh article of the bill

quantitative and qualitative perspective. Further research is required towards exploring and exploiting this potential of CSAV, covering different countries and cultures, types of laws, citizens' groups and tools.

References

1. OECD, Citizens as Partners – Information, Consultation and Public Participation in Policy-Making, Organisation for Economic Cooperation and Development, Paris (2003)
2. OECD, Promise and Problems of e-Democracy: Challenges of Online Citizen Engagement, Organisation for Economic Cooperation and Development, Paris (2004)
3. Macintosh, A.: Characterizing E-Participation in Policy Making. In: Proceedings of the 37th Hawaii International Conference on System Sciences (2004)
4. Timmers, P.: Agenda for eDemocracy – an EU perspective. European Commission (2007)
5. Rittel, H.W.J., Weber, M.M.: Dilemmas in a general theory of planning. Policy Sciences 4, 155–169 (1973)
6. Kirschner, P., Buckingham Shum, S., Carr, C.: Visualizing Argumentation: Software Tools for Collaborative and Educational Sense-Making. Springer, London (2003)

7. Renton, A.: Seeing the point of politics: exploring the use of CSAV techniques as aids to understanding the content of political debates in the Scottish Parliament. Artificial Intelligence and Law 14, 277–304 (2006)
8. Renton, A., Macintosh, A.: Computer Supported Argument Maps as a Policy Memory. Information Society Journal 23(2), m125–m133 (2007)
9. Ohl, R.: Computer Supported Argument Visualisation: Modelling in Consultative Democracy around Wicked Problems. In: Okada, A., Buckingham Shum, S., Sherborne, T. (eds.) Knowledge Cartography: Software Tools and Mapping Techniques. Springer, London (2008)
10. Loukis, E., Wimmer, M., Charalabidis, Y., Triantafillou, A., Gatautis, R.: Argumentation Systems and Ontologies for Enhancing Public Participation in the Legislation Process. In: EGOV 2007 International Conference, September 3-7, 2007. Regensburg, Germany (2007)
11. Wingmore, H.J.A.: The Principles of Judicial Proof as Given by Logic, Psychology, and General Experience and Illustrated in Judicial Trials. Little Brown, Boston (1913)
12. Toulmin, S.: The uses of argument. University Press, Cambridge (1958)
13. Kunz, W., Rittel, H.: Issues as Elements of Information Systems, Working Paper No. 131, California: Berkley (1979),
    http://www-iurd.ced.berkeley.edu/pub/WP-131.pdf
14. Conklin, J., Begeman, M.: gIBIS: A tool for all reasons. Journal of the American Society for Information Science 40(3), 200–213 (1989)
15. Conklin, J.: Dialog Mapping: Reflections on an Industrial Strength Case Study. In: Kirschner, P., Buckingham Shum, S., Carr, C. (eds.) Visualizing Argumentation: Software Tools for Collaborative and Educational Sense-Making. Springer, London (2003)
16. Davis, F.D.: Perceived Usefulness, Perceived Ease of Use and User Acceptance of Information Technology. MIS Quarterly 13(3), 319–340 (1989)
17. Davis, F.D., Bagozzi, R.P., Warshaw, P.R.: User Acceptance of Computer Technology: A Comparison of two Theoretical Models. Management Science 35(8), 982–1003 (1989)
18. Georgadis, A.: General Principles of Civil Law. Sakkoulas Publications, Athens (1997) (in Greek language)
19. Lingeropoulos, A.: Lectures of Roman Law, Classical Legal Library, vol. 32. Sakkoulas Publications, Athens (2002) (in Greek language)

Automated Analysis of e-Participation Data by Utilizing Associative Networks, Spreading Activation and Unsupervised Learning

Peter Teufl[1], Udo Payer[1], and Peter Parycek[2]

[1] Institute for Applied Information Processing and Communications -IAIK,
Graz University of Technology
[2] Donau Universitaet Krems

Abstract. According to [1], the term e-participation is defined as "the use of information and communication technologies to broaden and deepen political participation by enabling citizens to connect with one another and with their elected representatives". This definition sounds quite simple and logical, but when considering the implementation of such a service in a real world scenario, it is obvious that it is not possible to evaluate messages, which are generated by thousands of citizens, by hand. Such documents need to be read and analyzed by experts with the required in-depth domain knowledge. In order to enable this analysis process and thereby to increase the number of possible e-particpation applications, we need to provide these experts with automated analysis tools that cluster, pre-screen and pre-evaluate public opinions and public contributions. In this paper we present a framework based on Machine Learning-(ML) and Artificial Intelligence-(AI) techniques that are capable of various analysis mechanisms such as unsupervised clustering of yet unread documents, searching for related concepts within documents and the description of relations between terms. To finish, we show how the proposed framework can be applied to real world data taken from the Austrian e-participation platform mitmachen.at.

1 Introduction

E-participation presents an important possibility for citizens to actively take part in democracy. As a fundamental principle of democracy, participation in the broader sense includes engagement in acts of representative democracy. Public participation in its different forms can be legally institutionalized in all governmental powers: for example, petitions for a referendum in legislation, lay judges, juries in jurisdiction, and in large-scale administration projects which require official approval (as can be seen with planning laws or building regulations). Beside these regulated forms, there are various types of informal participation to be found; particularly in public administration, where individuals and lobby groups are engaged in projects, regional planning and developments in the public sector.

The main problem when dealing with large-scale, nationwide projects which lead to an enormous number of texts, is that they are simply too abundant to be analyzed without the use of technology. This framework was designed in order to gain a better

A. Macintosh and E. Tambouris (Eds.): ePart 2009, LNCS 5694, pp. 139–150, 2009.
© Springer-Verlag Berlin Heidelberg 2009

picture of texts dealing with similar topics yet using different semantic structures. One main research focus was real time data analysis for e-participation platforms.

In 2006, the Working Group for e-democracy and e-participation was founded by the Austrian Federal Chancellery with the aim of collecting and comparing e-participation projects in Austria in order to develop a general policy. An e-democracy policy and strategy were developed in 2008 displaying standardized e-participation methods. This policy can be used for a wide range of participation projects ranging from local, neighbourhood projects to nation-wide involvement. Standardization and reusability are important issues for a number of reasons: It is easier for public administration to build on the experience of successful methods. Every completed project leads to further improvement and the users become accustomed to certain formats and procedures. Reuse of existing platforms brings financial advantages and projects can be initiated quickly and with greater ease. Especially nationwide projects need automated analysis of e-participation data. More Austrian projects will be launched in 2009, and the coming years will show the extent to which citizens want to become politically involved and make use of the new technologies for this purpose. All in all, we will know soon whether technology can actually change democracy. One main research focus is the real time data analysis of e-participation information. As the first result of this research focus, we propose a framework for the automated analysis of e-participation data. The framework employs different algorithms from the areas of Machine Learning (ML) techniques and Artificial Intelligence (AI) and introduces so-called *activation patterns* that are used to represent sentences and documents. These *activation patterns* take the semantic relation between terms into account and thereby improve the quality of the analysis. We show the capabilities of the framework by analyzing data from the Austrian e-participation project mitmachen.at.

2   *mitmachen.at*

This section gives a short introduction to the e-participation project *mitmachen.at*. For a more detailed report on the project we refer to [2]. Enabling democratic political processes requires (1) a relationship and a dialogue between politics and citizens, and (2), citizens who are willing to participate in a democratic process [3]). The project mitmachen.at – move your future, is a youth e-participation project led by the Austrian Federal Computing Centre (BRZ, Bundesrechenzentrum) with the aim of motivating young people to participate in a political discussion about important topics for the future in Austria. In Austria, 90.8% of young people believe in the value and importance of their political participation, but only 25.4% actually know how to join in [4]. The name of the project reveals the objective: in German, the verb mitmachen means to join in, to participate. It was directed at providing young people aged 15-25 in Austria with the opportunity to participate in a 4-step process of presenting and voicing their concerns about the future using the Internet. Mitmachen.at was one of the biggest e-participation projects in Austria. The BRZ worked together with different organisations including youth institutions, software companies, various Think Tanks, and the relevant public authorities to develop a democratic participation process. Aside from revealing a number of interesting results and conclusions, the actual project itself proves that e-participation represents a cross sectional subject, which can be part of a procedure on its own, but could also be useful in many other areas of application [5]. The aim of this project was to investigate and test the general electronic participation processes, but it also examined the technical implementation and the (technical) framework, which make such participation processes possible. Portals are important for simplifying the vertical and horizontal integration of e-government [6]. The virtual portal used for this project included both the necessary instruments for participation as well as two different user levels (administrative and end-user).

3 Algorithms and Techniques

Semantic/Associative networks: The concept of associative or semantic networks was presented in 1968 by Quillain [7]. Such networks are directed or undirected graphs that store information in the network nodes and use edges to present the relation between these nodes. Good examples for semantic networks are WordNet [8] for the English language and Germanet [9] for the German language. Both networks store relations between synonym sets (synsets), which are cognitive synonyms that group nouns, verbs, adjectives and adverbs. Synsets are interlinked by means of conceptual-semantic and lexical relations. Examples for such links are hypernymy/hyponomy, antonyms and derivationally related forms. Associative networks represent a more general concept than semantic networks, since they use unlabeled links to represent relations between nodes. Typically, these links are weighted according to the strength of associations. In this paper, we use the frequency between two co-occurring nodes as weight. Spreading Activation (SA): Spreading activation (SA) algorithms are used for searching associative or semantic networks. In order to do so, one or more nodes are activated within the network. This activation is then spread over the network to neighboring nodes within one or more iterations. The optimal number of iterations depends on the data that is represented by the underlying network and the type of search operation. The activation values of neighboring nodes depend on the weights of the links to these nodes and the employed activation function. The results gained from SA algorithms are influenced by the employed strategies:

-**Activation function, activation threshold:** The activation value of a node is determined by the input it receives from neighboring nodes. The decision if the node fires and therefore spreads its activation value during the next iteration depends on the employed activation function and a pre-set activation threshold.

-**Decay, Iterations:** During each iteration, the activation spreads further over the network. In order to avoid the activation of a large part of the network, we need to constrain the spreading by employing a decay factor that reduces the activation energy during each iteration or limiting the number of iterations.

-**Fanout:** Nodes that are connected to a large number of other nodes (e.g. the term **be**) do not provide information and decrease the accuracy of the analysis process. Their influence needs to be constrained by utilizing a fanout factor.

Activation patterns: Given is an associative/semantic network with n nodes and an arbitrary number of edges that describe the relations between these nodes. In addition, let us assume to activate a sub-set of these nodes by using the SA algorithm to spread the activation. Then, we define an activation pattern as a vector that contains the activation values of the n nodes stored within the associative/semantic network. In the area of text classification, such an activation pattern represents a concept that is based on the relations between different terms. By defining an arbitrary distance measurement between these activation patterns, we are able to calculate the similarity between different concepts and can use this similarity to run unsupervised clustering and searching mechanisms to search for related concepts.

Unsupervised learning: For the automated analysis of e-participation data, unsupervised learning algorithms play an important role. Due to their unsupervised nature, they are able to find clusters of related documents without requiring any label/class information for these documents. In general, we can apply any unsupervised learning algorithm to the activation patterns extracted from the associative network. Examples for such algorithms are Neural Gas based algorithms [10]), Self Organizing Maps (SOM), Hierachical Agglomerative Clustering (HAC), or Expectation Maximation (EM). For the unsupervised analysis of the mitmachen.at activation patterns we employ the Robust Growing Neural Gas algorithm (RGNG) [10]. should be capitalized (i.e., nouns, verbs, and all other words except articles, prepositions, and conjunctions should be set with an initial capital) and should, with the exception of the title, be aligned to the left. Words joined by a hyphen are subject to a special rule. If the first word can stand alone, the second word should be capitalized. The font sizes are given in Table 1.

4   Framework for the Analysis of e-Participation Data

For the evaluation of the *mitmachen.at* data and the development of the framework we use the following strategy:

Finding suitable unsupervised learning algorithms: Typically, it is difficult to evaluate the quality of unsupervised learning algorithms since we do not have any label information for the analyzed data, that could be used for the evaluation of the performance. Furthermore, due to the high dimensionality of text data, we require an algorithm to have a model that is easy to understand and visualize. The visualization of the trained data is a vital component, since it helps to analyze unknown data. Therefore, in the first step we create simple bag-of-words models[1] and evaluated the suitability of unsupervised models. Neural Gas based algorithms are employed due to their simple model and the ability to visualize such models. The results of the first unsupervised analysis of the bag-of-words data with such an algorithm is visualized by employing an Actionscript[2] animation[3]. The clusters and the distances are extracted directly from the trained Neural Gas model. Integration of semantic information: The first results showed us that the simple bag-of-words approach is adequate for rough

---

[1] In such a model each document is presented by an *n*-dimensional vector that stores the frequency of each term within the document. n is the number of distinct terms within the whole data-set.

[2] http://www.adobe.com/devnet/actionscript/

[3] http://apps.egiz.gv.at/Mitmachen/bin/DocumentVisualizerNew.swf

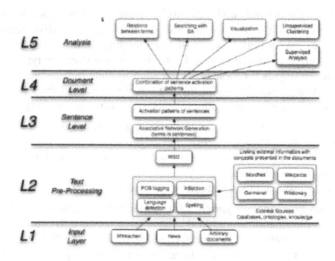

Fig. 1. Overview over the analysis framework

unsupervised clustering but cannot not be used for accurate searching within the data-set. The reason is that the bag-of-words approach does not cover any relations between the terms within the sentences or documents and thus, we are limited to simple keyword matching for finding related concepts within the data.

The results of the initial *mitmachen.at* analysis lead to the development of the presented framework that is depicted in Figure 1 and described in detail within the subsequent sections.

L1 -Input/L2 -Text pre-processing: The input layer consists of various input plug-ins that read documents from arbitrary sources. Before we can utilize sophisticated techniques for the analysis of the given text, we apply several preprocessing steps in L2:

–POS tagging: In order to decide which terms should be used for the subsequent analysis, we need to determine their part-of-speech (POS) tags. Such tags provide more information about the way a term is used within a sentence and how it is related to other terms. Currently, we only use a limited number of tags for the subsequent analysis: nouns, verbs, adjectives and adverbs. All other terms are dropped.

–Word Sense Disambiguation (WSD): WSD is the process of finding the sense of a term within a given sentence. Typically, WSD algorithms take the other terms within the sentence into consideration in order to determine the sense of the term.

–Lexical analysis: Currently, we only use a limited number of POS tags for the subsequent analysis. However, for future versions we plan to integrate the structural information about sentences gained by lexical parsers. A good example for such a parser is the Stanford parser [11].

L3 -Sentence Processing: This layer analyzes each sentence, generates an associative network that stores the relation between terms within sentences and generates the *activation patterns* for all sentences.

Generation of the associative network/semantic network: For each different term (sense) within the analyzed text corpus we create a node within the associative network. The edges between nodes and their weights are determined in the following way: All senses within a sentence are linked within the associative network. Newly generated edges get an initial weight of 1. Every time senses co-occur together, we increase the weight of their edges by 1. In addition, we store the type of connection for each edge. Examples for these types are noun-to-noun links, noun-to-verb links or adjective-to-adverb links. By using this information when applying SA algorithms, we are able to constrain the spreading of activation values to certain types of terms.

Network processing: The output of the last step is an associative network with nodes representing the disambiguated terms and edges representing the relation between terms. The weight of the edges is determined by the number of times terms co-occur within sentences. In order to apply SA algorithms to this network, these weights need to be normalized, so that the maximum weight is equal to 1.0.

Determination of *activation patterns* for sentences: We can now utilize SA algorithms and the information stored in the associative network to extract the *activation patterns* from the sentences. For each sentence we have the POS tagged senses of nouns, verbs, adjectives and verbs[4]. The terms (senses) correspond to nodes within the network and get an initial activation value of 1.0. We apply the SA algorithm to the associative network for at maximum two iterations and extract the *activation patterns* from the associative network.

L4 -Document processing: We could now apply unsupervised clustering algorithms or search algorithms based on SA to the extracted *activation patterns*. However, these patterns only represent information on the sentence level and we still need a method that allows us to represent whole documents. In order to do this, we simply sum up the *activation patterns* of each sentence within a document and use the resulting pattern as a representation for the given document. While we are able to achieve good results with this technique, this may be due the relatively short length of the analyzed *mitmachen.at* documents. We need to revise this process for larger documents that contain various different concepts.

L5 -Analysis: The *activation patterns* generated in the previous layers are the basis for applying supervised and unsupervised Machine Learning algorithms. Furthermore, we can implement search algorithms that are based on SA algorithms.

Unsupervised analysis: Unsupervised analysis plays an important role for the analysis of text, since it allows us to cluster unread documents according to their content.

Search with Spreading Activation (SA): In order to search for related concepts within the analyzed text sources, we apply the following procedures:

1. The user enters the search query, which could be a combination of terms, a complete sentence or even a document containing multiple sentences.
2. We determine the POS tags for every term within the search query.
3. Optionally, we now make use of an external knowledge source (e.g. Word-Net or Germanet) to find related terms and concepts for the terms in the query. Since, we currently do not employ WSD techniques we need to be careful when selecting the appropriate synsets from the external sources.

---

[4] Depending on the analysis we could filter out various types and constrain spreading to certain links.

4. We activate the nodes corresponding to the terms of the search query and the related terms extracted from the external knowledge source.
5. We use the SA algorithm to spread the activation over the associative network.
6. We extract the *activation pattern* of the associative network and compare it to the document or sentence patterns that were extracted during the training process. The patterns are sorted according to their similarity with the search pattern.

Relations between terms: The associative network trained in L3 contains information about relations between terms that co-occur within sentences. By activating one or more nodes within this network and applying the SA algorithm, we can find related terms.

5 Evaluation of the mitmachen.at Dataset

For the evaluation of the *mitmachen.at* data, we have applied the presented framework[5]:

–L1 -Input: Each *mitmachen.at* entry is stored in an XML file, that is read by an input plugin. Several transformations are applied to the raw text which include the replacement of characters specific to the German language and the removal of punction marks, other than period.

–L2 -Text preprocessing: For each sentence we apply:

• **POS tagging:** For POS tagging we use the LingPipe[6] API trained with text from Tiger Corpus [12]. Only nouns, verbs and adjectives are kept.

• **Lemmatization:** For each term we determine the lemma by using information extracted from the morphological analyzer MORPHY [13].

• **WSD:** Currently, we do not apply a WSD algorithm. However, we plan to integrate the WSD technique presented in [14]. It uses Wordnet to disambiguate English terms, but can easily be adapted to the German language by replacing Wordnet with Germanet.

–L3 -Sentence Level: We generate the associative network and the *activation patterns* for the sentences according to the procedures described before.

–L4 -Document Level: For each *mitmachen.at* entry (considered as document here), we generate an *activation pattern* by summing up the *activation patterns* of its sentences.

–L5 -Analysis: The *activation patterns* for each *mitmachen.at* entry and the associative network generated in L3 can now be analyzed by applying different techniques described in the subsequent sections.

5.1 Unsupervised Analysis-Clustering

In this section, we analyze the *activation patterns* of the *mitmachen.at* entries (generated in L4) by applying the RGNG algorithm. Users of the *mitmachen.at* platform

---

[5] The complete results can be downloaded from http://apps.egiz.gv.at/eparticipation.tar.gz

[6] LingPipe -http://alias-i.com/lingpipe/index.html

were able to create or join discussions on 8 topics: **environment, health, education, security, infrastructure, social system, political system, employment**. The results of the unsupervised clustering are shown in Table 1. As excepted the found clusters broadly cover these di☐erent topics. Since the trained model contains more than 400 documents, we only provide a short description for the clusters. The column *German terms* contains keywords that were automatically extracted from the clusters. The English translation of these keywords is available in column *English terms*. The column *topics* contains the *mitmachen.at* topics that describe the documents contained in the cluster. These topics were manually assigned in order to see the type of clusters the algorithm is able to find. The last column – *summary* – contains a short summary of the documents contained in the clusters. This summary was manually added in order to give a short description of the cluster. For the complete document cluster data we refer to *cluster-results.txt*. By taking a closer look at the found clusters we make the following observations:

–We are able to find clusters that are correlated with the topics available in *mitmachen.at*. Several topics, such as health, environment partly have similar contents and can be found together in single clusters.

–**Cluster 1:** This cluster contains discussions related to security, the social system and employment. The reason for the combination of these topics is the term security since it plays a role for security in terms of social security and in terms of security provided by the police and the military. This is a good example why WSD algorithms make sense, since the term security has two different senses here. Furthermore, the problem might have been avoided by employing a fanout factor (see the discussion on cluster 10 for more details).

–**Cluster 6:** This cluster contains documents that are related to the discussion of the *mitmachen.at* project itself.

–**Cluster 10:** This cluster contains documents from various topics. By inspecting the documents we can see that the term **Meinung** (opinion) is quite frequent within these documents. Since one can have an opinion on every topic, it is connected to a large number of nodes within the associative network which is depicted in Figure 2(b). Thus, the documents containing this term cause the activation of a large number of other nodes of arbitrary topics and therefore end up in the same cluster. This is a perfect example for the requirement of a fanout factor. Such a factor would simply penalize this node and suppress the activation energy spread by the node.

5.2 Search for Related Patterns

The *activation patterns* of the *mitmachen.at* data are represented by 5755-dimensional vectors. Given the *activation pattern* of an *mitmachen.at* entry, we can find related patterns by calculating the distance to the other *activation patterns* and sort the results according to similarity. For determining the distance we employ the cosine similarity.

Relations between terms: In order to find the relations of one or more input terms, we activate the corresponding nodes in the associative network and spread the activation by applying the SA algorithm. The strength of the activation of the other terms indicate the strength of the association with the input term. As example we use the term **Fahrzeug (vehicle)** and show the related terms in Figure 2(a). Some examples for related terms are: **Verschmutzung (pollution), Klimawandel (climate change)**, **Automobil (car), Fussgaenger (pedestrian)** and **Fussgaengeruebergang (pedestrian crossing)**.

Searching for related entries: In this case we select an existing document and calculate the distance to the other documents within the data-set. The other documents are then listed according to similarity. As example we use an input document that deals with the necessity to reduce the ticket price for public transport and the need to introduce a time schedule with shorter intervals. The complete list of related documents is available in *search-related.txt* and shows that the framework is able to retrieve similar documents that deal with issues related to traffic and public transport.

Finding relations/Searching without external knowledge: For this example we use the search query vehicle but do not employ Germanet to find related terms.

Table 1. Summarizing the 15 clusters found by the RGNG algorithm

	Docs	German terms	English terms	Topics	Summary
1	12	Sicherheit Bundesheer Oesterreich	security army Austria	security social system	social security issues security related to public places crime, army
2	22	Sicherheit Polizei Land Bundesheer	security police country army	security	army related issues discussion about police crime
3	30	Umwelt Wasser	environment water	environment infrastructure	pollution of the environment, alternative energy, fossil fuels, global warming, transport
4	3	Abgas Luft	exhaust air	environment health	health related issuest protection of the environment
5	17	Automobil Transportmittel Strasse Bus Eisenbahn	exhaust vehicle road bus train	environment infrastructure	CO_2 emissions solar energy fossil fuel quality of public transport traffic (trucks, cars)
6	4	Projekt Textanalyse	project text analysis	-	*mitmachen.at discussion*
7	26	Politik Mensch Politiker Umwelt	politics human politician	political system social system	discussion about politics, politicians

Table 1. (*continued*)

			environment		(un)employment political deciscions regarding health system, environment and
8	26	Bildung	education	education	university, schools, teachers
		Lehrer	teachers	social system	problems at schools
		Ausbildung	specific education		costs of the education system
9	34	Schule	school	education	discussion about schools and teachers
10	23	Meinung Schueler Lehrer	opinion pupils teacher		various topics
11	10	Arzt	doctor	health	discussions about health
		Medizin Patient	medicine		and the health
		Geld	patient money		system
12	6	Gesundheit	health	health	discussions about health
		Medizin	medicine		and the health
		Gesundheitssyste m Geld	health system money		system
13	13	Kosten	costs	health	discussions about health
		Medizin	medicine		and the health
		Problem	problem		system
14	12	Kosten	health	health	discussions about health
		Eltern	parents	social system	and the health
		Mensch	human		system
15	9	Kinder	children	social system	discussions about health
		Eltern	parents	education	the social system, children
		Geld	money		

We activate the node representing **vehicle** within the associative network and spread the activation. This results in the activation of other terms such as **pedestrian, car, road, price of resources**. The activation value depends on the strength of the relation between the terms. By taking a closer look at the activated terms we can draw several conclusions: Due to the co-occurence of **car** and **vehicle** within one or more sentences the term **car** is activated even if Germanet is not employed. Other terms such as **pedestrian or price of resources** are also found, since they co-occur with **vehicle** within sentences. Such relations could not be found with Germanet since they represent relations that are specific for the analyzed data.

The *activation pattern* generated out of the search query includes semantic information that is stored in the associative network. Now, we compare this pattern to the patterns of the other *mitmachen.at* documents and sort the results according to similarity. The analyis of the results (see *fahrzeug-without-germanet.txt*) shows that we are also able to find documents, that do not contain **vehicle** but related terms.

Finding relations/Searching by including Germanet: In this case we specify a search query consisting of one or more terms and apply an SA algorithm to Germanet in order to find related terms. Germanet employs various semantic pointers[7] that define the relations between different synsets. For our search query expansion we only use the hyponym relation which links more general concepts to instances of these concepts. Again, we use the term **vehicle** as search query. By activating the node for **vehicle** within Germanet and applying the SA algorithm, we are able to find additional terms related to **vehicle: airplane, helicopter** and **car**. All of these terms are within the *mitmachen.at* data. Other instances of **vehicle** are not taken since they are not within the analyzed documents. Now, we activate the nodes corresponding to the three terms within the associative network and spread the activation. Due to the activation of the terms found by Germanet additional terms are activated: **air, air pollution, greenhouse effect.** Due to **helicopter** we also get activations for **Galtuer** and **Eurofighter. Galtuer** is a village in Austria that was hit by avanlanches in 1999. After this event there were discussions about military helicopters that could be used for rescue and relieve efforts. In the *mitmachen.at* data, there is a reference to this discussion, therefore the name of the village is linked to **helicopter**. Such relations cannot be found with Germanet. The complete search results are available in *fahrzeug-with-germanet.txt*.

(a) Fahrzeug (vehicle) (b) Meinung (opinion)

Fig. 2. Two examples for terms and their related terms

6   Conclusions and Outlook

We have proposed an analysis framework for e-participation data, that combines various algorithms from the areas of Machine Learning and Artificial Intelligence and we have introduced *activation patterns* representing documents and sentences. We the applied the

---

[7] See http://www.sfs.uni-tuebingen.de/GermaNet/Pointers.html for a complete list and detailed description.

framework to real data from the Austrian e-participation project *mitmachen.at* and provided examples for unsupervised clustering, searching for related concepts and the analysis of relations between terms. The analysis of the results shows that the inclusion of semantic information and external knowledge sources is of great importance for the quality of the results. In future, we want to include further techniques such as fanout factors for the associative networks, WSD algorithms and improved versions of the RGNG algorithm in the framework. Furthermore, we plan to apply the framework to various e-participation related data-sets and integrate it into a website that offers a support forum for the Austrian Citizen Card. By applying the framework to different data-sets we will be able to gain more knowledge that allows us to improve the current techniques.

References

1. Macintosh, A.: Eparticipation in policy-making: the research and the challenges. In: Exploiting the Knowledge Economy: Issues, Applications and Case Studies, pp. 364–369. IOS press, Amsterdam (2006)
2. Edelmann, N., Krimmer, R., Parycek, P.: Engaging youth through deliberative e-participation: a case study. International Journal of Electronic Governance 1/4, 385–399 (2008)
3. Lerberghe, V.: Are we moving towards a more participatory representative democracy? In: Proceedings of the Eastern European e-Gov Days 2007: Best Practice and Innovation (2007)
4. Serloth, A., Maerki, O.: Partizipation und information -ergebnisse einer jugendbefragung. Technical report, Austrian Ministry of Social Security Generations and Consumer Protection (2004)
5. Piswanger, C.M.: The participatory e-government strategy of the austrian federal computing centre. In: Proceedings of the Eastern European e-Gov Days 2007: Best Practice and Innovation (2007)
6. Moon, M.J.: The evolution of e-government among municipalities: Rhetoric or reality? Public Administration Review 62, 424–433 (2002)
7. Quillian, M.R.: Semantic memory (1968)
8. Fellbaum, C.: Wordnet: An electronic lexical database (language, speech, and communication). Hardcover (May 1998)
9. Hamp, B., Feldweg, H.: Germanet -a lexical-semantic net for german. In: Proceedings of ACL workshop Automatic Information Extraction and Building of Lexical Semantic Resources for NLP Applications, pp. 9–15 (1997)
10. Qin, A.K., Suganthan, P.N.: Robust growing neural gas algorithm with application in cluster analysis. Neural Netw 17(8-9), 1135–1148 (2004)
11. Klein, D., Manning, C.D.: Fast exact inference with a factored model for natural language parsing. In: Advances in Neural Information Processing Systems, NIPS, vol. 15, pp. 3–10. MIT Press, Cambridge (2002)
12. Brants, S., Dipper, S., Hansen, S., Lezius, W., Smith, G.: The TIGER treebank. In: Proceedings of the Workshop on Treebanks and Linguistic Theories, Sozopol (2002)
13. Lezius, W., Rapp, R., Wettler, M.: A freely available morphological analyzer, disambiguator and context sensitive lemmatizer for german. In: Proceedings of the 17th international conference on Computational linguistics, Morristown, NJ, USA, pp. 743–748. Association for Computational Linguistics (1998)
14. Tsatsaronis, G., Vazirgiannis, M., Androutsopoulos, I.: Word sense disambiguation with spreading activation networks generated from thesauri (January 2007)

Enabling eParticipation of the Youth in the Public Debate on Legislation in Austria: A Critical Reflection

Sabrina Scherer[1], Christoph Neuroth[1], Günther Schefbeck[2], and Maria A. Wimmer[1]

[1] University of Koblenz-Landau, Universitätsstraße 1, 56070 Koblenz, Germany
{scherer,neurothc,wimmer}@uni-koblenz.de
[2] Austrian Parliamentary Administration, Dr. Karl Renner-Ring 3, 1017 Vienna, Austria
guenther.schefbeck@parlament.gv.at

Abstract. Legislation formation is an area of democracy, in which participation of target groups (citizens, companies, interest groups, experts) plays a crucial role. With the emergence of the Internet and the growing maturity of more recent technologies a new potential emerged for supporting participation in the legislation process. The use of ICT does, however, not automatically enhance the participation in democratic processes and may even impose new [technically based] barriers. Therefore, software development of legislative eParticipation applications should carefully investigate and bear in mind the specific targeted users. It is not feasible to just provide the necessary ICT and the legislative documents in order to start a consultation, especially with young citizens. When introducing not only a new tool but even a new procedure, the whole process needs to be planned in detail and accompanied by an expert team. In this respect, the paper at hand describes the implementation of a pilot within the LEX-IS project that aimed to facilitate and enable participation of the youth in the public debate on legislation in Austria. The subject of online discussion via the platform was a ministerial draft bill and the formulation of a comment statement based on the previous discussions to be uploaded on the Austrian Parliament's platform. The paper introduces the evaluation methodology and the results of the pilot regarding the use of the argumentation support system, participation of the youth and potential impact on the Austrian legislature. Finally, concluding remarks are provided.

Keywords: eParticipation, legislative debate, eConsultation.

1 Introduction

Electronic means are and will be more than just "technical" support for consultation processes: Indeed, since the beginning of the "world wide web era" in the 1990s, a new quality of procedural transparency has already been achieved by making procedural information, which until then had only been accessible at a few spots and, in practice, to a few actors, universally available, by providing space-independent access (and, intentionally, time-independent access, as well) to everybody (availing of the required technical infrastructure). A further qualitative step towards democratic participation is to be made by making use of the interactive capacity of the new

A. Macintosh and E. Tambouris (Eds.): ePart 2009, LNCS 5694, pp. 151–162, 2009.
© Springer-Verlag Berlin Heidelberg 2009

technologies, thus not only giving the citizens the opportunity to keep themselves informed about law-making processes but also to get actively involved. Electronic means will enhance such involvement but not be sufficient to make it part of political culture.

In this respect, the overall aim of LEX-IS project[1] was to facilitate and enable participation of the youth in the public debate of legislation among Parliaments, Citizens and Businesses in the EU. Therefore two pilots have been implemented: one in Austria (http://at.lex-is.eu) and one in Greece (http://hep.lex-is.eu).

The paper at hand describes and analyses the Austrian pilot implementation. The topic of online discussion of the Austrian pilot via the LEX-IS platform was a ministerial draft bill and the development/formulation of a comment statement based on the previous discussions to be uploaded on the Austrian Parliament's platform. In order to reach young people and give them an understanding of eParticipation, the Austrian pilot implemented a project in cooperation with schools. Young people got the task to discuss a ministerial draft bill offline and online and then to draft an official opinion/statement with the help of their teachers. Finally this official statement has been uploaded on the Austrian Parliament's website.

Next section introduces the LEX-IS platform. Section 3 describes the Austrian legislative process and the embedment of the pilot. Section 4 introduces the evaluation methodology and the results of the pilot regarding the use of the argumentation support system, participation of the youth and impact on Austrian legislative. In section 5 concluding remarks are provided.

2 The LEX-IS Platform

The main objective of the LEX-IS project was to improve the legislative process in National Parliaments through enhancing public participation on the preparatory stages (legislation proposal formation and debate on draft legislation) with the use of state-of-the-art ICT-based tools and methodologies, specifically focusing in enhancing the participation of younger citizens. [1, 2].

The LEX-IS platform consists of a simply structured website with a specific type of forum [3]. At the top level the major discussion units ("Topics"), which specify a general category (e.g. a specific draft bill), are visible. Each discussion unit can contain one or more threads, which are more specific discussions under the same topic. Both can only be created by administrators and contain relevant information about the discussion (subject, summary, dates, legal documents, etc). In each thread, any user is able to create a discussion-tree, where all participants can post comments/opinions/entries and attach files. These discussion-trees are of two types [3]:

- Issue-Alternative: Participants can choose between the five posting categories Issue, Alternative, Pro Argument, Con Argument and Comment. There are specific relations between these posting categories (i.e. under each posting category there are constraints about the next posting):
  - At the root level only an Issue can be posted
  - Only an Alternative or a Comment can be posted after an Issue

---

[1] See http://www.lex-is.eu/

- Only a Comment can be posted after a Comment
- Only a Pro/Con Argument can be posted after an Alternative or an Argument
• Question-Answer: The three posting categories Question, Answer and Comment can be chosen by the user. Again this forum has specific constraints:
  - At the root level there is only a Question
  - Only an Answer or a Comment can be posted after a Question
  - Only a Comment can be posted after an Answer or a Comment

3 The Austrian Legislative Process

The first stage of Austrian legislation is the submission of a bill containing the proposed legislation to the National Council. Such bills can only be submitted by persons or bodies explicitly entitled to do so under the Austrian Constitution. The majority of bills are submitted by the Federal Government. Submission of bills can only be done by the government as an entity, but not by individual ministers. Such bills must be approved by the Council of Ministers before they are submitted to the National Council. Before draft bills are submitted to the Council of Ministers by the Federal Minister responsible for the respective matter, they are undergoing a consultation procedure, in the course of which the Federal Ministries, the Provincial Administrations, and specific interest groups are invited to comment on the respective draft bill[2].

In 1999, the Austrian Parliament has published the ministerial draft bills with explanations on its website for the first time. Thereby it started to bring more transparency into the pre-parliamentary consultation procedure. Since then, it is common practice in Austria that the statements on legal drafts (uploaded on the parliamentary website) are the most important means for community groups to impact legislation during the consultation phase. In this general pre-parliamentary consultation phase, however, Members of the Austrian Parliament do not participate actively in consultation processes. Hence, so far there is no formal and bi-directional consultation procedure between "stakeholders" on the one hand and MPs on the other hand. The parliamentary groups, however, are kept informed about these consultation processes, and MPs regularly would show an explicit interest in receiving the respective documents without any delay.

In order to get sophisticated comments on draft bills, formal invitations for consultation are issued to specific interest groups such as trade unions, chambers, etc. Individual citizens may, however, also submit comments but are not formally invited to do so; in practice, only a few individual citizens would use this opportunity.

In any case, after the phase of consultation, the comments provided are processed by the responsible government officials, i.e. brought into a synopsis made available to the responsible Federal Minister, and, if the Minister so decides, an update draft bill to be presented to the Council of Ministers.

Figure 1 visualises the overall Austrian legislative process. The discussions in the LEX-IS pilot took place after the ministerial draft bill and the invitation for statements have been published on the Parliament's website.

---

[2] See the more detailed description of this consultation procedure, along with some conceptual perspectives, in [13, 14, 15].

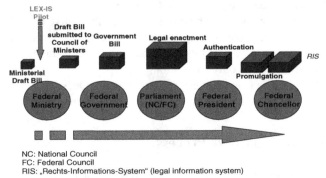

NC: National Council
FC: Federal Council
RIS: „Rechts-Informations-System" (legal information system)

Fig. 1. Austrian legislative process and the position of the LEX-IS pilot

4 Enabling Participation of the Youth in Austria – Pilot Organisation

The use of ICT does not automatically enhance the participation in democratic processes and may even impose new (technically based) barriers. Therefore, software development in legislative eParticipation applications should carefully investigate and bear in mind the specifically targeted users. Development of new technical features is not the most important criterion for success. Reasons are that on the one hand citizens do not have to use such software. On the other hand, staff from public authorities may be forced to. Besides, young people are pessimistic regarding political participation and wondering what will happen with their voice and what is the result [4]. Hence, people need motivational assets to use the technology. In consequence, tools to support the legislation drafting and formation processes should support and motivate the users and particularly consider their needs. It is not feasible to just provide the necessary ICT and the draft bill in order to start a consultation, especially with young citizens [5, 6]. The whole process needs to be planned in detail, accompanied by an expert team and have a defined result.

In order to reach young people and give them an understanding of eParticipation, the Austrian pilot implemented a project in cooperation with schools. The subject of online discussion within the Austrian pilot via the LEX-IS platform was a ministerial draft bill. The pilot aimed at the development/formulation of a statement based on the previous discussions to be uploaded on the Austrian Parliament's platform. A draft bill has been selected that directly affects and/or extends young citizens' knowledge on their own rights: the "Child and Youth Welfare Act" (Bundes-Kinder- und Jugendhilfegesetz 2009)[3].

---

[3] The ministerial draft bill which was discussed was not a draft amendment of an existing law but was to wholly replace the existing law regulating the respective matter, so that, unlike draft amendments, no text comparison was part of the draft bill. The draft bill consists of 45 sections divided into two parts (i.e. a rather complex structure from young people's point of view).

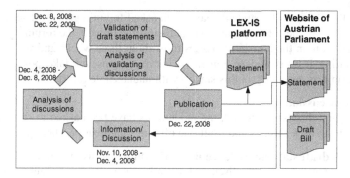

Fig. 2. Participation process of LEX-IS pilot

Different from mitmachen.at[4], a project that focussed on the general deliberation of future key issues [7, 8], the LEX-IS pilot directly addressed the deliberation of a specific draft bill in Austria. Nonetheless, the LEX-IS pilot implementation (see Figure 2) based on similar eParticipation phases, i.e. information and communication, analysis, validation, and publication. Thereby, the LEX-IS pilot combined analysis and validation as described below in the seventh step. Overall, the Austrian pilot was organised as follows:

Information / Discussions
1. When setting up the Austrian pilot, an invitation was sent to schools of different types to participate in the LEX-IS pilot.
2. Preparation of comprehensive and easy understandable information material suitable for young students (e.g. about the legislative process and the particular draft bill in Austria) was an important pilot aspect. The students needed to catch up on concepts (such as democracy) and the legislative process in Austria as well as on eParticipation. Some teachers used this material and prepared the students before the kick-start of the participation. In retrospect, it was easier for these young citizens to actively participate in the discussions.
3. The project team analysed the draft bill in order to identify legislative issues of interest to the target group and to draft an initial forum structure. Finally, nine discussion threads were initiated where different sections of the draft bill were taken into account[5]. One thread contained the compilation of the final statements of the seven successful threads towards one unique statement. Obviously the initial threads influenced the final discussions. Yet, the young citizens needed to be motivated to form their opinion on the law on the basis of presenting small understandable pieces of the draft bill.
4. The pilot started in the schools with a short presentation to introduce the pilot and give some background information. After that, an initial moderated discussion took

---

[4] See http://www.mitmachen.at (in German).
[5] The threads contained a description and some supporting documents as the specific paragraph. First, seven threads were initiated, and on later stages two threads were added upon users' remarks. These threads have however barely been elaborated further by the students, i.e. in the end, discussion went on in the seven threads opened at the beginning.

place in the classes. The students have been asked to build groups, discuss the legislative issues in these groups and to post their reflections in the forum.[6]

5. The discussion on the legislative issues took about three weeks and was conducted online during lessons and at home. To prevent misuse or fake postings, online moderation was necessary in this stage - with manageable effort.

Analysis of discussions

6. After the first discussion period, the moderators have been asked to summarise the discussions in their threads and draft one official statement per thread.

Validation of draft statements & Analysis of validating discussions

7. These statements have been discussed again in a period of one week in a separate thread. Although only few students participated in this stage, these suggestions and complaints were well to the point. They have been incorporated by the moderators into updates of their statements and have been validated again[7].

Publication

8. At the end of these discussions, the project team formulated the final statement. It was decided to have one statement in the name of all participating schools in order to have a "louder voice". The overall pilot phase ended with the upload of the statement to the Austrian Parliament's website on 22nd December, 2008.

5   Results

In order to evaluate the Austrian Pilot an evaluation methodology was applied based on the framework described in [9]. It takes into account the three evaluation perspectives process, system, context and outcomes. The overall evaluation methodology of LEX-IS bases on several aspects[8]:

- End user surveys for students and moderators investigating if the user is reached or not, and if he or she is reached to identify if the platform could attract his or her interest regularly. Several questions investigate the interrelations and interdependencies between platform attributes, a positive or negative attitude, and the behaviour of users to continue the use of the platform[9] [10].
- Website and user statistics have been tracked from starting with the pilot. Through these statistics, the behaviour of the platform visitors could be analysed.
- Interviews with students and moderators and the discussions during the initial workshop sessions were used in the qualitative analysis.
- Analysis of the quantity and quality of the users' contributions:

---

[6] It was necessary to motivate their participation and to take away their fear of bad phrasing and "stupid" posts. Beyond this, the project team tried to motivate teachers or students to take over the role of moderation for individual threads in order to integrate them better in the discussions.

[7] This is one of the aforementioned differences to the mitmachen.at participation process.

[8] The overall LEX-IS evaluation has been conducted by the AEGEAN University for the Greek LEX-IS pilot, too.

[9] The questionnaire is based on the end-user questionnaire developed within the MOMENTUM project (http://www.ep-momentum.eu). It is described in detail in [16].

- How many postings have been entered in total, per type, and per level?
- What percentage of the postings have been assigned a mistaken type (e.g. postings entered as 'key issues' are something else, e.g. 'alternatives', or postings entered as 'alternatives' are 'pro-arguments' or 'contra-arguments')
- What percentage of the postings are trivial, i.e. just 'agree' or 'disagree' without something more.

By combining all these aspects, coherence has been observed and the following pilot aspects of the Austrian case have been analysed:

- Use of the argumentation support system
- Participation of the Youth
- Impact to Austrian legislation

The pilot finally reached 8 participating classes from different types of school (vocational and general secondary schools), as well as from different geographic regions. Altogether, they formed a good sample of Austrian students of the age intended. To sum up, key figures of the Austrian pilot (duration about 1 month) are:

- approx. 120 registered and active young citizens (students) of age 14 to 19,
- 8 teachers, 1 student and 2 participants from LEX-IS who acted as moderators,
- 253 posts (of which about 230 stem from the students)
- 10 discussion threads (8 of which containing postings)
- 1 official final statement delivered to the Austrian Parliament's Portal[10] and
- about 12000 visits.

37 of the 120 participants completed the online survey, whereas 10 participants submitted only incomplete results which were not included in the evaluation process. Beyond, 3 students and 1 moderator have been interviewed.

With the Austrian pilot, about 120 young citizens could learn how to make use of their possibilities of citizen participation in drafting bills by participating via online communication means in the specific consultation procedure. They realized that they may have a potential impact on what their legal representatives will decide. Another positive side effect for the young citizens was the learning-by-doing effect with regard to experiencing political participation. They could learn how to participate in (political) opinion-forming processes by applying new technologies, and how to access information about ministerial draft bills as well as the whole work of their parliament. The overall user acceptance of the Austrian pilot was good; this assessment is supported by the following figures from the end-user questionnaire.

- More than 80% of the participants would like to come back after the end of the project, whereby nearly 62% of the participants would like to continue using the platform.
- More than 80% rated that the platform is easy use to use.
- For more than 75% the discussed topic was interesting.

---

[10] See http://www.parlinkom.gv.at/PG/DE/XXIII/ME/ME_00231_63/pmh.shtml

Main critical points which have been addressed by the participants were the inflexible forum structure through the constraints of the argumentation support system, the short time frame and the hard understandable draft bill.

5.1 Use of the Argumentation Support System

The inflexible structure of the forum (i.e. some posting types could only be used in combination with another posting type) was criticized by some of the participants. The design of the forum led to a high number of comments, i.e. students decided to choose the "comment" instead of pro- and contra-arguments or questions and answers[11]. Foremost, in some of the threads participants used almost only comments to submit their opinion. This behaviour can be argued as follows:

- Young participants do not think about their statement before typing. They choose one possible entry type and start to write their statement. They do not mind if it can be a pro or contra statement, an alternative or an answer at a first glance.
- Participants could be afraid of writing an alternative or answer because they think that the text they need to write should be of very good quality. The fear of too much attention is another reason for the non-usage of alternatives and answers.

Anyway, a more flexible forum structure allowing to more freely combining the different types of posts may be desired.

Another conclusion can be drawn by comparing the depths of the discussion threads: If a discussion has a higher depth, the interaction between the participants was greater. In summary, discussions in the threads of forum type issue – alternative reached a higher depth. This can be explained by the bigger interaction through the usage of pro and contra arguments. On the one hand these argument types improve the interactive discussions among the participants. Yet, on the other hand this results in a number of redundant posts caused by entries containing more or less only "I agree" or "I disagree". Through the implementation of a rating mechanism this redundancy may be reduced.

As explained above, many participants have simply chosen the entry type comment instead of answer or alternative, or instead of pro or con arguments. This happened most time in discussion threads with a high depth. One reason can be the complexity and therefore limited readability of these threads. Another reason can be the problem of iterating pro and contra arguments so that the participants do not know whether to use a pro or a contra argument to get their statement clear.

The fact that most of the participants rated the platform as easy to use shows that they did not think about this special argumentation support feature. However, the high number of comments in the forum made it difficult to sum up the threads in the final statement. The argumentation support feature was nearly useless.

5.2 Participation of the Youth

First of all, it can be observed that the vast majority of postings is characterized by honest efforts to keep to the issue of discussion and reasonably deal with it. In a very

---

[11] 40% in forum type issue-alternative and 15% in forum type question-answer, overall 55% of all entries were comments.

few cases, one might wonder whether a posting was treating the subject with irony, but it was not to be observed that postings were obviously malevolent or nonsense. Thus, one of the arguments often used against consultation of individual citizens, namely that evaluation of the results would be impeded by lots of irrelevant statements, can, once again, be deemed refuted. The publication of their statements on the parliamentary websites was an important motivating factor. However, we have, of course, to have in mind that the discussion took place under conditions of social control within classroom environments. This is also important as young people prefer debating in organised groups [11].

Secondly, turning to the knowledge base of the postings and their argumentative structure, the overall majority of postings would refer to individual experience and what might be called common sense but not to inter-subjectively available data and stringent argumentative figures. Thus, the discussion more or less consists of individual positions put opposite each other but not of dialectic structures leading to synthetic results. In this regard, the discussion resembles "political" debates on public fora like parliamentary plena, the important difference being the lack of that severe conflict-orientation that usually would characterize debates of that kind. Nevertheless, the lack of dialectic discussion structures is the reason for which it has been quite difficult to derive from the discussion a common final statement summarizing its results, which would be appropriate to form an input to the political decision-making process.

Finally, it should be mentioned that most of the postings, of course, show lacking of being embedded in the context of the overall legal system. In a few cases, there are references to other legal sources, in particular to the UN Convention on the Rights of the Child, obviously due to this Convention having been dealt with in the classes. In the long run, this issue might be one of the key success factors for public consultation processes, and this seems to be a challenge to the educational system as well as to IT applications supporting such processes: The potential impact of comments given in the course of such process to some extent will depend on how much they take into account the legal system context, and this implies, as prerequisites, some basic knowledge on the legal system being imparted already on young people at school, as well as tools enabling people to easily get access to legal material pertinent to a specific issue put to consultation.

Summarising the impression is that the alternatives discussed were already promoted or provoked by formulating the discussion threads, and this was done by the moderators, in advance of the classroom discussion itself; to nearly no extent, the discussion went beyond the scope staked out by the moderators.

5.3 Impact to Austrian Legislation

To implement LEX-IS in Austria, the pilot process had to be set up within the framework of the Austrian formal legislative procedure, or more precisely of the pre-parliamentary consultation procedure. This means that a more active participation of MPs (as participating stakeholders in the discussion) is (until now) not feasible due to the traditional procedure as explained above (even it was not possible for the trial of LEX-IS). In accordance with practical experience, the contributions may give the political decision-makers merely some "atmospheric" impression of how young people are thinking on legal issues pertinent to them, and on the role they would ascribe to the public authorities in the field covered by the draft bill.

The attention that the political decision-makers are paying to the results of consultation processes has traditionally been directed towards the contributions of organized interests, and among them in particular of the large and powerful organizations like chambers of commerce, trade unions, etc. There is no tradition of paying attention to public discussion processes, which have taken place in a very few exceptional cases only, so that the comment drafted within the school project in question cannot be expected to have a major impact. Political culture would undergo slow changes only.

At times when eConsultations will be more common practice and will result in high quality statements from the stakeholders' side, it might, however, be an option that MPs actively involve themselves in this consultation procedure, too. This would require a change in tradition and culture in the Austrian legislative process. Another approach might be to perceive the MPs' role as that of "interest brokers" building in their decision-making processes on the results of societal opinion-making processes taking place in advance of parliamentary procedure.

The Austrian LEX-IS pilot coincided with the intermediate phase of Austrian politics between the premature general elections and the formation of a new federal government. The draft bill used for piloting, of course, originated from the old government, a circumstance implying some uncertainty about the further destiny of the bill. Anyway, it will take some time till the new federal government will start dealing with the issue again, so that any kind of evaluation of the pilot's impact on real legislative decisions will be possible afterwards only.

6 Conclusion

The most encouraging result of the pilot can be seen in the experience made, once again, that young people are interested in getting involved in opinion-making processes as to public affairs, that they are ready to invest some time in participating in such processes (though this time it was merely classroom time), and that they are able to participate in a very serious manner [7, 8].

On the other hand, the pilot also showed the substantial limitations public consultation in general, and consulting young people in particular, is facing: The discussion was predetermined by the thread structure and thread issues defined by the moderators, and there would not have been a compact and computable result if not drafted by the moderators, as well. One might expect (or at least hope) that chances for developing an autonomous discussion structure would be better if more time was available, but in political reality the period of time available for a particular consultation process would not be much longer than a few weeks, too. Furthermore, drafting a compact text representing the results of a discussion process and accepted by its participants will always remain a challenge.

To turn "consumer democracy" into "participative democracy" educational efforts and learning effects will be required on the part of all (potential) actors of the political system: Citizens will have to be ready to invest more time into informing themselves and publicly expressing their opinions, and political decision-makers will have to learn that better democratic legitimization for public decisions will relieve them from some burden of responsibility. This means also that decision makers take over action as a result of serious participation to motivate young people (as Coleman suggests [12]) and other citizens, as well.

Nevertheless, of course, the technical capacity of the tools available will also be of major importance: Tools will have to be more flexible than simple web fora, they will have to offer knowledge management support in dealing with legal issues put to public consultation, and they will have to support social networking within consultation processes. Finally, they also will have to offer some benefits to the administrative users responsible for evaluating the results of such processes, in order to make it attractive for them to promote the use of these tools, and to speed up all administrative processes accompanying the mere discussion process itself.

Acknowledgments. LEX-IS is co-funded by the EC within the eParticipation Preparatory Action, grant agreement n° 2006/01/018. The authors are very grateful to the participants of the Austrian LEX-IS pilot and the project partners for their discussions and contributions, which provide the knowledge basis for the work at hand.

References

1. Loukis, E., Wimmer, M.A., Charalabidis, Y., Triantafillou, A., Gatautis, R.: Argumentation Systems and Ontologies for Enhancing Public Participation in the Legislation Process. In: Grönlund, A., Scholl, H.J., Wimmer, M.A. (eds.) Electronic Government. Proceedings of ongoing research, projects and workshop contributions, Linz, Trauner, September 2007. Informatik, vol. 24, pp. 19–28 (2007)
2. Loukis, E., Wimmer, M.A., Triantafillou, A., Charalabidis, Y., Gionis, G., Gatautis, R.: Development of Legislation through Electronic Support of Participation: LEX-IS. In: Cunningham, P., Cunningham, M. (eds.) Expanding the Knowledge Society: Issues, Applications, Case Studies. Number Part 1, October 2007, pp. 447–487. IOS Press, Amsterdam (2007)
3. Kountourakis, G.: LEX-IS Forum Manual. Technical report, ATC (July 2008)
4. Livingstone, S., Bober, M., Helsper, E.: Active participation or just more information?: young people's take up of opportunities to act and interact on the internet. LSE Research (2005), http://eprints.lse.ac.uk/1014
5. Coleman, S., Gøtze, J.: Bowling Together: Online Public Engagement in Policy Deliberation. Report (2002)
6. Macintosh, A., Coleman, S.: Promise and Problems of E-Democracy, Challenges of online citizen engagement. Technical report, OECD (2004)
7. Edelmann, N., Krimmer, R., Parycek, P.: Engaging youth through deliberative e-participation: a case study. International Journal of Electronic Governance 1(4), 385–399 (2008)
8. Krimmer, R., Makolm, J., Parycek, P., Steininger, S., Kripp, M.: Politik zum Mitmachen. Arbeitspapiere zu elektronischen Wahlen und Partizipation, Editor: Kompetenzzentrum für elektronische Wahlen und Partizipation, E-Voting.CC (2007)
9. Loukis, E., Xenakis, A.: A Framework for Evaluating eParticipation in the Legislation Development Process. In: Ferro, E., Scholl, H.J., Wimmer, M.A. (eds.) Electronic Government: Proceedings of ongoing research and projects of EGOV 2008. 7th International Conference, EGOV 2008, September 2008. Informatik, vol. 27, pp. 89–98. Trauner, Linz (2008)

10. Loukis, E., Xenakis, A., Triantafyllou, A., Koundourakis, G., Charalabidis, Y., Scherer, S., Neuroth, C., Wimmer, M.A., Schefbeck, G.: D3.2 System Evaluation Report. Deliverable, LEX-IS (2009)
11. Smith, E., Macintosh, A., Whyte, A.: Organised Use of eDemocracy Tools for Young People. In: Grönlund, A., Scholl, H.J., Andersen, K.V., Wimmer, M.A. (eds.) Electronic Government: Communication Proceedings of the Fifth International EGOV Conference 2006, Krakow, Poland, September 4-8, 2006. Schriftenreihe Informatik, vol. 18, pp. 260–267. Trauner Verlag, Linz (2006)
12. Coleman, S.: A Tale of Two Houses: the House of Commons, the Big Brother house and the people at home. Parliamentary Affairs 56(4), 733–758 (2003)
13. Schefbeck, G.: E-Partizipation und vorparlamentarische Konsultation. In: Schweighofer, E., Geist, A., Heindl, G. (eds.) 10 Jahre IRIS: Bilanz und Ausblick. Tagungsband des 10. Internationalen Rechtsinformatik-Symposions IRIS 2007, Boorberg, Stuttgart, pp. 134–142 (2007)
14. Schefbeck, G.: Auf dem Weg zur E-Konsultation? Zur Praxis deliberativer Politik in Österreich. In: Prosser, A., Parycek, P. (eds.) Elektronische Demokratie in Österreich. Proceedings der EDem 2007, Wien. OCG, Wien, pp. 43–59 (2007)
15. Schefbeck, G.: E-Partizipation und elektronisches Begutachtungsverfahren. In: Bildungsprotokolle Band 15: 5. Klagenfurter Legistik-Gespräche 2007, Verwaltungsakademie, Klagenfurt, pp. 7–29 (2008)
16. Bicking, M., Wimmer, M.A.: Deliverable 2.5: E-Participation Projects Evaluation Methodology. MOMENTUM Deliverable (2008)

eParticipation for Adolescent Citizens (in Austria)

Noella Edelmann[1], Johann Hoechtl[1], and Peter Parycek[2]

[1] Center for E-Government, Danube University Krems
Dr.-Karl-Dorrek-Strasse 30, Krems, Austria
{noella.edelmann,johann.hoechtl}@donau-uni.ac.at
[2] Austrian Federal Chancellery, Vienna, Austria
peter.parycek@bka.gv.at

Abstract. In Austria, two recent eParticipation projects focused on adolescent citizens. The first project, "mitmachen.at – move your future" was to provide initial experiences with an eParticipation tool. The second project, "Jugend2help", applied the lessons learned from the "mitmachen.at" project to improve the Austrian public administration web portal for adolescent citizens. In both projects, the results indicate that web portals and eParticpation seems to suit the adolescents' information and communication needs. Involving the users is central to the development of an eParticipation process or platform so that the users' specific characteristics (age, skills), needs and interests are included appropriately. The target users' characteristics are also important for developing a marketing strategy which is able to reach them. Other issues which must also be considered in eParticipation are accessibility, inclusion and possibly gender.

Keywords: eParticipation, eGovernment, deliberation, user groups, adolescents.

1 Introduction: eParticipation by Austrian Adolescents

Digital networks can support all forms and stages of public involvement and empowerment, ranging from simply providing information to actual decision-making [1]. The collaboration between public administration and all sectors of civic society includes integration in policy-making and the co-development of public services, so in the long run, eParticipation can contribute to the process of democratisation in both state and society. The internet not only enables groups with specific needs to participate (citizens with special needs, commuters or immigrants), but the anonymity of the web also facilitates discussions about sensitive subjects (such as drugs, HIV-prevention, child sexual abuse or domestic violence), and seeking advice from experts or peers.

Adolescents, often described as the „online generation", need to be recognised as a significant eGovernment and eParticipation target group; their interests include education, employment, social support programs and travel. In Austria, 95% of 14-18-year-olds use the internet [2] so online-based participation projects are possible. A common prejudice is that young citizens are not interested in politics at all, yet a survey in 2006 [3] reveals that 86.7% of all adolescents do want to be involved in

A. Macintosh and E. Tambouris (Eds.): ePart 2009, LNCS 5694, pp. 163–174, 2009.
© Springer-Verlag Berlin Heidelberg 2009

political decisions, and 92.5% believe that political engagement is beneficial to their personal development. But only 50.9% of the adolescents are actually willing to contribute politically. Whilst 25.4% of the adolescents questioned know about any participant programmes for young people, only 15% participate. This shows that there is a big discrepancy between the value attributed to participation and the actual level of engagement, particularly in traditional or party politics. Such statistics are alarming as young users are important both for the further development of eSkills as well as disseminators/teachers of digital skills and knowledge in their families and communities, a role which is particularly important in marginalised groups.

Young people have advanced digital skills and they want to be involved: these are the basic assumptions for the two nation-wide eParticipation projects conducted in Austria 2007-2008. This paper describes the two projects, the results obtained and the lessons learned for eParticipation with adolescent citizens. The first youth eParticipation project "mitmachen.at – move your future" was initiated as a "test" to gain experiences in eParticipation. The second project "Jugend2help", invited adolescents to participate in defining the content of their own space (the "youth" section) on the Austrian eGovernment www.help.gv.at platform.

2   eParticipation Projects in Austria

2.1 "mitmachen.at – move your future" (2007)

Online portals are important for simplifying the vertical and horizontal integration of eGovernment [4] and the virtual portal used for the "mitmachen.at – move your future" (www.mitmachen.at) project included the necessary instruments for participation and two different user levels (administration, citizen) to simulate the eGovernment process. "Mitmachen.at" was an eParticipation project aimed at getting young Austrians to participate in a political discussion about a range of topics.

If democratic political processes are to function, and for eGovernment to be successful, there needs to be a relationship and a dialogue between politics and citizens, and citizens must actually participate in the democratic process [5]. The name of the project reveals the objective: in German, the verb 'mitmachen' means 'to participate', and the project provided young citizens aged 15–25 living in Austria the opportunity to use the internet and voice their concerns and ideas about the future. It was the first eParticipation project that went beyond simply offering useful services and information to young people in Austria[1]. The project was led by the Austrian Federal Computing Centre (Bundesrechenzentrum BRZ[2]), supported by the Danube University Krems and involved youth institutions, software companies, various Think Tanks and the relevant public authorities so as to develop and achieve a democratic participation process. The main aims were to test the general electronic participation processes, the technical implementation and the (technical) framework which make online participation processes possible. Further aims included studying online participation, participant involvement, the relationships that developed between participants and, at a meta-level, how participants felt about online participation. The project and the results

---

[1] see www.yourchoiceinfo.at and www.politikkabine.at
[2] www.brz.gv.at

obtained were analysed as a case study, to show the opportunities and limitations of the project, and to understand how and to what extent deliberation can be implemented as a way of increasing citizen engagement and reducing citizen apathy ([6][7]). The project revealed a number of interesting results and valuable conclusions, but it is the actual project itself that proves that "eParticipation represents a cross-sectional subject, which can be part of a procedure on its own, but could also be useful in many other areas of application" [8].

The adolescents were reached using a number of different channels and emails were sent to pupils in all secondary schools. Information about the project was disseminated by youth institutions, state education authorities, IT-teachers, the school-IT organisation 'Education Highway', Austrian job centres and the Austrian Ministry of Education, Department of Political Education.

The project consisted of 4 phases (based on [9]): public participation, classification of the postings, a public poll and public presentation of the results. This provided the participants with a schedule and an outline of what they were required to do, and, at the same time, ensured the transparency of the project. The project "mitmachen.at" was the first eParticipation project to add the fourth phase, i.e. publishing all results and making recommendations (in the form of a report) available to the public, political decision makers, members of the public administration and the Austrian Federal Youth Council (the report and all results are still available on the project website). The "mitmachen.at" portal employed a moderator to ensure a minimum quality of the contributions (ensuring that comments were not off-topic; clarifying issues or answering questions; providing information) and censoring contributions which were racist, sexist, rude or used foul language.

During the first phase, the participants were asked to first rate eight pre-set topics (environment, employment, education, health, social system, infrastructure, safety, political system, from [10]) in terms of importance to themselves, then discuss the topics. Although the discussion process was governed by these eight topics, the participants had the opportunity to state their opinions about anything else they considered important. As can be seen from Table 1, the topics "environment", "employment" and "education" were those considered most important, whilst "safety" and "political system" were rated as least important. Interestingly though, it is "political system" which generated the highest number of postings (see Table 2), which clearly displayed the participants' frustration with politics and reflected the results obtained from the first part of this phase. The language used and how the comments were made in this category meant that the moderator often decided not to publish the comments made. Given the relation between comments made (414)/ comments published (168) raises the issue of the moderator's role in an eParticipation process. Some participants wanted to know more about the Austrian political system and politics, but, in general, the comments made in the category "political system" were derisive and very superficial. A small number of participants displayed interest in the project itself, the results to be obtained from the project and how opinions and results would be used. A participant declared: "The politicians should read this ..."[3] The other categories which generated the greatest number of postings were environment and health.

---

[3] Post made on www.mitmachen.at

Table 1. "mitmachen.at": rating the topics (Phase 1)

Topics	Very Important (3 points)	Rather Important (2 points)	Rather Unimportant (1 point)	Not Important (0 points)	Total Score
Environment	514	192	44	13	1970
Employment	474	225	53	11	1925
Education	472	215	61	15	1907
Health	446	250	59	8	1897
Social System	428	261	65	9	1871
Infrastructure	295	307	133	28	1632
Safety	233	262	217	51	1440
Political System	221	269	208	65	1409

Table 2. "mitmachen.at": postings made and published (Phase 1)

Topics	Total Postings	%	Published Postings	%
Environment	397	19.10%	289	20.29%
Health	237	11.40%	169	11.87%
Education	312	15.01%	245	17.21%
Safety	229	11.01%	181	12.71%
Infrastructure	134	6.45%	118	8.29%
Social System	126	6.06%	106	7.44%
Political System	414	19.91%	168	11.80%
Employment	154	7.41%	103	7.23%
My Opinion	76	3.66%	45	3.16%
Total	2079	100%	1424	100%

During Phase 2, the postings were collected, analysed and reformulated into 174 short statements by an expert panel (experts came from youth institutions, software companies, Think Tanks, education and public authorities). These statements were rated during the third phase, deliberation, i.e. the validation and prioritisation of the statements. The fourth phase collected the experiences and results gained from the project and made them available to the public, public administration and Government.

2.2 The Project Jugend2help (2008)

The project "Jugend2help" (www.jugend2help.gv.at) was largely influenced by valuable information gained from the project mitmachen.at ([11][12]). Therefore, a central aim was to collect new eParticipation and collaboration experiences and data, to examine the way a public Web 2.0 project works and to find out to what extent young citizens can be engaged in public decision-making processes. The cooperation between civic society, public administration and various partners (from schools to unemployment agencies) was to improve the online public services on the web platform www.help.gv.at.

The nationwide project was open to all adolescent Austrian residents, and the participants were invited to determine the content of their section ("youth") of the public www.help.gv.at web portal. The project "Jugend2help" was divided into four distinct phases; two of the phases (I and III) were available to the public on the internet platform www.jugend2help.gv.at, whilst phase II consisted of face-to-face discussions held in a number of schools. In Phase IV a report containing adolescents' ideas and recommendations was made public and presented to the Austrian Government. The recommendations are being implemented into the relevant section of the public portal www.help.gv.at:

Phase I: Public Participation - adolescent citizens were asked about their needs and attitudes towards public administration and the platform www.help.gv.at.
Phase II: Consultation - small groups of pupils from secondary schools discussed the input gained from Phase I and re-formulated them into statements or slogans.
Phase III: Public Poll - the statements from Phase II were posted on the web platform, and adolescents were asked to vote for or against the statements.
Phase IV: Implementation - the results of Phase III were analysed and implemented into the youth section on www.help.gv.at.

The main goals of Phase I were to identify the best channels public administration should use to reach young people and to find out what topics they are interested in. The results below (Table 3) show that adolescent participants would prefer to use discussion platforms or newsletters, but not podcasts or second life as electronic channels of communications for eGovernment and eParticipation. The results would indicate that the participants would use "e-" media channels, but prefer the more established forms or the ones they are most familiar with. Print media is no longer interesting, but it is interesting to note that schools are seen as an important channel for information (Table 4), as adolescents seem to still trust this institution. An alternative to schools are youth portals, as discussion and participation here can be anonymous.

The topics which adolescents consider to be most important are training and education, employment, support programs and travel (Table 5). This is not surprising, as

Table 3. Channels www.help.gv.at should provide, considered as very important

Channels	Nr.Votes
Newsletter	43
SMS	28
Live Broadcasts	35
Moderated Wiki	36
Discussion Forum	max 68
Moderated Chat	32
Second Life	min 16
Instant Messaging	27
Podcasts	20
Videos	37
Infotainment	36

Table 4. What media would you prefer to offer you information and service?

Media preferred	Nr. Votes
Dedicated Youth Portal (excl. www.help.gv.at)	48
Telephone Hotline	33
Print Media	min 27
Helpdesk / Offices	58
School	max 62
Youth Clubs and Organisations	55

Table 5. Topics participants require more information

Topics	Nr. Votes
Environmental Protection	47
Travelling Abroad	63
Policy-making in Austria and the EU	54
Work and Employment Laws	77
Training and Education	max 84
Support Programmes	73
Leisure, Welfare, Sport	54
Health, Addiction, HIV Prevention	51
Relationships, Personal Problems	42
Voluntary Work	44
New Media and Technologies, PC-games	36
Information Concerning the EU	min 34

these are topics which adolescents are confronted with at this stage of their lives and determine their future.

3   The Adolescents' View on eParticipation and eGovernment

Besides obtaining correlations between the users and their eGovernment needs, the researchers also investigated the adolescents' understanding of eParticipation and eGovernment.

In both projects, the adolescents were interested in the eParticipation process, and the results showed that a web portal can be a method for communication, participation and deliberation which is both accepted and will be used by adolescent citizens. The online discussions and the offline consultations revealed that participants tend to be sceptical of their generation, believing that "other" adolescents are simply not interested in politics and unaware as to what happening to them, society and "in the world"[4]. In the "Jugend2help" project, several participants stated that they were glad to have this opportunity to partici- pate, have their say and shape the public environment and services offered on www.help.gv.at. Adolescents will contribute and participate, but they do expect to be listened to and want politicians and public administration to act/react to their suggestions.

---

[4] Comment made by a participant / Phase II

The postings and discussions indicate that the adolescents would accept and use online platforms for a range of different subjects such as further education, information about public transport, driving schools and housing. But they requested "serious" platforms for such topics, and such platforms should neither reflect party politics nor contain advertising. They stress that they would like to receive "serious" information from all the political parties, and would like to learn more about politics, as the "Social Studies" class at school does not provide enough and is often presented in a "boring" and uninteresting way. There seems to be another problem too – whilst adolescents say that politicians and the public administration take no interest or do not listen to them, politicians and the public administration think that young people take no interest in politics and public institutions. Yet a member of the expert panel from the project "mitmachen.at" believed that the ideas and contents generated by the users can be used by Government or public administration as they provide a "mini-governmental program determined by young Austrians".

When participants in the "Jugend2help" project were asked what they knew about eGovernment, their answers included "something to do with the Government"[5], and "an opportunity to look into the state's finances and expenditure"[6]. They know little about eGovernment and the digitalisation processes occurring at state level, and they show some scepticism about eParticipation and eGovernment. Still, they responded positively to it and do want to be involved, as they strongly believe in the value of communicating and sharing. They recognised the project as an opportunity to participate in Government and public administration processes. The adolescents liked the idea of finding all the Government and public administration information electronically; they belong to the generation that is growing up expecting to find everything on the internet [13] and want to integrate their eParticipation and eGovernment needs seamlessly into their work and personal lives.

How important is it for sixteen year olds to vote? In the "Jugend2help" discussions about voting and eVoting, one group of adolescents immediately looked for a YouTube video popular during the Kerry-Bush US Elections in 2004[7]. Some of them knew about the Austrian web portal www.politikkabine.at which provides adolescents information and guidelines on politics and voting in Austria. The adolescents involved in these discussions do not believe that eVoting is particularly important, though politics is often a somewhat difficult issue to discuss with younger people as they see it as more of a "manipulative process... (they) recognise and dismiss the slick, clever presentations that pass for political debate. They know a spin doctor when they see one and have the most sophisticated spin detectors of all" [13].

4 Lessons Learned

The "mitmachen.at" project was the first of its kind in Austria, and provided valuable lessons for the "Jugend2help" project in particular and future eParticipation projects in general. "Jugend2help" specifically resulted in involving citizens in the development of the Austrian eGovernment web portal, but both projects produced results

---

[5] Ibid.

[6] Ibid.

[7] http://www.youtube.com/watch?v=L5l9X3laNoM

valuable for future eParticipation projects geared towards younger citizens. The results obtained, although small in scale, were generally positive and showed that there is interest in online deliberation and that the internet certainly offers a new way of involving citizens. The projects' weaknesses must also be considered, as these too can help improve future eParticipation processes. Given the possibility and the means, citizens will get involved, but they do need to be encouraged to overcome their scepticism - eParticipation is a way of being involved and may represent the future of eDemocracy.

The project "mitmachen.at" followed a top-down approach, and the discussion topics were given to the participants at the beginning. Participants' discussion was to remain focused on the topics and this meant only little leeway for discussing other issues. This approach has the advantage that it directs the participants' focus of attention, but, at the same time, has the disadvantage that it sets boundaries and reduces the extent of the discussion. Although the top-down approach does not influence the actual form and procedure of participation, it may influence the participants' behaviour and distort how they really feel, the way they discuss or rate certain topics. This top-down approach also means that any topics not considered by the project team were not included and discussed. Citizens do expect bottom-up approaches in participatory systems: the internet enables many-to-many-communication, and participants want to use the technology available to change their environment, organisations and society [14]. But a bottom-up approach will usually be resisted by political actors as it allows for criticism and oppositional voices.

In the "mitmachen.at" project young people were involved only as users. The project showed that involving young people throughout all four phases of the project would have been very valuable, and was a lesson learned both for the "Jugend2help" project as well as future eParticipation projects. The lack of young citizens' involvement in the organisational side of the project may have also encouraged the strong 'we' vs. 'them' mentality reflected in some of the comments. Some participants expected censorship, expressed disbelief that results from this particular eParticipation project and generally any participation processes would be taken seriously at the political and administration levels. Skepticism in the project and eParticipation may have also been strengthened by the fact that a moderator decided which postings to publish (even though the extent of the moderator's interventions way clearly explained to the users). Many web portals and discussion lists have moderators who can decide on the postings made, but this still remains an issue to be analysed for future eParticipation projects. The lack of trust reflects what adults / public administration / politics believe adolescents to have [3] but is a feeling which is not uncommon throughout the whole of society: "while citizens are not alienated to politics and the life of their communities, they are more and more distrusting their mainstream representatives" [5]. At same time, the participants did express some optimism: they do want this form of participation to be made possible; they want such projects to be politically supported; results should be made available to the general public and politicians. Citizens and political/public actors do have a wide range of media and ICT tools to assist them with complex processes such as participation, but they must be able to "enhance representative democracy, whilst creating a vibrant, inclusive, transparent and responsive Knowledge-based Democratic Society and not just be a new form of political communication" [5]. Lessons from the mitmachen.at project were applied to the "Jugend2help" project. Adolescents were involved during all 4 phases of the project – the Phase II expert panel from the "mitmachen.at" project was replaced with face-to-face discussions with adolescents, who categorized the postings and contributions made in Phase I. Involving the adolescents at this stage can certainly increase the credibility of an eParticipation process.

eParticipation projects must clearly define the age bracket of the intended users before starting the project. Youth eParticipation will require a specific definition of the category "young people", that may vary in different countries – the Austrian Census Office[8], for example, defines a "youth" as a person up to 19 years of age. The means and channels of participation must be adapted to the target group's characteristics, and age will determine the design and structure of the platform or portal, the participation process, the choice of topics, the language used etc. Certain topics, language and terms used for older participants may not be appropriate or understood by younger participants, and they may, therefore, not understand what they are required to do. Age is an important factor which needs to be considered, as different age groups will have different needs and skills (for example senior citizens: the electronic process may have to be designed differently as they may have different digital skills or attitudes to the way public discussions ought to be held).

The age bracket chosen will also determine the marketing strategy necessary to reach and encourage citizens to participate. The results from the projects clearly show that better marketing of eParticipation platforms will achieve more discussions and greater involvement. The projects could have been reached more participants by using more information channels and timing the participation process to the target group's needs. The choice of communication channels (i.e. the ones users really like and use) and institutions (i.e. the ones they trust or are in contact with) can help reach the users. Adolescents are attracted to electronic networks and platforms (e.g. YouTube, MySpace, Twitter, Facebook), and should be used to either direct the participants to the discussions or as a tool for participation, although it must be considered carefully as not all participants may have access to the technology or the tools. The users' responses obtained during the various stages of the two projects will be used in future to develop a customised marketing and PR strategy, and a partnership with Austrian youth platforms and institutions will be expanded. Obviously trends need to be monitored, and the suitability of electronic media has to be considered. Some institutions exert strong influence on adolescents – the consultation phase of "Jugend2help" showed that schools are still one of the most trusted institutions, and are often the providers the digital equipment for digital participation.

Accessibility is an issue, and the Austrian Government aims to achieve it: "No citizen shall be denied the use of Governmental services due to physical restrictions." This is not a mere stance, but part of several Governmental acts such as the Austrian eGovernment Act or the Principle of Equality ("Gleichstellungsgrundsatz"). Since 2008, any public internet site must be accessible and free of barriers and obstacles which might constitute a hindrance for a citizen. While no reference to any standard or convention is provided as to how this should be achieved, it is widely understood that it should adhere to WAI (Web Accessibility Initiative) requirements[9]. The

---

[8] www.statistik.at/web_de/statistiken/bevoelkerung/index.html
[9] http://www.w3.org/WAI

www.help.gv.at platform is WAI-AAA conformant[10], so the "Jugend2help" project's underlying framework was per se WAI conformant, which made it easy to achieve a high degree of accessibility (WAI-AAA). The underlying www.help.gv.at platform has repeatedly proven to be resistant to hack attacks, but vandalism during the course of the project still had to be prevented as far as possible. Any form of personal identification (login/password, personal identification card, Austrian Citizen Card), though an effective way to avoid vandalism, had to be abandoned in advance as entry to the platform had to be anonymous. Captchas were used as an entrance barrier although these conflict with the goal of being as open as possible so as to attract users. For the project "Jugend2help", it was decided to enhance the captcha with an audio file which "speaks out" the letters, which in turn, can be entered by citizens with visual impairments. This provided the project with a sensible trade-off between security, accessibility and openness, but in future other methods will have to be found to ensure a high degree of accessibility.

In terms of eInclusion, all young Austrian citizens must have equal access to the public offers and services, and, in terms of internet access, website accessibility and usability. Website texts will be reviewed by pupils from all school forms, so that all users, including those with special needs, can understand and use them. Given a gender gap in the use of technology to communicate [15] - male adolescents prefer the PC whilst female adolescents use SMS (short message service, texting) significantly more - other forms of media technology (e.g. mobile phones) may have to be considered.

Finally, the societal context in which eParticipation processes occur will have to be considered when interpreting any results. The topics which generated the greatest interest and discussion in "mitmachen.at", e.g. environment and education, were strongly present in the Austrian media. During the course of the project the ORF (Österreichischer Rundfunk, the Austrian public broadcasting corporation) was showing a number of TV-programs about climate change. In the last couple of years the media has contained numerous discussions about the education system and employment rates in Austria. There may be a correlation between the prominence of a topic in the media and the high number of ratings and discussions in an eParticipation process. The results from participatory processes must always be evaluated, analysed and understood in the context of the society and the media: "You may find it difficult to understand the events in a particular period of time without knowledge of what went before and what may follow" [16].

5 Conclusions

At the beginning of 2007, the Austrian parliament reformed the voting laws and the voting age was set to 16 years. This means that political education is more important than ever before, and adolescents must be well informed in order to be able to take good decisions. It is well known that political education needs to include a practical approach; so, beside the right to vote, youth participation programmes should encourage young people to engage in politics. Public administration also needs a policy and guidelines for online citizen participation – such a policy should have standardised

---

[10] Ibid.

eParticipation methods, so that it can then be used for a wide range of future participation projects ranging from local, neighbourhood projects to nation-wide involvement.

The "Jugend2help" project recommendations are presently being integrated into the web portal www.help.gv.at (for example, the discussion forum). More Austrian projects will be launched in 2009, and the coming years will show the extent to which citizens want to become politically involved and make use of the new technologies for this purpose. In general, the results from "mitmachen.at" and "Jugend2help" show that most young Austrians have a positive attitude towards online deliberation, new methods and opportunities to participate. But questions remain, including: Will adolescents use the new resources extensively when they are neither "told to do so" by their teachers nor motivated by a PR/marketing campaigns? Can adolescents obtain the skills to deal with the online information flood, judging and selecting useful offers from the useless and the dangerous, and so make effective use of public administration services?

References

1. Parycek, P., et al.: EDEM. In: Positionspapier zu E-Democracy und E-Participation in Österreich (2008)
2. GFK AUSTRIA, Online Monitor 3. Quartal, GfK Austria (2007)
3. Serloth, A., Maerki, O.M.: Partizipation und Information – Ergebnisse einer Jugendbefragung, Study conducted for the Austrian Ministry of Social Security Generations and Consumer Protection, das Fernlicht, Vienna (2004)
4. Moon, M.J.: The evolution of e-government among municipalities: rhetoric or reality? Public Administration Review 62(4), 424–433 (2002)
5. van Lerberghe, D.: Are we moving towards a more participatory representative democracy? In: Proceedings of the Eastern European eIGov Days 2007: Best Practice and Innovation, OCG Band, Vienna, vol. 222, pp. 197–204 (2007)
6. Blumler, J.G., Coleman, S.: Realizing Democracy Online: A Civic Commons in Cyberspace. IPPR, London (2001)
7. Klein, H.: Tocqueville in cyberspace: using the internet for citizen asssociations. Information Society 15(4), 213–220 (1999)
8. Piswanger, C.M.: The participatory e-government strategy of the Austrian federal computing centre. In: Proceedings of the Eastern European eIGov Days 2007: Best Practice and Innovation, OCG Band, Vienna, vol. 222, pp. 205–210 (2007)
9. Piswanger, C.-M.: E-Participation bei kommunalen Planungsprozessen. Skizzierung von Einflussfaktoren und Verfahren, Master Thesis, Danube University Krems, Krems (2004)
10. Mahrer, H.: Österreich 2050 – Visionen und Werte für Österreichs Zukunft. Czernin Verlag (2006)
11. Edelmann, N., Krimmer, R., Parycek, P.: Engaging youth through deliberative e-participation: a case study. Int. J. Electronic Governance 1(4), 385–399 (2008)
12. Krimmer, R., Makolm, J., Parycek, P., Steininger, I., Kripp, M.: Politik zum Mitmachen, Jugenddeliberation im Internet, Arbeitspapiere zu elektronischen Wahlen und Partizipation, pp. 69–78 (2007)
13. Codrington, G., Grant-Marshall, S.: Mind the gap! Penguin South Africa (2005)

14. Fuchs, C.: eParticipation Research: A Case Study on Political Online Debate in Austria, ICT&S Center, Research Paper No. 1, University of Salzburg, Salzburg (2006), http://icts.uni-salzburg.at/media/pdf/pdf1060.pdf (accessed September 21, 2007)
15. Döring, N.: HandyKids. Wozu brauchen sie das Mobiltelefon? Machen Computer Kinder dumm? Wirkung interaktiver, digitaler Medien auf Kinder und Jugendliche aus medienpsychologischer und mediendidaktischer Sicht, pp. 45–66 (2006)
16. Hussey, J., Hussey, R.: Business Research, A Practical Guide for Undergraduates and Postgraduate Students. Palgrave, New York (1997)

Democracy to Come: Active Forums as Indicator Suites for e-Participation and e-Governance

Debbie Rodan[1] and Mark Balnaves[2]

[1] School of Communications and Arts
Edith Cowan University, Perth, Western Australia
d.rodan@ecu.edu.au
[2] Department of Internet Studies, Curtin University of Technology, Perth,
Western Australia
School of Communications and Arts
Edith Cowan University, Perth, Western Australia
m.balnaves@ecu.edu.au

Abstract. There is in modern industrial societies a 'civic deficit' Civic engagement in the traditional sense of community values and civic participation is declining (Putman 2000). What has not been examined is the ways in which various media including new media may provide real options for participatory cultures and participatory democracy now and in the future. Undoubtedly there are differences between participatory cultures that are considered a 'genuine' contribution to representational democracy and those that are not. This paper, based on initial research into Internet activism, will examine GetUp! as a specific example of an active forum that the authors argue enable participatory citizenship through media participation. While there are very few examples of active forums that might be considered a 'genuine' contribution to representational democracy there are clear signals that activism through active forums is maturing into a potent democratic force.

1 Media Activism

Derrida used the expression 'democracy to come' to describe his views on both the idea and ideal of democracy. Democracy, for Derrida welcomes strangers, accepts diversity, and enhances participation (Lucy & Mickler 2006). Democracy is ongoing. The authors have examined one activist group that has used and does use 'many media' to mobilise public opinion on key social issues and who see them self as democratic as well as contributing to the democratic process.

   In this paper the authors will examine a media active forum which they argue enhances participatory citizenship. The author's identify GetUp! as one specific example of an active forum which they consider enable participatory citizenship from the aspect of media participation. GetUp! is an Australian not-for-profit, grass-roots community advocacy organisation that relies on public donations. It began in 2005 and the aim is to build an accountable and progressive Australian Parliament and for this reason GetUp! does not support any particular political party (Get Up!, Annual Report 2005-2006, p. 5). The authors regard Get Up!'s forum to be an example of

A. Macintosh and E. Tambouris (Eds.): ePart 2009, LNCS 5694, pp. 175–185, 2009.
© Springer-Verlag Berlin Heidelberg 2009

media activism that fosters participation in decision making—that is, an activity which involves active participation as opposed to merely attendance at a group activity (see Pateman,1970, pp.68-69).

To begin, activism presupposes a policy, doctrine or agenda that shapes or defines action, while action refers to the condition of acting, exerting influence or 'doing'. In the broadest sense, activism may be seen as both a belief in an agenda for action as well as the process of taking action. Thus activism is not "synonymous with direct action" and there are "practices or forms of activism that are less direct action driven and operate more within the dominant political and judicial system" (Cammaerts, 2007, p.217). Cammaerts claims that central to a definition of activism are the notions of agency and possibility of re-making society: from this viewpoint activism "represents the practice of struggling for change and can be fueled by reactionary tendencies and aims, as well as progressive" (Cammaerts, 2007, p.217). He cites Wikipedia's defining of activism "as an 'intentional action to bring about social or political change' " as appropriate and exactly right. Wikipedia is considered an appropriate source because "in its own right" it is "a form of media activism, driven by the copyleft Creative Commons ideals". Cammaert (2007, p.217) along with Meikle (2002, p.4) include "electronic advocacy, hacktivism, and culture jamming" as well as "corporate saboteurs to established political parties" as other forms of media activism.

Meikle marks out Internet activism as a form of political activism that applies to various uses of the Net which attempt "to effect social, cultural or political change" both online and offline (2002, p.4). From this viewpoint media activism refers to an array of activities rather than a singular set of properties or practices. Activities and practices that could be described as examples of media activism are more likely to be characterised by affiliation than the sharing of common traits. Concerning Meikle's projects, media activism constitutes clusters or sets of features that intersect and overlap within the context of media use and production. In this regard, the conjunction of 'media' and 'activism' allows for a range of meanings to emerge.

The author's argue that GetUp! is a media activist forum that can be viewed as a confluence of media and activism. Members can access and use a range of media to inform themselves about issues, to participate in campaigns and to educate themselves about the parliamentary process. GetUp!'s forums also assist members to develop opportunities as well as skills for purposes of political engagement. Affiliates can engage in the political process by contacting members of parliament, participating in activist events and assisting in the production of advertisements. The forum functions in ways that allow genuine engagement with representational democracy. What the authors mean by genuine engagement is that it is the experience of the participation in decision-making in wider fields that leaves an individual with cognitive, emotional and intellectual skill development to participate in other forums in the future.

Recently GetUp! emailed members in each state inviting them to participate in the government's National Human Rights Consultations held in May 2009 (Get Up! Perth Human Rights Consultations, 2009). The consultations were not widely advertised in the community. When GetUp! asked members to register, they also outlined what was expected, how much time it would take, and where the consultations were being held. GetUp! also highlighted that attendees did not need "any special knowledge" in order to participate (personal communication, May 6, 2009). Registration was a matter of typing in your name and email address; confirmation of registrations was also by email. Encouraging members to attend through simple email requests does not necessarily translate into activism in the way Meikle defines it (2002); however it does contribute to increasing the participation of Australian's as well developing citizen's skills to participate further in other forums.

Media activism for Carroll and Hackett (2006) is not characterised as a specific activity or singular entity rather it is an emerging praxis of new social movements—in this sense media activism is a set of activities or practices whose resemblance resides in their tendency to be unfinished, intercreative, conversational and responsive to context (also see Meikle, 2002, p.33). Carroll and Hackett point to the resurgence of media activism within civil society since the mid-1990s which they see as: "organized 'grassroots' efforts directed to creating or influencing media practices and strategies, whether as a primary objective, or as a by-product of other campaigns (for example, efforts to change public opinion on environmental issues)" (2006, p.84). They found that different media activist groups used distinct "action repertoires and modes of organization" as well as the kinds of interventions varied (2006, pp.86, 90). Their findings underline a key fact "that media activism is indeed a diverse field of collective action" (2006, p.90). In the contemporary Anglo-American context, Carroll and Hackett's perspective implies that meaning is not embedded or fixed, but emerges through processes in context and practices of use.

Among the conclusions drawn by Carroll and Hackett (2006) is the idea that contemporary media activism problematise aspects of social movement theory. Geert Lovink draws attention to the problem of the metaphor of the social "movement" in the contemporary context of media activism (cited in Boler, 2008b, p.126). For Lovink, "Movement might suggest too much unity and continuity to describe today's event on the streets and the Net" (2005, p.13). He argues that the concept of social movement may not adequately reflect what is occurring today because although the word "movement" suggests progress or moving "something" in a particular direction: "movements are deeply temporary and heterogeneous experiences, all geared toward creating a political event as an almost metaphysical statement. It can be easy to create media events, but they are not by definition political events, since they do not necessarily make much difference" (cited in Boler, 2008b, p.126).

Having a presence online, creating a media event etc however can begin the process of mobilising members to take action and to participate in political events. Jenny Pickerill (2006, p.271) points out "one of the key functions of activists' presence online has been to mobilize others to take part in or support particular campaigns and actions". A good example is a recent campaign by GetUp! that started with an online petition to the Australian Communications Minister Senator Conroy to Save The NET (GetUp! Save The NET, n.d.). An email alert was sent to members; members signed the petition by typing their email address into a box. An easy to print Fact Sheet on Internet Censorship (a similar format to the government ones) was provided which members could forward with the petition to a friend. Because it takes 5 minutes to participate, GetUp! are more likely to involve citizens in the most minimal way. As Pickerill points out mobilising online in this way can trigger an individual's commitment to active support for campaigns which has the potential to promote further action "off-line" (2006, p.271).

For Lovink the Internet generates social activism through the activities of social movements (cited in Boler, 2008b, p.124). Activists tend to use the Internet as a 'tool' and to-date the Internet is not transformative in the sense of movements grow-ing out of the Internet (Lovink, 2008a; cited in Boler, 2008b, p.124). Clearly it is time-efficient to use the Internet: for instance, Lovink points out that activists use clips on YouTube which could transform into something more political. So there is scope, but activists need a much more sophisticated multi-media approach (Lovink, 2008a). In the past activist groups and social movements relied too much on email, which goes back to the mid-1980s; but at very early stages activist groups found the use of email turned against them. At present activists are using the Internet, YouTube etc as a tool for spreading information and groups of people sharing information. Nonetheless some activist groups are very suspicious of using any electronic media because the monitoring and surveillance of electronic media is legal and very easy to do even at the gathering stage (Lovink, 2008a).

For Lovink activism has to be effective, and the Internet in theory is ideally a huge accelerator; it rapidly connects people into issues (2008a). Furthermore at the back of the Internet there are a lot of tools activist groups can use. Online groups, including activist ones, as Lovink points out have shortened life spans and that activists have to experiment with campaigns as well as how to sustain a group before they know what works (2008a).

Cammaerts, Meikle, Carroll and Hackett's writing about media activism reveals that while contemporary meanings of media activism may share some of the associa-tions of social movements of the past, media activists today are highly contextualised within current socio-political frameworks. Thus they represent different sets of fea-tures and emerging intersections of meaning. As a set of activities that do not neces-sarily cohere, media activism reflects the tenor of contemporary social experience, and reveals its capacity to function and evolve within contextualised cultural and technological parameters (see Lovink cited in Boler, 2008b, p.126; Bennett, 2003).

GetUP! shares few associations with social movements of the past. The authors claim that GetUP! reflects more the social experience of media activism in that it is about 'intensive' networking, connecting and mobilizing through geographi-cal/physical expanse and reach it . Thus the organization does not just use the Internet as an add-on tool (Bennett, 2003); the Internet is used in an expansive way which is evident in that GetUp!'s website is core to the network governance of the group. For GetUp! online the aim is, in Pickerill's (2006, p.274) words, to "attract participation" of individuals considered to strengthen campaigns—a target that is rife with uncer-tainty with regard to mobilizing members to action.

Because it is not possible to know how many (if any) people are mobilised to act for some GetUp! is considered to be a 'pressure group' which focuses on key issues; others consider it to fit between a pressure group and informed citizenship. Others consider sites/grassroots organisations like GetUp! as 'call to action' posts in order to achieve two things: first, to influence legislation; and second, to facilitate online/offline civic engagement to change 'norms'. In terms of currency of engage-ment, the online activism GetUp! offers members is a different form to that of local civic organizations like APEX. In APEX people earned their speaking position by being a member of APEX for many years—GetUp! allows another way of participat-ing to emerge that does not necessarily replace offline civic participatory groups. Thus the author's argue that GetUp! has the potential to enhance participation in civic groups. Despite the limits of mobilizing online, GetUp! does offer an opportunity to revisit the whole issue of participatory democracy. Our earlier example of the governments National Human Rights Consultation exemplifies this point.

The methodology for the authors' analysis of web sites is based on the notion of *indicator suites* (Anheier & Isar, 2008) and Foucault's (1977) concept of discursive practices. The basic idea of indicator suites is not a statistical one but a conceptual one – to draw together different indicators, quantitative or qualitative, about a phenomenon that can provide a picture of what might be happening (Anheier 2006). For example indicators on cultural tourism in terms of demand and spending, or destinations and travel patterns across the world may not necessarily be straightforwardly comparable from a statistical point of view, because they were constructed with different measurements in mind. However, conceptual interpretations are still possible.

Discursive practices, by extension, are group of statements which provide a language for talking about a particular topic at a particular historical moment (Foucault 1977). Each discursive practice implies a play of prescriptions that designate exclusions and choices. Activist web sites have their own statements about who they are, what they do, and then actions that may or not correlate with what they say and do.

The authors have combined the methodologies and analysed a selection of web sites that nominated themselves as activist. A detailed analysis of the discursive practices of over 30 sites and their claims enabled the researchers to come up with preliminary classifications of activities. These activities and claims were then explored in the detailed activity of one specific site.

In analysing the activists websites the authors considered not only the ways "the producer shapes the text but the text, and its conventions" and how these shape "its production" (Richardson, 2007, p.41). Clearly activists emphasise one view over another, certain links over others, and specific kinds of editorial processes etc. In analysing activist websites the authors focused on how individuals could participate in campaigns and activism as well as how interactive and conversational the spaces (as described by Meikle in *Future Active*, 2002, pp.12-13). Media activist websites are shaped by the encoded practices of website production and the open source movement; what is considered in the latter is how interactive and accessible websites are for multiple users. The authors were also mindful that "the point of consumption" (Richardson, 2007, p.41) is part of the production of discursive practices. How members access information, interact with hyperlinks, blogs etc upload texts/video as well as how they were informed about campaigns contributes to the production of media activism. In this sense consumers of the website do not simply read the information and take it on board; they tend to also "decode texts" (Condit cited in Richardson, 2007, p.41). For these reasons both the production and the consumption of activist websites play a part in what is considered the discursive practice of participatory democracy especially in the way it is 'lived'.

We make five points to exemplify how GetUp!'s media activism forums constitute indicator suites and enable/facilitate participatory democracy skills for citizens—that is, how this organisation functions in ways that allow genuine engagement with representational democracy. GetUp!:

- Provides a diversity and surplus of information sources
- Exemplifies the principle of shared collaborative access
- Enables participation in decision making

- Develops skills necessary to participate in democracy
- Allows citizens to have an effect on governance

Provide a Diversity and Surplus of Information Sources

The activist organization GetUp! provides a diversity of information resources. The Media Coverage and Press Releases provides a detailed account of GetUp!'s activities in internet, in newspapers, on radio and TV media coverage. The GetUp! Campaigns (n.d.) section directs users to "past campaigns" and "achievements". Some of the current campaigns conducted by GetUp! include: "Do it for the Children" which targets paid parental leave; "Fuel Watch,"; "Equal Pay for Women," ;"Fix Transport"; "Buy Me a River", (centres on the Murray-Darling Basin), "Climate Action Now"; "Climate Torch Relay"; and "No Pulp Mill" (concerns the construction of Gunn's Tasmanian Pulp Mill).

Media activist spaces like GetUp! have quickly standardized in their use of technology. Standardisation is evident in that GetUp!'s campaigns are coordinated mainly via email and the internet. As technology use is standardised, so the media activist space becomes one directional like many other media outlets (Pickerill, 2004, p.179). Currently member's access is limited to retrieving information about activist campaigns, sending emails and/or making donations to campaigns. Despite this limitation, GetUp! do source a diversity of mediums such as YouTube, newspapers, radio and television (Get Up!, Annual Report 2005-2006, p.5). Members are also encouraged to participate in the production of the various media campaigns.

Exemplify the Principle of Shared Collaborative Access

Shared collaborative access is essential to GetUp!, Members of GetUp! when outlining ideas for possible campaigns are asked to: identify the target audience; the key message; desired outcomes; and specific action required for change (GetUp! About Us – FAQ. n.d.). In this regard, GetUp! follows the model of MoveOn.

While GetUp! members are asked for their input and to suggest campaigns a limited amount of ideas are actually taken up. Ideas suggested by members are put forward to a committee and the committee decides the campaigns in which to invest time and money. Information about who is on the committee and how participation in the formal organisation occurs is not available on the GetUp! website. Most GetUp! members then are doing grassroots agitation at a distance. Yet endless letters have put pressure on democratic governments and regimes have been shifted.

Enable Participation in Decision Making

GetUp! enable citizens to participate in processes of decision making. The particular forms of participation on the GetUp! site largely revolve around the sharing of information. The site claims that "GetUp members are always only ever asked to take targeted, coordinated and strategic action" (GetUp! About Us – FAQ. n.d.). GetUp!'s participation options include: receiving email updates about new campaigns; members can send emails or contact a member of parliament; engage with the media; sign petitions; attend an event; assist with the production of a TV advertisement; and/or provide financial support (GetUp! About Us – FAQ, n.d.). GetUP! produces advertisements for newspapers and television with the assistance of donations from the public. A recent example is the thirty second television message about human rights issues in China, planned to coincide with the television coverage of the opening ceremony of the 2008 Beijing Olympics (GetUp! Campaign Actions, Olympic silence is not golden, n.d.).

What may be happening with GetUP! is that in *theory* members do participate in decision-making, but in *practice* key people in the organization have control over the final decision. Pickerill found in her research that hierarchies can develop around an issue even with activist groups that are fairly non-hierarchical (2004, pp.178-181). She points to several issues in which hierarchies develop: to start with there is the issue of "who maintains and understands the online linkup" of the organisation; another issue is "who gains access to the limited number of computers" at an activist site (Pickerill, 2004, p.180). A further issue is "the process of editorial control"; that is, whether blogs are subject to editorial interference, what kinds of posts get removed etc (p.180). Finally, there are issues around what posts get linked to which sites—in short which sites are included and excluded on the web page.

Develop Skills Necessary to Participate in Democracy

A key priority for GetUp! is the development of skills necessary to participate in democracy. One example is GetUp!'s E-Democracy Project—the first phase of the project facilitates opportunities to learn about the role of the Australian senate and to become familiar with individual senators (GetUp! Project Democracy, n.d.). The project provides a range of tools to demystify mainstream political institutions and assists the development of participatory skills. For example a summary of the role and history of the senate is outlined on their website.

A list of the senators representing each state and territory can be accessed by clicking on individual sections of a map of Australia. The site features an interactive model of the Australian senate—by placing the cursor over the individuated seats in the model of the senate chamber this highlights a visual image and introductory details about the senator who occupies the seat (GetUp! Project Democracy: Your Senate, n.d.). Information available includes senators' Senate speeches, biographies, media reports and relevant blog posts making it easier to contact/engage with Senators about comments made etc.

Members can share thoughts about the senator's performance via the community blogposts or receive weekly email updates about their parliamentary statements and media appearances. A contact form is included to simplify access to individual senators for those who wish to email or write. As the process is atomized, the feature does facilitate a form of accountability from politicians.

In future, their E-democracy project will be expanded to incorporate a House of Representatives section. From GetUp!'s viewpoint by informing, educating and encouraging engagement with institutional mechanisms and ideas, the organisation empowers citizens and encourages participation (GetUp! Project Democracy, n.d.). This viewpoint is shared by others in the UK and Australia with the current call for the government to facilitate education about democracy and civic engagement in schools (NHRC, 2009; Crick, 2007). The call is for citizens to develop skills necessary to participate in democracy.

As discussed earlier central to a definition of activism is the notion of agency and possibility of re-making society (Cammaerts, 2007, p.217). Citizens in democracies like Australia need to understand the political process in order to access the politicians in meaningful ways. Information about democratic processes needs to be easily accessed and easily digested. Like Wikipedia's " 'intentional action to bring about social or political change' " (Cammaerts, 2007, p.217) by enabling accessible information, GetUp! can attempt to do the same.

But access does not guarantee participation. Access can at best enable individuals to be informed. Pickerill asserts that research to date "has concluded that it has been rare that online information alone has triggered the participation of those who had no other links into activism" (2006, p.272). However, online participation has enabled connection and coordinated communication between campaigns. And at the same time "encouraged those involved in more peripheral ways to increase their activism", that is, from just "reading emails online to attending a street protest" (p.272).

Allow Citizens to Have an Effect on Governance
The examples selected for discussion reveal how media participatory activism can enable citizens to have an effect on governance. The power to impact governance according to GetUp! is on-going. On their website they outline recent campaigns which GetUp! consider have had an effect on governance (GetUp! Campaigns, n.d.). After the election, GetUp! members gathered in hundreds of local meetings to discuss their top priorities for a "People's Agenda" much of which found its way into the high-profile of several Parliament member's "maiden speeches" (Brandzel, 2008, para. 20).

In February 2008, to coincide with the event of the Prime Minister's apology, GetUp! members indicated the primary significance of the occasion by illuminating the words "Sorry: the first step" in a display of candles outside parliament (Australia GetsUp! '07: Post Election Report, n.d). Subsequent initiatives included the provision of assistance to members of the stolen generation to travel to Canberra and the production of a song *From Little Things Big Things Grow* incorporating extracts from Prime Minister Kevin Rudd's address and Paul Keating (Australia GetsUp! '07: Post Election Report, n.d.).

GetUp!'s imaginative campaigning for reconciliation between indigenous and non-indigenous Australians is noted by Brandzel (2008) as an example of the way participation coordinated through sequential events can support social change and from our viewpoint impact on governance. In following months during 2007 over 350 "Reconciliation Get-Togethers" took place in local settings across Australia, the aim of which was to bring indigenous and non-indigenous Australian's together to discuss issues relating to reconciliation (Brandzel, 2008, para. 22). Brandzel concludes that by coordinating all these events:

It was a brilliant piece of political jujitsu, an illustration of how independent progressives can take the momentum of a government position of initiative, pull on it, and use the participation of ordinary people to transform the moment into something much bigger. Done right, this can ensure the government's initial bid and establish the floor, not the ceiling, for progressive reform (2008, para. 23).

GetUp! Try to Influence Public Policy Making through Activist Means
According to Putman in *Bowling Alone: The Collapse and Revival of American Community* (2000), the investment citizens of modern democracies are prepared to make in civic engagement appears to be declining. It may be that it is the traditional ways in which citizens engage that is declining—investment may be on the rise

through media activism. Frank Brennan, the Chair of the National Human Rights Consultative Committee stated that all of the human rights community consultations in Australia have been "very well attended around the country" (NHRC, 2009). While the authors cannot prove this was a result of GetUp!'s actions, we do argue that through GetUp!s media activism they contributed to increased participation in the campaign.

2 Conclusion

Groups like GetUp! are successful in mobilising its members and, indeed, giving them a feeling of 'sense of outcome' from its activities. Mueller and Page (2004) point out that media activism is about becoming an informed citizen. Community media, radical media and marginalized media are all attempts to provide communicative spaces for democratic dialogue and diversification of sources of opinion. Habermas (1984) made it foundational that people act in ways that distort communication but essentially humans want to know the truth. However people do not necessarily look for the truth—as exemplified in many forums on the web—often they look to support their own world view. In one sense post-modernity has revealed and illuminated for citizens that the truth is contextual and partial as opposed to absolute and definitive.

Access to the media is a vital component in the democratic process and an essential element of citizen participation. It is interesting and perhaps ironic that learning to be an active citizen is coming about outside the formal education system. The authors have argued that there are activities and structures that can be gleaned from these activist groups and their active forums that are potential guides for civic engagement.

References

Anheier, H., Isar, Y.R.: Introducing the cultures and globalization series and the cultural economy. In: Anheier, H., Isar, Y.R. (eds.) Cultures and globalization: The cultural economy, pp. 12–24. Sage, London (2008)

Anheier, H.: Globalization and social science data workshop. UCLA Center for Civil Society (2006), http://www.global.ucsb.edu/orfaleacenter/conferences/ngoconference/DataConference_Summary.pdf (retrieved May 20, 2009)

Australia GetsUp! 2007: Post Election Report (n.d.), GetUp! Action for Australia: and May 20 (2009), http://www.getup.org.au/about/faq/, http://www.getup.org.au/media/TheGetUpMob/ (retrieved November 28, 2008)

Bennett, W.: Communicating global activism. Information, Communication and Society 6(2), 143–168 (2003)

Brandzel, B.: Where do we move when America MovesOn? The American Prospect 19(9) (September 18, 2008), http://www.prospect.org/cs/archive/view_issue?issueId=293 (retrieved November 30, 2008)

Cammaerts, B.: Activism and media. In: Cammaerts, B., Carpentier, N. (eds.) Reclaiming the media: Communication rights and democratic media roles, vol. 3, pp. 217–224. European

Communication Research and Education Association (2007),
http://www.intellectbooks.co.uk/ppbooks.php?isbn=9781841501635
(retrieved April 29, 2007)

Carroll, W.K., Hackett, R.A.: Democratic media activism through the lens of social movement theory. Media, Culture & Society 28(1), 83–104 (2006)

Crick, B.: Citizenship: The political and the democratic. British Journal of Educational Studies 55(3), 235–248 (2007)

Foucault, M.: History of systems of thought. In: Bouchard, D.F. (ed.) Language, counter-memory, practice: Selected essays and interviews by Michel Foucault, pp. 119–204. Cornell University Press, Ithaca (1977) (Sherry Simon, Trans.)

GetUp! About Us – FAQ (n.d.), GetUP! Action, For Australia:
http://www.getup.org.au/about/faq/ (retrieved November 28, 2008)

GetUp! Annual Report 2005-2006 (n.d.) GetUp! (2008) Action for Australia:
http://www.getup.org.au/ (retrieved November 28, 2008)

GetUp! Campaigns (n.d.) GetUp! Action for Australia,
http://www.getup.org.au/campaigns/ (retrieved November 26, 2008)

Get Up! Campaign Actions. Olympic silence is not golden (n.d.) GetUp! Action for Australia Campaign Actions:
http://www.getup.org.au/campaign/OlympicSilenceIsNotGolden&id=373 (retrieved August 16, 2008)

Get Up! Perth Human Rights Consultations, Get Up! Action for Australia:
http://www.getup.org.au/campaign/rights/407 (retrieved May 06, 2009)

GetUp! Project Democracy (n.d.) Get Up! Action for Australia,
http://projectdemocracy.com/ (retrieved November 26, 2008)

GetUp! Project Democracy: Your senate (n.d.) Get Up! Action for Australia,
http://projectdemocracy.com/ (retrieved November 26, 2008)

GetUp! Save The NET (n.d.) Get Up! Action for Australia,
http://www.getup.org.au/campaign/SaveTheNet/442
(retrieved November 26, 2008)

Habermas, J.: The theory of communicative action vol. one: Reason and the rationalization of society (T. McCarthy, Trans.). Beacon Press, Boston (1984)

Lovink, G.: The principle of notworking: Concepts in critical internet culture. Public Lecture presented at Institute of Network Cultures, Amsterdam Media Research Centre, Hogschool van Amsterdam (February 2005)

Lovink, G.: Publish now: The cultural politics of blogs and web 2.0. Keynote address and Masterclass presented at Centre for Research in Entertainment, Arts, Technology, Education and Communications (CREATEC), December 2008a. Edith Cowan University, Perth, Western Australia (2008a)

Lovink, G.: Toward open and dense networks: An interview with Geert Lovink. In: Boler, M. (ed.) Digital media and democracy: Tactics in hard times, pp. 123–136. The MIT Press, Cambridge (2008b)

Lucy, N., Mickler, S.: The war on democracy: Conservative opinion in the Australian press. University of Western Australia Press, Crawley (2006)

Meikle, G.: Future active: Media activism and the Internet. Routledge / Pluto Press, New York / London (2002)

Mueller, M., Page, C.: Reinventing media activism: Public interest advocacy in the making of US Communication-Information Policy, 1960–2002, School of Information Studies. Syracuse University, Syracuse (2004)

National Human Rights Consultation, Human Rights Share Your Views. Attorney-General's Department, Barton, ACT, http://www.humanrightsconsultation.gov.au (retrieved May 19, 2009)

Pateman, C.: Participation and democratic theory. University Press, Cambridge (1970)

Pickerill, J.: Rethinking political participation: Experiments in internet activism in Australia and Britain. In: Gibson, R., Roemmele, A., Ward, S. (eds.) Electronic democracy: Mobilisation, organisation and participation via new ICTs, pp. 170–193. Routledge, London (2004)

Pickerill, J.: Radical politics on the net. Parliamentary Affairs 59(2), 266–282 (2006)

Putnam, R.: Bowling alone: The collapse and revival of American community. Simon & Schuster, New York (2000)

Richardson, J.E.: Analysing newspapers: An approach from critical discourse analysis. Palgrave MacMillan, Basingstoke (2007)

Author Index